Biblical Law Codes in Creative Tension

Biblical Hermeneutics Rediscovered

The Series as the name suggests will focus on Biblical Hermeneutics, i.e., literary works concerned with methods of interpreting the Old and New Testaments of Bible via different stream of topics like Literature & Poetry, Indigenous Philosophizing, Ethical response towards Ecology, Health & Healing, Science & Technology, Feminist Theology, Sociological approach towards Human Rights, Law & Politics, Arts, History of Ideas, Ancient Civilizations, Cultural Contiguity, Religious Cosmologies & Mysticism, Appraisal of various Theologians, World Peace & Harmony, Global Capitalism, Network Marketing, Cybertheology, Population & Demographics, Epigraphic Studies, Contextualized Education, and many others. We welcome a Mss. on any topic/s mentioned, whether they are original works, scholarly monographs, collections of conference papers, revised dissertations, or translations of historical documents. Through the Series we, the Publishers, are striving to put forward published works that may help Institutions, Academic Bodies, Researchers, Scholars and the World at large in furthering their respective knowledge and understanding on the concerned subject. We welcome your comments on our efforts and further suggestions on how we can enshrine new ray of analysing & explaining the written Texts through our upcoming books.

Biblical Hermeneutics Rediscovered - 1

Biblical Law Codes in Creative Tension

A Postcolonial Womanist Reading

Dr. Shiju Mathew
New Theological College, Dehradun

CWI
Christian World Imprints™

First Published in 2016 by

Christian World Imprints™
Christian Publishing & Books from India
H-12 Bali Nagar, **New Delhi-110015**
info@christianworldimprints.com
www.ChristianWorldImprints.com
Phone: +91 11 25465925

ISBN-13: 978-93-5148-127-0 ISBN-10: 93-5148-127-1

Cataloging in Publication Data--DK
Courtesy: D.K. Agencies (P) Ltd. <docinfo@dkagencies.com>

Mathew, Shiju, 1971- author.
Biblical law codes in creative tension : a postcolonial womanist reading / Dr. Shiju Mathew.
pages cm. -- (Biblical hermeneutics rediscovered ; 1)
Includes bibliographical references and index.
ISBN 9351481271
ISBN 9789351481270

1. Women (Jewish law) 2. Women in the Bible. I. Title. II. Series: Biblical hermeneutics rediscovered ; 1.

KBM526.M38 2016 DDC 296.18 23

Printed at D. K. Fine Art Press Pvt. Ltd.

Dedicated

to my parents, wife Clara and
children Freny and Reuel

The Book

The present book is about the Israelite law codes found in the Hebrew Bible. In Hebrew Bible there are casuistic laws and apodictic laws. Casuistic laws unlike apodictic are not in favor of all the weaker sections of the society especially Women. It focuses not only to identify the roots and further growth of the Biblical law system but also serves as a guiding tool in knowing the influence of AWA (Ancient West Asia) legal system on it.

The author has attempted to re-examine the position of the women in the Pentateuchal law codes especially Covenant code, to explore how the re-reading of the laws by employing postcolonial womanist approach can lead for a better and harmonious society and to seek a space where members of our differing worlds can be involved and be partakers in creating a world of freedom, world of balanced coexistence, and a world free from exploitation or suppression.

The projection of the book is to initially bring out the position of women in the Deuteronomic and Holiness codes and then to investigate how the position of women in the Book of the Covenant Code differs from that of the other two codes. Additionally, it provides a platform to re-read the legal text that affirms the right to independence & freedom and to explicate how the postcolonial womanist readings of the laws can contribute & promote a society for its betterment. This scholarly work is a must have for Lawmakers, Sociologists, Religious leaders, Christian Laity, Church Clergies, Institutions, Students and Researchers.

The Author

The author is an ordained minister of Christian Evangelistic Assemblies. His theological journey started in the year 1992. He did Bachelor of Divinity from Faith Theological Seminary, MTh (Old Testament) from Union Biblical Seminary, and Doctorate in Theology from United Theological College; all these Colleges and Seminaries being affiliated to the Senate of Serampore College (University).

The author served with Gospel for Asia in different capacities (1996-1999) and presently serving at New Theological College as Assistant Professor and Dean of Academic Affairs. Some of his articles are: Ruth, a Moabite Gentile Woman blessing the nation Israel: A Subaltern Reading; Qumran Interpretation of the Hebrew Bible and its significance in Christian writings. Few more of his works are in the pipeline and will be published in the near future like Deuteronomy and Women rights: A Subaltern reading; Kingship in Israel: Traditions in Conflict?

Acknowledgements

Hard work, prayer, commitment, and well wishes of many have contributed towards the success of this work. First of all, I thank God who made me experience His unique and universal grace and power throughout the course of writing this work. I would like to express my heart-felt gratitude to my gurus Dr. K. G. Jose, Dr. Paulson P., Dr. Eliya Mohol, Dr. Daniel Jones Muthunayagom, Dr. John Samuel Raj and Dr. David Joy and many others who contributed immensely during my theological journey. The constructive criticism, encouragement, and guidance, I received from them are of ineffably significance.

I praise God Almighty for the lovely people He had given in my life for completing this work. I am indebted to Founders (Uncle George and Auntie Leela), Managing Director (George C. Kuruvilla), Principal (Dr. Simon Samuel), Faculty, Staff and Student body of our college, Luther W. New Jr. Theological College (NTC) for their valuable prayer and support.

I am so grateful to my parents and siblings for instilling on me the fear of God and supported me throughout my life journey. My special thanks are due to my wife Clara for her advice and constant encouragement. I owe debt of gratitude to my friends and colleagues for everything they have contributed towards me despite all odds.

List of Abbreviations

AnBib - *AnalectaBiblica*
AV - Authorized Version
AWA - Ancient West Asia
AWAT - Ancient West Asian Text relating to the Old Testament
BA - The Biblical Archaeologist
BC - Book of the Covenant Code
BCE - Before the Common (or Christian) Era
BDB - F. Brown, S. R. Driver and C. A. Briggs Hebrew and English Lexicon of the Old Testament
BHS - Biblia Hebraica Stuttgartensia
BSAW - *Berichteüber die verhandlungen der sächsischenAkademie der wissenschaftenzu Leipzig*
CE - Common (or Christian) Era
C.f. - *Confer*, Compare
CH - Code of Hammurabi
Chr - Chronicles
Circa - about, approximately
Cor - Corinthians
D - "Deuteronomic" Source
DC - Deuteronomic Code
Deut - Deuteronomy

E	-	"Elohist" source
Ed.	-	editor (s)
EL	-	Laws of Eshnunna
Eng	-	English
Exod	-	Exodus
Ezek	-	Ezekiel
Gal	-	Galatians
Gen	-	Genesis
HC	-	Holiness Code
Heb	-	Hebrews
HL	-	Hittite laws
Hos	-	Hosea
Ibid.	-	*ibidem* (in the same place)
Isa	-	Isaiah
J	-	"Yahwist" source
JAOS	-	Journal of the American Oriental Society
JBL	-	Journal of Biblical Literature
JCS	-	Journal of Cuneiform studies
Jer	-	Jeremiah
Josh	-	Joshua
JSNT	-	Journal for the Study of the New Testament
JSOT	-	Journal for the Study of the Old Testament
JSOTS	-	Journal for the Study of the Old Testament Supplement series
JSS	-	Journal of Semitic Studies
Judg	-	Judges
KJV	-	King James Version
Lev	-	Leviticus
Lit.	-	literally
LXX	-	Septuagint
MAL	-	Middle Assyrian laws
Mic	-	Micah
MS	-	Manuscript

MT	-	Masoretic Text
NEB	-	New English Bible
Neh	-	Nehemiah
NRSV	-	New Revised Standard Version
Num	-	Numbers
OT	-	Old Testament
P	-	"Priestly" source
Pl.	-	Plural
Prov	-	Proverbs
RGG	-	Religion in *Geschichte und Gegenwart*
RSV	-	Revised Standard Version
Sam	-	Samuel
Tg J	-	*Targum Pseudo Jonathan*
*Tg*Mss	-	*Targum* manuscripts
VT	-	*Vetus Testamentum*
VTS	-	Vetus Testamentum Supplements
ZAW	-	*Zeitschriftfür die alttestamentliche Wissenschaft*

Abstract

The Israelite law system can be broadly divided into three law codes: (1) The Covenant Code (Ex. 20-23), (2) The Deuteronomic Code (Deut. 12-26) and (3) The Holiness Code (Lev. 17-26). The laws found in the Covenant Code are quite different from that of the Deuteronomic Code and Holiness Code.

Within the legal Codes of the Pentateuch, unlike male, the position of women has a bewildering variety. The position of women in the Covenant Code differs from the Deuteronomic Code. In the Covenant Code, male and female are subjected to different sets of rules. It enforces the degradation of women and inscribes male power. The legal terminology used when dealing with women and their sexuality is concerned far more with property than with gender. The laws in the Deuteronomy Code had a progressive and positive attitude to the legal status of women, which is not found in the Covenant Code. The laws in the Holiness Code are more or less ambivalent in nature.

Some of the areas attempted in this work are: How far the alien cultures and practices got enmeshed Israel? Had the existing law codes undergone a change or development in the course of her history? Did the changes occur due to the repeated foreign invasion in the course of her history? Is the language of female subordination limited to patriarchy only or is it impacted by colonialism also?

Good number of scholars studied the Israelite law system. These works shed light on the subordination of women in religious and other spheres of life. For example, Phyllis Bird sees the subordination of women as the result of patrilineal and patriarchy. She advocates for a reconstruction of traditional historiography. Cheryl B. Anderson argues by raising two important questions: Did the laws serve a legal purpose? Can Ancient Israelite society be reconstructed from the Biblical laws? She answers these questions by employing Gender and postmodern Feminist Legal theory. G. I. Emmersion emphasized the subordination of women in the Old Testament and argues that the women played a crucial role in the liberation and progression of Israel, but they were not given due credit like male. Victor Matthews' analyses the law and points out the protective and positive attitude towards women in the Deuteronomic law code. N. C. Habel advocates for sociological approach. His argument is to read the text by identifying with the oppressed group. G. C. Chirchigno's approach was more of a comparative analysis. The arguments of all these scholars in general are based on patrilineal and patriarchal ideology. They brought out the discrepancy in the law codes and expressed their reservation against domination both in class and gender. Many other scholars also contributed immensely on Israelite law system such as Bernard Levinson (Levinson argues for revision and interpolation).The issues raised by all these scholars and their contributions are immensely helpful to locate the reasons behind the degradation of the weaker sections in the society which includes slaves and women.

The issue before us is to find out whether the female subordination was exclusively due to patriarchal ideology or it has a colonial dimension also. As per our knowledge and readings, it seems there is not an exclusive work related to Israelite Law system in a Postcolonial Womanist approach. Hence, this work is important and distinct from the other works and this study may add a new dimension to the existing work.

Findings/Observations

Some of the main findings addressed in this work are:

1. The Empire/s and their strategies

2. Law: Is it an Independent Entity?
3. Cultures of Ancient West Asia: A Fusion
4. Land, Law and Gender: An Agriculture Setting
5. Discrepancies in the Pentateuchal Law Codes
6. Is the Biblical law Immutable?
7. Powerful and powerless: The power play behind the law

I argue in this work that the Covenant Code appears to have originated or codified during the Assyrian rule (8th century BCE), the Deuteronomic Code toward the end of the Assyrian colonialism and the rise of Babylonian colonial advent (7th century BCE) and the Holiness Code during the Persian colonial period (6th century BCE). So, all Israel's law system, at least their codifications took place under the colonial experiences of the people of God. These experiences vary in their intensity: the Assyrian conquest and colonial experience appears to be more intense than the other two. So, the Covenant Code that was codified under the Assyrian colonial times in Israel exhibit a rather more oppressive feature than the other two.

This is particularly seen in the way women are treated in these three law codes. The treatment of women in the Covenant code is comparatively more degrading than the Deuteronomic and the Holiness Code. I argue that this is because of the particular degrading colonial experience and the collaborative Israelite elements who supported the colonialism may perhaps be behind the composition or the codification of this law code. In this law code, women are degraded. I argue that not only patriarchy but also the colonial ideology led to this phenomenon.

I use Postcolonial Womanist approach for reading because in a colonial context the women of the colonists also turn out to be oppressors. So, the women of the subjected population experience a kind of double subjugation not only from the male colonists and the native men but also from the female colonists. A general feminist approach therefore is not useful for analyzing this specific experience of the colonized subject women population.

Introduction

The Biblical law codes like election and covenant is one of the fundamental and central realities in the life of the Hebrew people. They are apodictic and casuistic in style. The Casuistic laws are pre-dominant both in AWA (Middle Assyrian laws, Code of Hammurabi's etc) and Biblical laws. The laws instituted in the book of the Covenant Code (Exodus 20-23) especially casuistic laws are quite different from that of the Deuteronomic Code (Deuteronomy 12-26) and Holiness Code (Leviticus 17-26). Within the legal Codes of the Pentateuch, unlike male, the position of women varies. The position of women in the Covenant Code differs from the Deuteronomic Code[1]. The Covenant Code unlike the Deuteronomic Code enforces the degradation of women and inscribes male power. The legal terminology used when dealing with women and her sexuality is concerned far more with property than with gender. The Laws in the Deuteronomic Code had a progressive and positive attitude to the legal status of women, which is not found in the Covenant Code.

1 (a) Deuteronomy 22:28-29 and Exodus 22:15-16. In Deuteronomy the accused is forced to marry the girl and renounce his rights to divorce her, whereas in Exodus 22:15-16 the father was entitled to deny the marriage of his daughter. (b) Deuteronomy 15:12-18 and Exodus 21:2-11. In Deuteronomy the freedom was entitled both for male and female slave, whereas in Exodus 21:2-11, freedom is only for male slave

The author's attempt is to re-examine the position of the women in the Pentateuchal law codes especially Covenant code, to explore how the rereading of the laws by employing postcolonial womanist approach can lead for a better and harmonious society and to seek a space where members of our differing worlds can be involved and be partakers in creating a world of freedom, world of balanced co-existence, and a world free from exploitation or suppression.

Israel's history covers a long period of time going back to second millennium BCE. During this period, she encountered with a great variety of socio-economic and political situations. Her interactions with alien cultures were manifold.[2] These interactions perhaps affected her life and functioning, which includes the legal system. There is also a possibility that Israel mimicked the strategies adopted by her neighboring nations of wealth and production (agriculture), which affected both the land and women. The Biblical laws are complex and open to several interpretations.

Few Questions will put the problem into perspective: How far the alien cultures and practices enmeshed Israel? Had the existing law codes gone for a change or development in the course of her history? Had the changes occurred due to the repeated foreign invasion in the course of her history? Shall the subjugation of the land to increase wealth and productivity be equated with the subjugation of women to increase labor force/manpower?[3] What was the role of tradition/s (dominant tradition such as Judahite and Priestly tradition) in

---

2 The parallels between the Israelite law codes and Ancient West Asian law codes will be explored in detail in the following chapters (chapter three to five). The parallelism clearly suggests of an acceptance of cultural borrowing, which made a strong impact in the socio-religious life of Israel.

3 The gender roles and women's subjectivity are mentioned in detail in the works of Alison Blunt, *Travel Gender and Imperialism: Mary Kingsley and West Africa* (New York: Guildford, 1994). Laura Donaldson, *Decolonizing Feminisms: Race, Gender and Empire Building* (Chapel Hill: University of the North Carolina Press, 1992). and Homi K Bhabha, *The Location of Culture* (New York: Routledge, 1994). One of the imperialist strategies is the employment of female gender to legalize the relationships of subordination and domination. For Baba, hybridity can be envisioned as empowering for a woman's subjectivity as it has the potential to destabilize any form of authority (*Location of culture*, 1).

the final form of the legal text? Was the social position of women worse, equal or better than that of AWA? Is the language of female subordination limited to patriarchy or has power of colonialism behind it?

Scholars such as George Ernest Mendenhall[4], S. M. Paul[5], W. Preiser[6], L. Rost,[7] and many others indicate in their writings that the Israelite legal system had faced a drastic inner-development during the course of her life especially during second and third millennium BCE. So, the chief purpose of this book is to display the insufficiency of the legal stand concerning the weaker section of the society especially women in the Pentateuchal texts, as there are evidences which indicate that there are significant connections between substantial portions of the Pentateuchal law codes and the operative Ancient West Asian law. There are different strategies of the imperial world, and one among them is the strategy of imperializing texts, i.e., employment of female gender to authenticate relationships of subordination and domination. The use of female gender to describe the colonized serves the agendas of the colonizer and the imperial world.

Any law that cripples human growth in all its dimensions or forbids him/her of doing well to others is null and void. Human persons and their identity and survival are more important than mere observance of the Law.[8] The Legal disparity, which is believed to have been caused and taken final form by human hands, is one of the widely discussed issues today. The issues such as abuse of power, exploitation towards the weaker section through unjust means, deprivation of human rights etc are rampant and as a result of these

---

4 G. E. Mendenhall, "Law and Covenant in Israel and the Ancient near East," *BA* 17 (1954): 26-46.

5 Shalom Paul, "Studies in the Book of the Covenant in the Light of Cuneiform and Biblical Law," *VTS* 18 (1970): 78-83.

6 W. Preiser, "Vergeltung Und Sühne Im Altisraelitischen Strafrecht," *Festschrift für Eberhard Schmidt* (1961): 246.

7 L. Rost, "Das Bundesbuch," *ZAW* 77 (1965): 225-259.

8 Pauline Chakkalackal, "Law and Religion: A Feminist Biblical-Theological Critique," *Journal of Dharma* 32, no. 3 (2007): 241.

there is an increase of crime. Who is responsible for the breakup of the society? Is it religion, law or traditions?

Religion and Law

Religion and Law have been two connected powers in almost every human society. They represent two vital scopes of human existence. They are existential realities in the social and personal lives of human beings. They succeed in establishing and maintaining social orders leading to the formation of cultures and civilizations. Many factors, including human creativity and imagination have played an indispensable role in the development of religion which includes the Law. Though traditionally the biblical law has been considered and claimed as the product of the divine revelation, in reality its origin is debatable due to its contradiction in its style and nature. Most of the laws have possibly resulted into its final form from human influence (tradition) and its vested interest.[9] The distribution of the legal text in the Pentateuch, the composite character and nature of the laws (Apodictic and Casuistic laws) and its differences[10] and its resemblance with the Ancient West Asian codes (Code of Hammurabi, Eshnunna, Hittite and Middle Assyrian laws) make it impossible to attribute these legal materials to one particular period. The law probably does appear in a small way at the beginning of a state but as a result of various experiences and interactions within societies and outside forces, a final form took place. It took a formal shape at the culmination of the society, i.e., during the exilic/post exilic period. So, it points to a product of a long process of development. Against

9 Saju Chackalackal, "Religion and Law - Forces of Liberation?," *Journal of Dharma* 32 (2007): 221.

10 The character of casuistic law is its objective 'if-style' and the formulation is in third person. The form of the casuistic law is not genuine and exclusively Israelite form of law, rather it was known throughout the Ancient West Asian culture. Its setting is in social context and its content does not contain any laws concerning the cult and seems neutral with regard to religion. In short, it is confined to human relations and problems. The Apodictic laws are basically commandment and prohibitions. They aim at religious and ethical questions. They have direct and personal address (you) to the community unlike Casuistic laws which are objective and descriptive.

this background, how can we read the Biblical laws and its relation to the weaker section in general and women in particular?

The Biblical law written from the socio-cultural and religious perspectives of male authors to some extent has legitimized women's subordination and promotes directly or indirectly all forms of exploitation towards women and weaker sections of the society. There are ample evidences in the Law, which support the negative approach meted out to the women.

Some of the texts are: Women as man's property (Exodus 20:17, 21:2-11; Deut. 5:17-21); Women as deprived of inheritance right (Numbers 27:8); Women are culturally, socially and physically detested (Leviticus 12, 15).

Israel and Ancient West Asia

In order to understand the religion, culture, and practices (legal practices) of Ancient Israel, to a certain extent a general understanding of AWA religion, culture and practices must be known, as most of them, if not all, probably have influenced Israel. Either Israel would have borrowed some of their practices or reacted to some others. So, the Israelite history and tradition did not develop in an isolated vacuum. Geographically, Israel was part of the Ancient West Asia. History and archaeology inform us that it's political, commercial, and cultural relations with its neighbors were manifold and varied.[11] The question, before us is, to what extent and in what way have factors from outside Israel contributed to the Israelite history? There are many similarities between biblical ideas, practices, or narratives on the one hand and extra-biblical material on the other. There are, for instance, similarities in vocabulary which derive from the fact that Hebrew and the other Northwest Semitic languages are closely related. But problems arise when we deal with religious vocabulary, which includes the legal system.

---

11 Helmer Ringgren, "The Impact of the Ancient near East on Israelite Tradition," in *Tradition and Theology in the Old Testament*, ed. Douglas A. Knight (Philadelphia: Fortress Press, 1977), 31.

The Israelite covenant traditions exhibit striking similarities with Hittite vassal treaties.[12] The Israelite Laws are connected to the concept of the Covenant, which were modeled after the formal agreements or treaties that existed between the monarchs and their vassals in the political sphere of the world.[13] A careful study of the Hammurabi code clearly rectifies that, it is Hammurabi who enacts the laws. He turns to the gods only to ask them to give a good reward to him that will keep his statutes, and to inflict severe punishment on those who transgress the statutes. So, the whole content seems secular in color.[14] Now, among the Israelites, during the whole period preceding the destruction of the First temple, the sources of the official law were the secular statutes of the ruling authorities, whereas the Torah laws were regarded as religious and ethical requirements.[15] If we observe carefully, the Casuistic laws in particular do not contain any laws concerning the cult. The casuistic law on the whole seems to be neutral with regard to the religion and is confined to human relations and problems occurring between humans (secular). The casuistic law is dominant in the Covenant Code. The nature and style ofthe Covenant Code in a superficial reading appears to resemble closely with the Nuzi text, Hittite Laws[16], Code of Hammurabi[17]

---

12 Ibid., 36. The Decalogue has similarity with Hittite treaty form. The Preamble, historical prologue, stipulations, deposit and public reading, list of witnesses and the blessings and curses can be seen both in Decalogue and Hittite treaty form with much similarity.

13 Samuel Greengus, "Law," in *Anchor Bible Dictionary*, ed. David Noel Freedman (New York: Double day, 1992), 245.

14 U. Cassuto, *A Commentary on the Book of Exodus* (Jerusalem: The Magness Press, 1967), 259-260.

15 Ibid., 260.

16 Hittite laws are formulated as case laws-they start with a condition and a ruling follows.

17 For Taylor, under the Sumerian law, the punishment for crime was often a fine but under Hammurabi's law, the guideline was 'an eye for an eye". Punishment was also dependent on who was wronged. If a person puts out the eye of a slave, he would not lose his eye but could pay a fine. If that person puts out the eye of a noble man, he would lose his eye as punishment. Although the Code of Hammurabi was essentially humanitarian in its intent and orientation, it contained the 'eye for an eye' punishment, which is a barbaric application of

and the laws of Eshnunna[18].Scholars like John Bright, W. F. Albright, G.E. Mendenhall, Gerhard von Rad and others generally agree on the influence of AWA laws.[19]

After having a careful look into the internal factors[20] (differences in the law especially with regard to women) and external factors (resemblance in style and nature between Israelite Law and AWA, and scholars approach with regard to Israelite law and AWA), it is difficult to overlook the influence of AWA legal texts in Israelite legal system.

Discrepancies in the Israelite Law System: The Covenant Code and the Deuteronomic Code

For Eckart Otto, the laws found in Deuteronomic code protect the rights, dignity and identity of women, and are in an elevated position whereas the position of women in Covenant Code is of disadvantage and they are treated as property. Covenant Code portrays male dominance whereas the Deuteronomic code was deeply concerned with the restriction of male predominance (Deut 12:15-18// Exod 21:2-11; Deut 16:11-14).[21]

Scholars like Michael Fishbane *(Biblical Interpretation in Ancient Israel* [Oxford: Clarendon, 1985] 95), Dale Patrick, *Old Testament*

---

the concept making the punishment fit for the crime (Mary B. Taylor "Laws and Government- Hammurabi's Code).

18 The Laws of Eshnunna show signs of social stratification mainly focusing on two different classes - the *muskenum* and *awilum. Awilum* - free men and women and *Muskenum*- slave men and women.

19 See the exegetical chapters for their views.

20 For Internal factors compare the following passages (Exod. 21:2-11, 21:12-19; 21:20-21; 21:22; 21:26-27 and 22:16-17 with Deut. 15:12-18; 16:11-14; 22:13-21; 22:22-29; 23:17 and Lev. 18:6ff; 20:10ff; 25:6ff and 25:39-43). In the Book of the Covenant Code there are sharp differences between male and female whereas in Deuteronomic Code and Holiness Code, both male and female are given equal treatment.

21 Eckart Otto, "False Weights in the Scales of Biblical Justice? Different Views of Women from Patriarchal Hierarchy to Religious Equality in the Book of Deuteronomy," in *Gender and Law in the Hebrew Bible and the Ancient near East*, ed. Bernard M. Levinson Victor H. Matthews, and Tikva Frymer-Kensky (Sheffield: Sheffield Academic Press, 1998), 140. A detailed exegetical study to support this view can be seen in chapter three, four, and five.

Law (Atlanta: John Knox, 1985) 198; and James W. Watts, *Reading Law: The Rhetorical Shaping of the Pentateuch* (Biblical Seminar 59; Sheffield: Sheffield Academic Press, 1999) 136-37 agree that biblical law, as it is presented in the Pentateuch, functions to promote a religious agenda rather than to establish a full-fledged legal system.[22] Is there any hidden religious agenda or power play behind the legal system?

Dating of the Codes

The rationale behind this section is to figure out the period, when each code came to its final shape. For a postcolonial reading, the fixing of the period is essential to ascertain if there was any influence of neighboring nation in the final form of the codes.

There are mixed opinion among the scholars concerning the dating of the Book of the Covenant, Deuteronomic Code and the Holiness Code.

The Book of the Covenant Code

Martin Noth argues for a date after the settlement period, as certain parts of the Book of the Covenant resembles in form and content with the laws of Ancient West Asia.[23] For R. E. Clements, a precise date is not possible, as the laws relate to the everyday life of a typical settled life without direct reference to external political conditions. He places the date of the Book of the Covenant between 1200-1100 BCE. However, he agrees that like other codes, the Book of the Covenant underwent subsequent revision.[24] Werner H. Schmidt states that the collection of laws in Exodus 20-22-23:33 has been introduced at a later date into the Sinai Pericope by means of preceding and following narrative devices, and it is from this new setting that

---

22 Bruce Wells, "What Is Biblical Law? A Look at Pentateuchal Rules and near Eastern Practice," *The Catholic Biblical Quarterly* 70 (2008): 226.

23 Martin Noth, *Exodus* (London: SCM Press Ltd, 1962), 174. The Casuistic forms of Book of the Covenant are similar in form and content with the AWA Laws.

24 Ronald E. Clements, *Exodus* (Cambridge: Cambridge University Press, 1972), 128.

the Collection gets its name as the Book of the Covenant.[25] For Robert Gnuse, the law comes from the period of settlement in the land from the 13th to 10th centuries. The laws are perhaps Canaanite, and their adoption by Israel was in the early settlement period.[26] For Alan Cole, the Book of the Covenant deals with the problems of bronze-age society. And due to this, extreme critics favor for an early date for this section, the period of the Judges at the latest.[27] Albrect Alt suggested that the casuistic laws had its setting in the secular case law of the Ancient West Asia, whereas the apodictic laws arose out of the unique covenantal setting of early Israel. The subsequent fusion of legal material far from being a late literary activity reflected the institutional life of Israel during the early period of the Tribal league in which Israel appropriated common Ancient West Asian Law from the Canaanites and brought it under the control of her unique covenantal law.[28] Vasantha Rao argues that the collection of laws favors the early monarchic period. The compiler of the law 'either had access to the Ancient West Asian law codes or the laws that were compiled in Israel which manifested the common ethos of the Ancient West Asia'. He favors for 8th century BCE (722/721 BCE).[29] Van Seters argues that the Book of the Covenant Code is not the oldest legal collection in the bible, but arose centuries later as a law for the diaspora. For him, the laws in the Covenant Code that are similar to the Deuteronomic and Holiness Code are in fact later than both of these. He also argues that the Covenant Code must be placed in the context of the Babylonian exile.[30] Dale Patrick argues

25 Werner H. Schmidt, *Old Testament Introduction* (Mumbai: St. Pauls Publication, 1997), 134.

26 Robert Gnuse, *You Shall Not Steal: Community and Property in the Biblical Tradition* (New York: Orbis Books, 1985), 1.

27 R. Alan Cole, *Exodus* (London: The Tyndale Press, 1973), 162.

28 A. Alt, "The Origins of Israelite Law," in *Essays on Old Testament History and Religion* (Oxford: Oxford University Press, 1966), 81-132.

29 Chilkuri Vasantha Rao, *Ecological and Theological Aspects of Some Animal Laws in the Pentateuch* (Delhi: ISPCK, 2005), 15-16.

30 John van Seters, *A Law Book for the Diaspora: Revision in the Study of the Covenant Code* (New York: Oxford University Press, 2003). The author is not convinced with the argument of van Seters. The BC was the oldest law code and reworking took place in the course of history. Douglas A. Knight also

that the similarities between the Book of the Covenant code and the Deuteronomic code are due to the reworking of the chronologically earlier provisions of the Book of the Covenant code in the later work.[31]

A closer reading of the covenant code with the codes of the neighboring nations and taking into account the scholars observation, appears that the law though originated during pre-monarchic period, and developed through the monarchy period, had its final form in 8th century BCE.The reason behind this argument is that Israel being a newly formed nation got influenced by the policy of the neighboring nations. Eighth century was a period when Israel as a nation became politically and economically sound. It also appears that Israel mimicked the culture and practices of neighboring nations. These change of life styles probably affected the laws of Israel. The gap between the rich and the poor increased. Gender discrimination took place, which can be seen in the Book of the Covenant codes.

The Deuteronomic Code

Few scholars argue that the laws in Deuteronomy 12-26 were the product of Josiah's reform, but majority opines that they were part of the law book found in the temple.

For Gerhard von Rad, Deuteronomy unlike Book of the Covenant Code is 'not a divine law in codified form, but preaching about the commandments. It is very much interspersed with parenesis'. He further argues that the law carries an interpretation, and these interpretations must not be considered 'as legal sections or supplementary laws, but as homiletics'.[32] For G. T. Manley, many of the laws are ancient, going back to the beginning of Israel's existence as a nation. The Laws and exhortations of Deuteronomy were once delivered orally by Moses or Samuel or a group of Levites. The

---

argues for later dates for the Book of the Covenant Code [Douglas A. Knight, 'Village Law and the Book of the Covenant' in *A Wise Discerning Mind: Essays in Honor of Burke O. Long*, ed. Saul M. Olyan and Robert C. Culley (RI: Brown Judaic Studies, 2000), 103-119.]

31 Dale Patrick, *Old Testament Law* (Atlanta: John Knox Press, 1985), 9.

32 Gerhard von Rad, *Studies in Deuteronomy* (London: SCM Press, 1948; reprint, 1961), 15, 17.

oratorical style of the book, the introduction of time and place, the appeals to remember the past and relating to the present conditions all presume that Moses is the speaker.[33] For Robert Gnuse, the Laws in Deuteronomy 12-26 represent a 7th and 6th century revision of earlier laws for the new social, economic, and political condition of the country. The law reflects the critique of the 8th century prophets and their call for justice. The laws are more humane and reflect a more complex society than the Covenant Code.[34] According to A. C. Welch, Deuteronomy was given its literary form between the middle of the 8th century BCE and the seventh century BCE. He argues for the Northern kingdom and assumes that the book might have been brought to the southern kingdom and deposited in the temple in Jerusalem after the fall of Samaria. And during the restoration of the temple, it was found.[35] For D. L. Carmody, "The Book of Deuteronomy probably took shape in the seventh century BCE, was influential in the reforms of King Josiah, and received its present shape during or immediately following the exile (587- 539 BCE)."[36] According to Chilkuri Vasantha Rao, the Deuteronomic Code was written down in the 7th century BCE. However, he strongly feels that the Deuteronomic Code 'had its own pre-history, beginning at an earlier time, such as at the time of Hezekiah's reform. It underwent a gradual growth in successive periods, revising and contextualizing from earlier periods of history'.[37]

---

33 Manley, 70.

34 Gnuse, 14.

35 A. C. Welch, *The Code of Deuteronomy: A New Theory of Its Origin* (London: 1924), 3-8. Other scholars like H. Gressmann and A. Bentzen supports this view.

36 Denise Lardner Carmody, *Biblical Woman: Contemporary Reflection on Scriptural Texts* (New York: Crossroad, 1992), 22.

37 Rao, 16-17. Rao quotes Otto by stating that the Deuteronomic Code had a great impact of the Assyrian rule. Rao expresses that 'the Deuteronomic Code is a product of a common climate of literature. It was a time of renaissance throughout Ancient West Asia. Assurbanipal of Assyria showed special interest in collecting and copying ancient texts and writing new ones. This was also seen in Egypt. The reformation can be seen also in the reign of Hezekiah and Josiah' [Rao, 17. C.f. E. Otto, "Deuteronomium," *RGG* 2 (1999): 693-696.]

Among the scholars there is a large variety of hypotheses regarding the date of the work. It has been argued that the date of the Deuteronomic Code was from the time of Moses to Post-exilic period. The probable date can be fixed to 7th century BCE. During seventh century the issue of justice was given prime importance by the prophets. The ethical and moral principles were given utmost importance. The extended forms can be seen both in the Decalogue (Deut. 5:1-17 cf. Exod.20:1-17) and other laws.

Holiness Code

There are different views among the scholars concerning the date of Holiness code. The evangelical scholars like G. Archer, R. K. Harrison and others strongly argue for Mosaic authorship, whereas critical scholars like P. Cross, Vink and others argue for exilic and postexilic period.

Martin Noth concedes that the directions for Jubilee and restoration of the land to its owner are of the era, when Israel settled in Canaan, and concludes that it reached its present form in the exile[38]. According to James Limburg, the Holiness Code in Leviticus 17-26 appears to have taken shape during the 6th century, though many ancient cultic and civil laws are found in this Code.[39] For Roland De Vaux, the definitive form of Holiness Code was though drawn after the exile; however, it has very old elements. The Laws in 17-26 come from the period of monarchy.[40] Chilkuri Vasantha Rao argues that the Holiness Code was compiled during the time of the exile. During this period, priestly writing too was shaped.[41]

38 Martin Noth, *Leviticus* (Philadelphia: Westminster Press, 1965), 184-185.

39 James Limburg, "Human Rights in the Old Testament," *Concillium* (1979): 24.Lalfakzuala, *Human Rights in Deuteronomy: A Sociological Approach* (Delhi: ISPCK, 2004), 43. The other scholar who argues for sixth century BCE is P. Cross. For more reading on the origin of the book of Leviticus, refer John E. Hartley, "Leviticus," in *Word Biblical Commentary*, ed. John D. W. Watts (Texas: Word Books, 1992), xxxv-xliii.

40 Roland De Vaux, *The Bible and the Ancient near East*, trans. Damian Mchugh (New York: Doubleday& Company, 1971), 47.

41 Rao, 20-21. For Rao, 'the Priestly writer took the Holiness Code, redacted and incorporated it into his own composition, thus supporting his own theological stance…' (Rao, 21).

For Frank H. Gorman Jr, the contents in the book of the Leviticus belong to the priestly traditions located in the Babylonian exile, in the 6th century BCE. The Holiness code has a variety of genres focusing on holiness.[42]

Scholars generally agree that the Holiness code came to its present position during exile (6th century BCE). However, it has materials of earlier period.

There is no consensus among the scholars concerning the dating of the Codes. In the author's understanding, lot of developments took place in the legal codes, and the claim for one particular period for the whole Israelite Law Code is questionable and unreasonable. Each law code had its own history. It covers a long history of transmission. The oral form (a tradition that affirms on Yahweh's command/revelation to Moses) was augmented by the Israelite community through the centuries as per the changing social and political scenario. The Israelite society had a shift from tribal to monarchy; monarchy to divisions; kingship to high priest; and an independent and equally powerful nation to a nation under exile. These shift perhaps resulted in a modification in the codes. Hence, we may presume that the legal codes of Israel are of different origins and time.

The Covenant Code though took its initial shape in thirteenth/twelfth century BCE; it reached its final shape in 8th century BCE. Lot of changes and development took place during ninth and eighth century BCE. Assyria got revived under the rule of Assurnasirpal (883-859 BCE) and won victory during the reign of Shalmaneser III (858-824 BCE). However, between 783 and 745 BCE, Assyria became weak. In the latter part of eighth century, Assyria once again became strong under the rule of Tiglath-Pileser III (745-727 BCE). Egypt as a nation was weak both in 9th century and first half of the eighth century. Both Israel and Judah were at their best during the first half of the eighth century BCE under the reigns of Jeroboam II

42 Frank H. Gorman, "Divine Presence and Community: A Commentary on the Book of Leviticus," in *International Theological Commentary*, ed. Fredrick Carlson Holmgren and George A. F. Knight (Edinburgh: The Handsel Press Ltd, 1997), 2.

in Israel (786-746 BCE) and Uzziah of Judah (787-736 BCE)[43], the period when Assyrian empire was weak. They probably would have taken advantage of an enfeebled imperial control and made necessary amendments in their practices.

Eighth century BCE was a period when both Israel and Judah underwent great socio-political changes due to the presence of the colonial powers like Assyria and Babylon. On the one hand, both Israel and Judah were marching forward to a higher position in terms of economy, whereas on the other hand, the Assyrian king was moving forward to conquer other nations. Israel and Judah tried to compete, perhaps to mimick[44] the ideologies, politics and cultures of the colonial powers. It was a time when Israel and Judah reached in their Zenith both politically and economically. However, the religious and ethical/moral decay can be seen during this period. Land accumulation, extraction of taxes, building projects, enhancing military power, trades and commerce and various other practices of a colonial nation entered in the life of Israel and Judah. According to Premnath, the Israelite state got shifted from an agrarian economy to a market economy.[45] As a result, a great gap in economic terms was created between the rich and the poor, for which the prophets like Isaiah, Amos and Hosea attacked the ruling classes. The prophets denounced the upper classes represented by the landlords, officials, military men and merchants for drifting away from the way of

---

43 During the reign of Uzziah and Jeroboam, the life of Israel and Judah entered a prosperous period both politically and economically. They tackled their hostile neighbors. Trade in particular flourished. Foreign practices and customs got influxed in the life of Israel and Judah. C.f. Moshe Pearlman Teddy Kollek, *Jerusalem, Sacred City of Mankind: A History of Forty Centuries* (London: Weidenfeld and Nicolson, 1968), 57-58.

44 Israel as a nation perhaps got influenced by the impact of the Colonial power resulting into mimitizing the ideologies of the colonial power [Homi K Bhabha, "Of Mimicry and Men: The Ambivalence of Colonial Discourse," in *The Location of Culture* (London: 1994), 85-92; Homi K Bhabha, "Of Mimicry and Man: The Ambivalence of Colonial Discourse," in *Postcolonialisms: An Anthology of Cultural Theory and Criticism*, ed. Gaurav Desai and Supriya Nair (New Jersey: 2005), 125-133.]

45 D. N. Premnath, *Eighth Century Prophets: A Social Analysis* (St. Louis: Chalice Press, 2003), 20-42.

Yahweh and corrupting the judicial system.[46] They condemned the materialistic aspect, which was a threat both to religious and ethical values. Injustice was meted out by the powerful towards the weaker sections of the society. In order to increase wealth, perhaps laws were misused and altered, which in turn benefited the elite, thereby they could exploit the marginalized group. These characterizations of colonialism not only entered into the socio-political and religious life of Israel and Judah but also in their legal system. Hence, the Covenant Code, which can be located in this period, was not in favor of the weaker sections of the community, especially the women.

The Deuteronomic Code though had its own pre-history came to its final shape during seventh century BCE. This was the period, when reformation and renaissance took place throughout Ancient West Asia. The practice of collecting older writings and creating new set of laws took place throughout Ancient West Asia. Assurbanipal of Assyria (669-630 BCE) took keen interest to bring new laws by collecting and copying the ancient texts. Almost in parallel Hezekiah (716-687 BCE) and Josiah (640-609 BCE), kings of Judah took drastic steps to reform the life of Judah. The Deuteronomic Code underwent a radical revision. Its main reason was to improve the legal, social, economic and political situation of Israel and Judah, and also to restore freedom and equality.[47] Moreover, during this period, the Assyrian empire started deteriorating due to internal political dissension and problems[48] and became weak. Perhaps, Josiah, the reformer of Judah took advantage of the prevailing situation and tried to get rid of the Assyrian influence and step forward resulting to a new awakening in the life of the people that was marginalized by the powerful group within and outside Judah. This period was marked by a powerful political and religious revival. As a result, the

46 Daniel Jones Muthunayagom, "Globalization, Debt Burden and Debt Slavery: Response from a Biblical Perspective," in *Bible Speaks Today: Essays in Honour of Gnana Robinson*, ed. Daniel Jones Muthunayagom (Delhi: ISPCK, 2000), 123-124.

47 Ibid., 124-125.

48 The conflict between the two sons of Asshurbanipal (Ashuretililani and Shinsharishkun) to achieve the throne resulted in loss of many nations, thereby the empire became weak.

laws in Deuteronomic Code became more humane in nature, where voices of the voiceless were heard and the power of the powerful declined.

The Holiness Code deals with situations that reflect the settled life of Israel in Canaan, for instance ancient cultic and civil laws. It also contains temple, ritualistic worship and priesthood, which comes from the time of King Solomon and his successors. The temple of Solomon which was built in the 10th century was destroyed by Nebuchadnezzar, king of Babylon. It was during the rule of king Cyrus of Persia (539 BCE), the Judahites were encouraged to rebuild the temple. The temple was rebuilt during 520-515 BCE. After rebuilding the temple, the priests gathered together and gave importance to the aspect of 'holiness', which can be seen in the Holiness Code (Lev 17:9; 19:2; 20:7-8, 26; 21:6-8, 15, 23; 22:9, 16, 32).[49] It is generally agreed by almost all modern scholars that the Holiness Code was gradually put together over the centuries and the final form of the Holiness code took place in sixth century BCE. The Priestly writers reinterpreted the legal tradition 'to reinstate the original communitarian and egalitarian values of the Israelite society and to restore peace, joy and socio-economic equality in the Israelite community'.[50] Holiness code unlike the two extreme laws (Covenant and Deuteronomic code) is ambivalent in nature.

Thus, the final shaping of the laws[51] (BC, DC and HC) can be fixed from 8th to 6th century BCE.

---

49 George A. F. Knight, *Leviticus* (Philadelphia: The Westminster Press, 1981), 3-6; Allen P. Ross, *Holiness to the Lord* (Grand Rapids, Michigan: Baker Academic, 2002), 35-36.

50 Muthunayagom, 126.

51 The Covenant Code is the earliest law code followed by the Deuteronomic Code and the Holiness Code. The best example to support for this stance is the laws of Slavery, which will be dealt in detail in the exegetical sections. In Exodus 21:2-11 (BC), freedom is given to the male slave and not to female slave. The period of slavery is seven years. In Deuteronomy 15:12-18 (DC), freedom is given both to the male and female slave and the time frame is seven years. In Leviticus 25:39-46, freedom is given to male slave (Hebrew) and his children. Freedom for Female slave (Hebrew) is not specified (v. 41). The period of freedom specified is Jubilee (50th year). A distinction between Hebrew and non-Hebrew is stated in Holiness Code. The Deuteronomic Code is more

Previous Research

Phyllis Bird[52] sees the subordination of women as the result of patrilineal and patriarchy. She advocates for a reconstruction of traditional historiography. Anderson[53] argues by raising two important questions: Did the laws serve a legal purpose? Can Ancient Israelite society be reconstructed from the Biblical laws? She answers these questions by employing Gender and postmodern Feminist Legal theory. G. I. Emmersion[54] emphasized the subordination of women in the Old Testament and argues that the women played a crucial role in the liberation and progression of Israel, but they were not given due credit like male. Victor Matthews'[55] analyses the law and points out the protective and positive attitude towards women in the Deuteronomic law code. Habel[56] advocates for sociological approach. His argument is to read the text by identifying with the oppressed group. Chirchigno's[57] approach was more of a comparative analysis. The arguments of all these scholars in general are based on patrilineal and patriarchal ideology. They brought out the discrepancy in the

---

humane in nature, whereas the Holiness Code falls in between Covenant Code and Deuteronomic Code. Another example to support this view is 'eating meat' (Exod 22: 30[31]; Deut 14:21; Lev 17:15; c.f. Deut 12:16, 23, 24, 27). For detail on reading of 'eating meat' refer Rao, 38-39.

52 Phyllis Bird, "The Place of Women in the Israelite Cultus," in *Ancient Israelite Religion*, Miller Patrick (ed.), Philadelphia: Fortress Press, 1987, 397-419.

53 Cheryl B. Anderson. *Women, Ideology and Violence: Critical Theory and the Construction of the Gender in the Book of the Covenant and the Deuteronomic Law*. London: T& T Clark, 2004.

54 G. I. Emmerson, "Women in Ancient Israel." In *The World of Ancient Israel: Sociological, Anthropological and Political Perspectives,* R. E. Clement (ed.), Cambridge: Cambridge University Press, 1989, 371-394.

55 Victor H. Matthews, Bernard M. Levinson, and Tikva Frymer-Kensky. *Gender and Law in the Hebrew Bible and the Ancient Near East*. Sheffield: Sheffield Academic Press, 1998.

56 N. C. Habel. "The Future of Social Justice Researching the Hebrew Scriptures: Questions of Authority and Relevance." In *Old Testament Interpretation: Past, Present and Future,* London: T & T Clark, 1995, 277-291.

57 Gregory C. Chirichigno. *Debt-Slavery in Israel and the Ancient Near East*, Journal for the Study of the Old Testament Supplement Series 141. Sheffield: Sheffield Academic Press, 1993.

law codes and expressed their reservation against domination both in class and gender. Many other scholars also contributed immensely on Israelite law system such as Bernard Levinson (Levinson argues for revision and interpolation).The issues raised by all these scholars and their contributions are immensely helpful to locate the reasons behind the degradation of the weaker sections in the society which includes slaves and women.

The issue before us is to find out whether the female subordination was exclusively due to patriarchal ideology or it has a colonial dimension also. As per the author's knowledge and readings, it seems there is not an exclusive work related to Israelite Law system in a Postcolonial Womanist approach. The purpose of this book is (i) to examine in detail the role of the tradition/s and the socio-historical factors behind the formation of the Israelite legal system, (ii) to find out whether the present Israelite legal system had any influence from Ancient West Asia like Nuzi text, Code of Hammurabi, Laws of Eshnunna, Middle Assyrian laws, Hittite Laws , and (iii) whether there is any power play (Colonial interest) within and out of Israel in shaping/formation of the Israelite legal system, which affected the weaker sections of the society especially women.

The methodology applied in each of the previous work and the issues addressed will definitely contribute in our research work.

Methodology and Structure

The method employed for this work is postcolonial womanist approach[58], which is a combination of postcolonial and womanist approach.

Apart from introduction and conclusion, the whole work is divided into six chapters. The first chapter is on the contextual methods of reading the Bible with particular emphasis on postcolonial womanist reading.

The second chapter focuses on the position of women in Ancient West Asian laws. In this chapter, the importance of Ancient West Asian laws, the Ancient West Asian empires and the laws related to women is explored.

---

58 Postcolonial Womanist approach will be dealt in detail in the first chapter 'Contextual Methods of reading the Bible'.

The third, fourth and fifth chapter, which is the center of the work, is an exegetical study of the Deuteronomic, the Holiness and the Covenant Code with a postcolonial womanist perspective. The author attempted to bring out how the position of the Covenant Code differs from the Deuteronomic and the Holiness Code.

The sixth chapter is an evaluation of the work. In this chapter, the author brought out the observations and the findings.

The general conclusion highlights the summary of the whole book.

Aim of the Work

The aim of the book is to identify the origin and development of the Biblical law system and to explore whether it was influenced by AWA legal system. It will also unearth the role of the dominant tradition's (Judahite and Priestly) role in the final shaping of the Israelite legal system and how it affected the weaker sections of the society especially women. The author will also examine whether the subjugation of women has to with land and its productivity. The task therefore is to reread the legal texts that affirm the right to independence and freedom and to explicate how the postcolonial womanist readings of the laws can contribute and promote to a better society.

As mentioned earlier, the approach employed will be a combination of two approaches: Postcolonial and womanist, as it will reconfigure both postcolonial and womanist studies. The reason for applying both of these approaches is due to the fact that womanist approach deals with identity issues and postcolonial approach will go further to it, i.e., why woman are treated in an inferior way. Is there any hidden agenda behind the degradation? This approach will be dealt briefly in the second chapter 'Contextual Methods of Reading the Bible with particular emphasis on Postcolonial Womanist Reading.'

The book will be on the position of women in the Pentateuchal laws with special reference to the book of the Covenant code. The author in the exegetical sections will initially bring out the position of women in the Deuteronomic and Holiness code and will attempt to investigate how the position of women in the Book of the Covenant Code differs from that of the other two codes. Hence, for this work selected texts from the Book of Exodus, Leviticus and Deuteronomy will be taken into account.The selected passages are: Exod 20:8-10, 17; 21:2-11, 21:22-27; 22:16-17; and 23:12,17; Lev 12,15:16-31,19:20-22,29; 20:10-14, 17-21; and 25:39-46; Deut 15:12-18; 16:11-14; 20:10-14; 21:10-14; 22:13-29; 24:1-4; and 25:5-10.

Contents

Chapter 1

Contextual Methods of Reading the Bible

The purpose of this chapter is to present and analyze the various contextual methods employed in reading the Bible. The author strongly argues that each method has its own merits and demerits. The traditional theories and methods are helpful to understand the meaning behind the text but failed to address the contextual issues such as gender discrimination. The contextual methods address both the text and the context. The postcolonial womanist approach goes even further to locate the reasons behind the female subordination.

Methodological Survey: Past and Present

The rationale behind this chapter is to have an overall understanding of various contextual methods which have contributed immensely in the field of Biblical Studies. For decades, historical critical method dominated the field of Biblical studies where the author and historical background was given importance. However, in last few decades we could see a radical shift. The advent of approaches such as literary, structuralism, post-structuralism, postmodernism and postcolonial approaches challenged the historical critical method. All the above mentioned method played its role and contributed immensely based on the need of the hour. A clear shift can be seen from author centered approach to reader centered approach. The reader and his/her understanding of the text is what matters. The debate for decades are between the 'author and the text' and 'the readers who handle the text'.

The Query of Methods in Reading the Bible

Hermeneutics and Exegesis

Hermeneutics and exegesis complement each other within the task of interpretation. Exegesis brings out the meaning out of a text and hermeneutics in the most general terms can be described as the art of understanding and in narrower sense, a method to interpret the written texts.[59] In exegesis, we focus on the meaning of the text and try to find out its significance for its authors and their hearers. In a sense, we try to discover the objective meaning of the text. In hermeneutics we are not neglecting the objective meaning of the text but emphasize its significance and its relevance in our life and context.[60]

The author strongly advocates for the need of both hermeneutics and exegesis. The Bible unlike other religious books underwent various types of attack[61] right from its inception. The Scripture was misinterpreted, misquoted, and misrepresented or misused. For some, Old Testament is a book of failure, a book of miscarriage and so on. Some even consider that without knowing Old Testament, New Testament can be addressed to our community. A Chinese Christian in the use of the Old Testament states that "Reading the

---

59 Bernard C. Lategan, "Hermeneutics," in *The Anchor Bible Dictionary*, ed. David Noel Freedman (New York: Doubleday, 1997), 149. In theology, Hermeneutics is usually used in contrast to Exegesis. The former is a theory and the latter is the practice of interpretation.

60 J. Goldingay, "Hermeneutics," in *Dictionary of the Old Testament Pentateuch*, ed. T. Desmond Alexander and David W. Baker (Secunderabad: OM Authentic Books, 2003), 387.

61 Different heretical teachings and doctrines emerged from second and third century CE. It continued throughout the ages.

Old Testament is like eating a large crab; it turns out to be mostly shell, with very little meat in it".[62] Indian Christian theologian P. Chenchiah felt that it was not necessary to hold the Old Testament as an integral part of the Christian message. He was not convinced with the fact that Jesus was the fulfillment of the Old Testament. He was not in favor of the view that one needs to know the Old Testament in order to understand the new.[63] Why such a view is seen in and around the world particularly in the theological field? How can we reduce the misunderstanding among the so called critics? Which is the best possible method/s to bring the text closer to the reader?

If we go back into the history, from 18th century onwards, lot of shifts took place in the biblical field. Two different approaches prevailed for a longer period of time and even now they have been adopted and employed in the theological circle. They are synchronic and diachronic approach. Textual analysis was highly placed. A series of articles were published where text was examined closely and thereby related to the context. But now, changes can be seen where context is given more importance and text is used as a supporting tool, i.e., from context to text. The question before us is: Which is the right and best hermeneutical approach to make the text relevant to the present readers? What is the role of exegetical and hermeneutical studies?

The exegetical and hermeneutical study was given importance throughout the ages. It is the need of the hour because the scriptures are indistinctly understood in our Churches. The text was used and misused by the dominant group/colonial world for ages. Now, the situation is changing. The marginalized and silenced group took up the challenge to read the text in their context. And since the context of the contemporary world is changing, the interpretation of the Old Testament must be employed and needs to be adapted to the changing context of the interpreter.[64] In this section, the researcher will make an attempt to bring out some of the methodological

62 Cited by R. S. Sugirtharajah, *The Bible and Empire: Postcolonial Explorations* (Cambridge: Cambridge University Press, 2005), 145.

63 Ibid., 162.

64 Daniel Jones Muthunayagom, "Contemporary Approaches to Old Testament Interpretation," in *Interweaving Methodology and Praxis- Exploring Disciplinary*

approaches adopted in the past and present to interpret the Old Testament passages.

Differing Theories and Methods in Reading the Bible

The basic debate in hermeneutical circle is: Who can decide the meaning of the text? Is it the author, or the text, or the reader? If author, how we can discern his/her mind in order to know the real sense/logic of the text? If text, the question will be, can a text alone convey its meaning, if so, how? If a reader, whether the understanding of the text is important or the context in which he or she lives? There are few main theories[65], which will help us to know the nature of the text such as philosophical theories, literary theories, and linguistic theories.

I. Different Theories of Reading the Bible

The main three theories for reading a text are Philosophical, literary, and linguistic theories. The different methods employed in the theological studies can be placed in one of these theories. Each theory has placed a major role in identifying the nature and significance of the text.

A. Philosophical Theories

The Philosophical theories for decades have influenced in understanding the meaning of the text. Scholars such as Friedrich Schleiermacher, H. G. Gadamer, Paul Ricoeur and others have contributed a significant role in modern understanding of literature and its interpretation. This theory will uncover the thoughts, ideas and expressions of the author and seek to locate the meaning behind the text.

Options in Today's World, ed. Indukuri John Mohan Razu (Bangalore: BTESSC/SATHRI, 2007), 171.

65 Though there are scholars who provide us a space for other theories like postcolonialism, the researcher strongly feels that almost all other theories including postcolonial can be understood based on the theories mentioned. The Postcolonial theory has resemblance with philosophical, linguistic and literary theories.

(i) Friedrich Schleiermacher

Schleiermacher has done most distinctive contributions in the field of Hermeneutics. He is known as the 'father of modern Hermeneutics.' He is the one who formulated a clear hermeneutical goal, the aim of re-living and re-thinking the minds of an author. He saw hermeneutics as the problem of human understanding. He placed hermeneutics in the context of theories of knowledge. Based on the theories of knowledge, his query was not how an assumed understanding had been arrived rather what are the conditions under which human understanding could take place. He stresses a role of creative processes within the human mind within the process of understanding.[66] He writes:

> Understanding a text always involves two moments: to understand what is said in the context of the language with its possibilities and to understand it as a fact in the thinking of the speaker. These two hermeneutical tasks are completely equal, and it would be incorrect to label grammatical interpretation the 'lower' and psychological interpretation as the 'higher' task.[67]

Schleiermacher raised a few questions which contributed further in the field of hermeneutics: Can we interpret the meaning of the texts purely with reference to their language-situation and language –world out of which the text arose, or purely with the author who produced the text or does the meaning reside in the inter-relation or inter-action between both? Is rational reflection the only hermeneutical tool to understand the text?

(ii) Hans Georg Gadamer

Hans Georg Gadamer, a student of Husserl and Heidegger has contributed immensely in the field of hermeneutics since 1960s.

---

66 Anthony C. Thiselton, *New Horizons in Hermeneutics* (Grand Rapids, Michigan: Zondervan Publishing House, 1992), 204-206.

67 F. D. E. Schleiermacher, *Hermeneutics: The Handwritten Manuscripts,* 98-99 cited by Ibid., 206.Thiselton describes in length on Scheiermacher's understanding of Hermeneutics, 204-232.

His contribution involves in the interpretation of biblical texts. His work is also on the issue of the role of method in hermeneutics. His approach not only constitutes a point of transition towards a new paradigm of hermeneutical theory but also it places him firmly on the boundary line between modern and post-modern thought. As a result, he is recognized as the pivotal figure between modern and postmodern paradigms of thinking. His hermeneutical approach is 'ontological', i.e., all reality is hermeneutical. On one hand, 'Truth' comes to be only in their actualization as 'performance'. On the other hand, where there is no method, there remains a part to be played by human judgment. In the unveiling of truth, the interpreter may admit the reality. The first part is post-modern and the second is traditional.[68] His position is when we are not applying rule; Judgment and wisdom need to be employed. The concept of truth is basic to Gadamer's Philosophical hermeneutics.

The questions before us are: In the context of historical pluralism, how can we bring out truth? How can we bring out or recover the meaning of the text? Gadamer accepts the problem of historical pluralism and recognizes the reality of the historical construction world of the past. His position is that 'practical reason' may be advanced. He emphasizes the fact that 'the work belongs to our world, and therefore reading is not merely a past historical activity but a present conception of meaning. His suggestion for solution is dialogue, judgment and inter-subjective 'enculturalization'. For him dialogue is a vehicle out of which truth may surface.'[69] In the issue of recovering meaning, he argues that two factors are essential- the horizon of the text and the horizon of the reader. The dialectic of these two horizons produces meaning, which he calls 'the fusion of horizon'[70], and it is possible through dialogue and judgment.

---

68 Joel C. Weinsheimer, *Gadamer's Hermeneutics: A Reading of 'Truth and Method'* (New Haven: Yale University Press, 1985), 108. C.f. Craig G. Bartholomew, "Postmodernity and Biblical Interpretation," in *Dictionary for Theological Interpretation of the Bible*, ed. Kevin J. Vanhoozer (Grand Rapids, Michigan: Baker Academic, 2005), 601-602.

69 Thiselton, 315-317.

70 Hans-Georg Gadamer, *Truth and Method* (London: Sheed and Ward, 1981), 273-274.

Besides the problem of historical pluralism, Gadamer gave due importance to language as it too constitutes a hermeneutical problem. For him, 'our understanding is restricted by the boundaries of our language. Language provides positive hermeneutical conditions for understanding. Language is "where 'I" and world meet" and gives hermeneutics an ontological turn. Hence, it has a universal dimension.'[71]

(iii) Paul Ricoeur

In post-Gadamerian hermeneutics, the text is treated as an independent body free from the author.

Paul Ricoeur's understanding of the text is different from Schleiermacher's and Gadamer's position. He argues that the text is autonomous with respect to the intention of the author. In other words, what the text signifies no longer coincides with what the author meant.[72] He asserts: "The reader is absent from the act of writing; the writer is absent from the act of reading. The text thus produces a double eclipse of the reader and the writer. It thereby replaces the relation of dialogue, which directly connects the voice of one to the hearing of the other". [73] His approach gives due importance to the text as it stands, rather than to the issue what lies behind the text.

Ricoeur seeks to bring together the two major areas of hermeneutics: explanation and understanding. His hermeneutics is to bring out the importance of both explanation and understanding in the context of human subjectivity, as humankind is fundamentally finite and deeply fallible yet able to reach 'beyond'. He argues that explanation alone can be reductive and understanding alone remains defenseless. A sound hermeneutics must and should remain as a metacritical discipline, which embodies both the unmasking function of explanation and the creative function of understanding.[74]

---

71 Thiselton, 322-323.

72 Paul Ricoeur, *Hermenuetics and the Human Sciences* (Cambridge: Cambridge University Press, 1981), 139.

73 Ibid., 147.

74 Thiselton, 344. Explanation is critical and understanding functions at a post-critical level. Explanation entails the willingness to expose and to abolish idols which are merely projections of human will (Scientific knowledge)

Ricoeur's hermeneutical approach disagrees with Gadamer's approach. Gadamer argues for the historical nature of understanding. In contrast to Gadamer, Ricoeur seeks to bring together explanation and understanding. For Ricoeur explanation alongside understanding are the two key axes of hermeneutical enquiry. Gadamer elaborately rejected *explanation* which he described it as *method.* His position is to choose between truth and method, for which he advocates truth. Ricoeur argues for a dialectical relationship between explanation (method) and understanding (truth).[75]

B. Literary Theories

Most modern Biblical scholars are influenced and have brought up various arguments in favor of literary theories. M. H. Abrams[76] in his classic work *The Mirror and the Lamp* classifies different schools of literary theory namely *mimetic, pragmatic, expressive and objective* theories. Though his work mainly deals with romantic poetry in English poetry and literature, biblical interpreters are influenced by his writings. Abrams introduces his work with an introductory chapter called 'The Orientation of critical theories' in which he provides a fourfold points which is a model for a critical theory. They are (1) work; (2) the artist who made it; (3) its subject matter, i.e., universe and (4) its audience. In this, the work is the centre and the other three are radiating from it.[77] He classifies literary theories into four major critical theories, which are important in the history of criticism.

---

and understanding helps to listen with openness to symbols and to indirect language (participatory apprehension).

75 Ibid., 348.

76 M. H. Abrams, *The Mirror and the Lamp: Romantic Theory and the Critical Tradition* (New York: OUP, 1953), 3-29. C.f. John Barton, "Classifying Biblical Criticism," *JSOT* 29 (1984): 19-35.

77 Barton: 20.

(i) Mimetic Theory

The oldest critical theory takes the 'universe' as its crucial coordinate, which is known as mimetic theory. This theory treats literary art[78] 'as essentially an imitation of aspects of the Universe.' In this theory any work is evaluated in terms of truth or accuracy of its imitation or representation.[79]

(ii) Pragmatic Theory

This theory, which concentrates on the audience, relates the aim of the artist and the character of the work to the nature, the needs and the springs of pleasure in the audience.[80] In this theory, the literary art is judged by its success in persuading its readers. This theory is a dominant theory.

(iii) Expressive Theory

It is an author centered theory, where a literary art is essentially the internal expression of an author and are his/her perceptions, thoughts and feelings.[81] In this theory, the importance given is the success of art in communicating the feeling of the artist/author. Here, we enter into the author's experience and reconstruct it in ourselves.[82]

(iv) Objective Theory

It is a text centered approach, where it regards the work of art in isolation from all external points of reference and analyzes it as a self-sufficient unit constituted by its parts in their internal relations, and sets out to judge it solely by criteria inherent to its own mode of being.[83] Here, the interest is centered on the work itself, i.e., text, where neither author nor reader exercises any control or command.

---

78 Art is defined as imitation, an imitation of the external world. The imitation should be a primary concern of the artist cf. Ibid.: 21.

79 Abrams, 8.

80 Ibid., 20-21.

81 Ibid., 26.

82 Barton: 22.

83 Abrams, 26. This theory is more concerned with the internal relations within a text rather than with its relation to the author, reader or the external world.

If we observe all present methods of biblical interpretation, each method falls in line with any one of the above mentioned four categories.

C. Linguistic Theories

Linguistic theories have played a major contributory role in reading the Biblical texts. These theories explain how language works in a given text. Good numbers of scholars have played a major role in the development of these hermeneutical theories. The prominent among those are Jacques Derrida and Ferdinand de Saussure.

The two major methods that sprang out are Structuralism and Deconstruction method. Hermeneutically, structuralism focuses on the deep structure in a given literary work whereas deconstruction is a reaction to the structuralism's claim that meaning lies in the structure of the text.

(i) Structuralism

Ferdinand de Saussure advocated for structuralism. The structuralism is more interested in analyzing the art or structure in the biblical text rather than giving importance in investigating the documents that lie behind the biblical text. Instead of seeking the meaning of a text by asking what its author meant by, it read texts as they stand. The structure which is used by structuralists does not refer to the internal structure but rather the structure which is applied from outside the text such as semantic, linguistic, narrative and mythical. The meaning of a text is derived from the language itself. This approach unlike philosophical theories and literal theories is centered entirely on structure. It attempts to uncover the linguistic structures of the text. It will also help in checking the critical method's tendency to split the text into different layers such as original text, later additions etc.[84]

---

84 Joseph Abraham, "Re-Reading the Old Testament: A Study of Feminist Readings of Genesis 1-3," (UK: Coventry University through Wycliffe Hall Oxford, 1996), 17-18. C.f. Barton: 28-29.

(ii) Deconstruction

Deconstruction, a critical analysis was developed as a reaction to structuralism. It also involves a critique of western philosophy. The proponent of this method is an Algerian born French Philosopher Jacques Derrida (1930-2004). He derived the term 'deconstruction' from Heidegger's *Destruktion*. The word *Destruktion* means not destruction rather 'destructuring that dismantles the structural layers...'[85] According to this approach there is no determinate or purely 'ideal' meaning in any text. It advocates that every text is divided against itself or deconstructs itself, resulting in multiple meanings and so it is not possible to obtain any original meaning from any text. There is not a dominant meaning in a text; instead meaning in a text is determined in its difference from other texts.[86] Reading differs from one culture to another and from one person to another. It will be actualized in different ways by different readers and different cultures.

a. Derrida and Deconstruction

For Derrida, Deconstruction is not a method. It is a strategy of critical analysis. Unlike other methods or theories, it cannot be defined with a clear set of objectives. He questioned the truth claims of Western philosophy.[87]

In connection with the meaning of a text, Derrida argues that 'the process of making meaning is structured in terms of how signs differ from other signs: a thing is defined in relation to what it is not. The meaning is always perpetually deferred across a spatial and temporal axis, so that a final point of stable meaning and knowledge is never reached in any signifying system'.[88]

---

85 Craig G. Bartholomew, "Deconstruction," in *Dictionary for Theological Interpretations of the Bible*, ed. Kevin J. Vanhoozer (Grand Rapids, Michigan: Baker Academic, 2005), 163.

86 Abraham,19.

87 Stephen Morton, *Gayatri Chakravorty Spivak* (London and New York: Routledge, 2003), 26.

88 Ibid. Derrida coined a word 'Difference' from the French verb 'Differer' to point out that meaning is unstable and subjected to change. The word *difference* means 'to differ', 'to defer' and also 'to supplement'. For him signs differ from

Hence, for Derrida, texts defer meaning depending on the reader's socio-religious-cultural-political location. The meaning of texts never comes to an end due to differing standpoints in relation to the contexts.

b. Paul de Man and Deconstruction

Along with Derrida, Paul de Man is one of the prominent advocates for deconstructive postmodernism during 1960s and 1970s. For de Man 'the meaning of a literary text is not stable or transparent, but is radically indeterminate, hence always open to further questioning'.[89] He further argues that 'the texts contain blind spots which always and inevitably lead to errors and misreading'.[90]

c. Postcolonialism: Is it a theory?

Postcolonialism is not a separate theory like philosophical, linguistic and literary theories, rather a theoretical structure within which we can analyze and figure out the past and the ongoing bequest of colonialism.

The pertinent questions to be addressed are: Is Postcolonialism an aftermath of Colonialism? How is it unique to other methods?

Postcolonialism must not be seen exclusively as a viewpoint born due to colonial forces. For Loomba "In the term 'postcolonialism' 'post' is not merely a sequential prefix or polarity, but suggests a theoretical standpoint set at a distance from the phenomenon of colonialism, giving a wholesome view of all factors involved. It does not seek to divide events into the colonial past and the non-colonial present, but seeks to look at the 'subordinating and the subjectivity

---

other signs, it is incomplete within itself and always needs additional terms to complete it.

89 Ibid., 4.

90 Ibid.

discourses and practices."[91] For Bhabha, the term 'Post' points to the very act of going 'beyond'.[92]

Postcolonialism confronts classical historical methodology that looks at historical events and processes as clean, clear, linear progressions. Postcolonialism may also be mistaken to be a distinct theory like the above mentioned theories, but in reality it occupies spaces in a vast number of disciplines ranging from literary criticism to ethnography. Postcolonialism is heterogeneous in nature, involving all these fields and interlinking them, creating a diverse and fluid body of work. [93]

Postcolonialism seeks to expose the created body of theory and practice and the systematic knowledge about the Orient which seems to affect the subjectivity and consciousness of the East, Asia which includes India. Postcolonial theory confronts the unchallenged centrality of European consciousness which appears to define, construct and imagine other cultures, other people and other events.[94]

---

91 Ania Loomba, *Colonialism/Postcolonialism* (New York: Routledge, 2007), 12. For Laura Chrisman, 'Postcolonialism is the analysis of the phenomenon of imperialism and its aftermath: Slavery, Colonialism, nationalism, independence and migration'. Laura in her writings brought two views on colonial encounters. The Materialistic and Deconstructionist scholars expressed their respective out views. For Materialistic postcolonial scholars, 'Colonialism is a territorial expression of politic-economic expansion', whose goal is 'domination, appropriation and exploitation'. Here the colonizer and the colonized are antagonistic in relationship. The Deconstructionist understands colonialism as a 'cultural, epistemological, or psychological condition'. They regard the antagonistic relationship between the colonized and the colonizer, i.e., Fanon's 'mancheanism' as a 'binary opposition' which requires a break up. Hence, for them 'the colonial dynamics is ambivalent, indeterminate or negotiated' [Laura Chrisman, "Postcolonial Studies," in *New Dictionary of the History of Ideas*, ed. Maryanne Cline Horowitz (London: Gale Cengage Learning, 2005), 1857-1858.]

92 Bhabha, 4.

93 George Oommen, *A Historian's Interaction with Postcolonialism and Subaltern Theories, UTC, Bangalore, 2004, 1 (1-12).*

94 Ibid., 2.

II. Different Contextual Methods of Reading the Bible

For more than two centuries, biblical interpretation was mainly focused and based on historical-critical approach as they tried to interpret and understand the text with the help of historical background, the context in which it came into existence, and moreover the background and intention of the author. However, for the last few decades this method is losing ground with the emergence of new approaches. Historical critical method, which grew out of a Euro-centric culture, which dominated the theological field for centuries and still occupies a prominent place particularly in the west, is not enough for Indian context as it seldom speaks to the actual needs of the community. It is a past enlightenment resulted western thought and does not justify the Indian values and concerns. However, this method is employed as it helps out in bringing out the meaning of the text in its final form. This method will complement the new methods and lead to perfection. This method should be used in order to identify the socio-historical setting of the given text.

A. Contextual Methods

The untold plights of the marginalized and weaker section and their ongoing struggle by the so called hierarchical system have forced them to have their own voice resulting into the emergence of different movements (Subaltern, Dalit, feminist, womanist). For them, through the rereading of the Bible, the past becomes alive and can illumine the present with new possibilities, thereby resulting in personal and social transformation.

The historical critical method which dominated the theological field for more than two centuries is shifted to contextual approaches which can be addressed or known as people's approach. The reason for a shift is due to the fact that the historical questions raised by this method may be too limiting for people in other contexts. The understanding of western culture is different from Asian cultures. So, a western historical criticism cannot be and should not be taken as universally binding and valid. David J. A. Clines notes this shift as a shift from author to text to reader.[95] The fundamental hermeneutical

95 D. J. A. Clines, *What Does Eve Do to Help? And Other Readerly Questions to the Old Testament* (Sheffield: JSOT Press, 1990), 9-10.

question is where the meaning lies in a literary work? Is it with the mind of the author, text or the reader? The answers to these questions can be known on one's understanding of the nature of the text and one's own reading process. This will help us to know the insights of other cultures and thereby broaden our understanding.

(i) Subaltern Reading[96]

In the second half of the 20th century, there has been a powerful and unswerving resistance from the people of the voiceless group to redefine the elitist historiography which was written by the so called influential groups. Subsequently the writings became a people centered one.[97] This approach is the voice of the people who belongs to the subordinate social groups. It is a hermeneutics from below. It refers to a situation of inferior rank. It emerges from out of the lowly, inferiorly or marginally placed situation of any group in society. [98] They refute, reject or disown all the religious interpretation of the dominant groups and bring out the picture and words of forced marginalization and powerlessness. This approach re-reads and re-interprets the events which have been written from an elitistic perspective. Hence, this study is an effort to hear/listen to the people and their voices which were silenced by the colonial and

---

96 The term 'Subaltern' was coined by the Italian political theorist (Marxist) Antonio Gramsci (1891-1937). The term 'subaltern' generally means subordinate social groups. R. Guha has contributed richly in the area of Subaltern studies. For him, the colonist, nationalist and Marxist historiography ignored the importance and contribution of the peasants and tribals in South Asia. Spivak focuses primarily on the experiences of the subaltern women whose voices and social locations were ignored by both the colonial and the elite social groups. She points out that the active involvements of women against British colonialism were ignored to keep the male dominant. For further readings refer Gayatri Chakravorty Spivak, "Postcolonial Theory and Literature," in *New Dictionary of the History of Ideas*, ed. Maryanne Cline Horowitz (London: Gale Cengage Learning, 2005), 1863.

97 C. I. David Joy, "The Social and Religious Origins of the Gospel of Mark and Its Hermeneutical Implications: A Post-Colonial Critique," *Bangalore Theological Forum* 33, no. 1 (2001): 11-12.

98 Felix Wilfred, "Towards a Subaltern Hermeneutics: Beyond the Contemporary Polarities in the Interpretation of Religious Tradition," *Jeeva Dhara* 26, no. 151 (1996): 46.

dominant groups. It enables them to converse in their own language, the language of remonstration, resistance and repudiation. It has commonality with Postcolonial approach which will be discussed later.

The prominent people who advocated for subaltern readings are the Italian Marxist thinker Antonio Gramsci, Gayatri Chakravorty Spivak and Ranajit Guha. Gramsci employed the term 'subaltern' primarily for the oppressed rural peasant group in South Italy. The rural peasant groups were disposed to the ruling groups and their ideas and culture. He also used this term interchangeably with 'subordinate' and the 'non-hegemonic groups or classes'. [99] Both Guha and Spivak went beyond Gramsci's class ideology and opted for class, caste and gender. Both of them questioned and attacked the National Independence movement and the Western critical theory adopted by the Indian historians. Spivak raised a crucial question: Why Indian nationalism failed to represent the majority of India's population? Her argument is based on the contribution of the Subaltern groups to Mahatma Gandhi in the policy of resistance against the British colonial rule. It was the subaltern groups and not merely the small educated middle class who joined Gandhi to resist the British colonial rule. She advocated rewriting history from below, as the subaltern resistance to colonial rule and oppression are unrecorded in the records of official history.[100] Spivak also questioned the rationale behind the adoption of Western critical theory and Western Marxist model. For her, the Western Marxist model will not help to recover and address the complex histories of the Subaltern especially the resistance made by the Subalterns.[101] She also argued that 'the everyday lives of many Third world women are so complex and unsystematic that they cannot be known or represented by the vocabularies of western critical theory'.[102] She also went further to say that the lives and struggles of the 'Third World' women will be 'silenced and restricted within the technical vocabulary of the

99 Antonio Gramsci, *Selection from Prison Notebooks*, trans. Quintin Hoare and Geoffrey Nowell Smith (London: Lawrence and Wishart, 1978), xiv.

100 Morton, 6.

101 Ibid., 7.

102 Ibid.

Western critical theory'. [103] She also questioned the classic Marxist approach which overlooked the lives and struggles of the third world women. Similarly, Ranajit Guha, the Subaltern Studies historian questioned the national independence movement. For him, the small groups of educated middle-class men dominated and controlled the political and economic realm giving no benefit whatsoever to the rural peasant laborers.[104]

The Subaltern reading advocates writing history from below as they strongly feels that the histories of the rural peasantry, working class, and women were documented first by the British colonial powers and then rewritten by the elite social groups to meet their terms and interest.

(ii) Feminist Reading

Women are deprived of all rights and are considered as an epitaph of suffering. Her position in the society is inferior to men socially, economically, psychologically, physically and religiously. In light of these, feminist movement emerged. In 1882, Hubertine Auclert coined the term 'feminism' to address the struggle of women to gain political rights in a male dominated society.[105]

The term 'feminist' is commonly used today to address those who take initiatives to remove women's subordination and marginalization.[106] Feminist approach starts from women's experience of life, especially their experience of subjugation by men. Feminists consider women equal to men intellectually, morally and spiritually. They reexamine the biblical text and strongly feel that the scriptures were manipulated to justify male headship upon women, and thus suggest that the interpretation of the scriptures has been affected by patriarchalism.[107] They used various tools to dismantle

---

103 Ibid.

104 Ibid., 6-7.

105 Anne M. Clifford, *Introducing Feminist Theology* (New York: Orbis Books, 2001), 11.

106 Elisabeth Schussler Fiorenza, "Feminist Hermeneutics," in *Anchor Bible Dictionary*, ed. David Noel Freedman (New York: Doubleday, 1992), 783-784.

107 Goldingay, 392.

the male prejudiced text and one among those is the hermeneutics of suspicion. Using this method they critiqued many traditional claims regarding the Bible and its androcentric bias.

The 'root experience' of feminism is women's realization that cultural common sense, dominant perspective, scientific theories, and historical knowledge are androcentric, and therefore not objective, but ideological. [108] In protest of this ideological construction, there arose the feminist movement. However, it must be noted that, the feminists were concerned with the white women, and were not bothered about the black women and women of other color, and did not consider them in their category.

Feminist Movement

There are three waves[109] of feminism:

First Wave of Feminism

In the first wave of feminism, the issues raised by feminists are anti-slavery and political rights. The proponents of this wave are Elizabeth Cady Stanton (1815-1902), Lucretia Mott (1793-1880) and Susan B. Anthony (1820-1906). This movement declined due to Second World War.

Second Wave of Feminism

In 1960s a drastic change took place among the women, especially in Western Europe and United States. During this time, majority of the spokeswomen were well-educated, white middle class women, who failed to acknowledge the experiences of women of color.

Third Wave of Feminism

The women of color have been critical to the white feminists for universalizing their experience and thereby ignoring the experiences unique to them. It was the period during which the black female was considered as mere chattel, a thing or an animal. So, in late 1970s a new development took place, which drew attention to difference in

---

108 Fiorenza, 783-784.

109 Clifford, 11-25; bell hooks, *Ain't I a Woman: Black Woman and Feminism* (Boston: South End Press, 1981), 159.

race and social class of women. This wave is called as the Third-world Feminism.

According to womanist theologian Delores William, the main three things that the white women used in their methods, which were a thorn and barrier for the black women to associate with the white women, are their theory, argument and the privilege. Since the black people could not attend the white university, there was no way to disclaim the researcher's theories about life in black community. They never did anything about the poverty and suffering they witnessed. The white merely composed theories.[110] So, the question raised by the blacks is, whose liberation does feminist theory serve? The white consider that they are having some kind of privileges, which the blacks have not. And because of the racist attitude of many white feminists, black women have generally been forced to the realization that they need their own brand, based on their voices and experiences. This thinking resulted into Womanist movement.

(iii) Womanist Reading

During the Third Wave of feminism, as mentioned earlier, the white women considered the women of color as chattel and creatures unworthy, and the black women were dehumanized. In this context of racial discrimination emerged the Womanist[111] movement. The word 'Womanism' was coined by Alice Walker, the Afro-American author in her book 'In search of our Mother's Garden: Womanist prose". She used the word to describe the perspective and experience of 'women of color'.

For Walker, to be womanist, is to be independent, in charge and grown up, above all, determined to be her own woman-person, to be her own mouthpiece, and to speak her mind.[112] The womanist

---

110 Delores S. Williams, "Womanist-Feminist Dialogue: Problems and Possibilities," *Journal of Feminist Studies in Religion* 9, no. 2 (1993): 68-71.

111 The word 'Womanist' is a word play on the popular folk term 'womanish'. It means a young woman who displays self-assertive or willful behavior, judged unsuitable for black women because of the place society has assigned to them (Clifford, 25.).

112 Alice Walker, "To the Editors of Ms Magazine," in *Search of Our Mothers' Gardens* (New York: Harcourt Brace Jovanovick, 1983), 352.

does not depend on or allow white women or men of any race to rule and govern, or control her life. She is self-determined and capable of thinking, speaking, and acting for herself whenever she deems it necessary.

Alice walker describes 'Womanism' as the specificity of black feminism and contrasts it to what she sees as an ethnocentric and separatist white feminism.[113] Womanist are all those who consider women as women and fight and stand for their right cause. The author strongly advocates for womanist as opposed to feminist, because the issues like color and class are a significant part of our life and society. This movement unlike feminist are concerned with and committed to the survival of entire people, whether it is male, female and of every race and ethnicity.

While feminist scholarship gives importance in detecting the androcentric language and patriarchal contextualization of male stream theory and biblical interpretation, womanist addresses the issue of linguistic sexism and their interpretation are four-fold, i.e., gender, race, class and language. The best text to support their methodological position is Hagar-Sarah episode found in Genesis 16 and 21.

B. Reader's Response Method

The field of biblical interpretation has shifted from author centered historical critical methods to the text centered literary critical methods to the reader centered approach (readers and to reading communities). Earlier the author and the text were given importance but the trend is shifted. The present trend is reader oriented approach. The reader is the one who is more active and can interpret the text in a more meaningful way. According to Anthony C. Thiselton,

> Reader –response theories call attention to the active role of communities of readers in constructing what counts for them as 'what the text means'.[114]

---

113 Sonya Andermahr, *A Glossary of Feminist Theory* (New York: Oxford University Press, 2000), 289.

114 Thiselton, 515.

The reader is the one who looks at the texts not merely as collections of meaning which he/she inertly takes in. For Mulloor, 'The text is a catalog to meaning which must be actively and dynamically evoked, construed and articulated through the process of reading, through the reader's resources. This approach is a summons to Semantic realization through the interaction by the reader.'[115] So, the text does not have any determinant meaning at all, but the meaning is created and determined by the readers who read the text.

In Reader response method, there are radical theory and moderate one. The radical theory emphasizes that the reader can create meaning and determines the interpretation. Stanley Fish is a radical theorist. For Fish 'The idea that meaning resides *in* the text or that texts exercise control over the interpretation is an illusion.'[116] The reader can determine the meaning. Moderate theory falls 'in between the claim that a text means only one thing and the claim that a text can mean anything'.[117] The former theory is problematic, as it can pose a threat of the text being misused and the latter a challenging one as it creates space for the 'Others'.

The positive point and the advantage of the reader's response method is the open ended affair. The reader is having the freedom to read, interpret and apply the text to his or her context. The reader is active. As a result, the text and context is taken into consideration with a dialogue or interaction. This interaction will help to locate the socio-cultural factors that played a dominant role against the will of a true liberating God.

C. Postcolonial Reading

Before defining Postcolonialism and its importance in Biblical studies, a brief section on postcolonialist triads will be highlighted. The progenitors of the postcolonial theory are Edward Said[118],

---

115 Mulloor: 349.

116 Robin Parry, "Reader-Response Criticism," in *Dictionary for Theological Interpretation of the Bible*, ed. Kevin J. Vanhoozer (Grand Rapids, Michigan: Baker Academic, 2005), 659.

117 Ibid.

118 Edward W. Said, *Orientalism* (Penguin: Harmondsworth, 1985).

Gayatri Chakravorty Spivak[119] and Homi Bhabha[120]. Robert J. C. Young refers to them as the 'Holy Trinity' of Postcolonial theory.[121]

(i) Edward Said

Edward W. Said (1935-2003) who is regarded and recognized as the icon of the postcolonial theory and whose master piece work 'Orientalism' made an entry of Postcolonial Studies in Europe and United States,was born in Jerusalem. He had his education at Victoria College, Cairo, Mount Hermon school, Massachusetts, and at Princeton and Harvard Universities.

a. Said and Postcolonialism

For Said, the understanding of the word 'post' in Postcolonialism is unique. For him, the prefix 'post' in postcolonialism suggests not so much a 'sense of going beyond but rather continuities and discontinuities'.[122] Said's two mind-blowing and ground-breaking works are '*Orientalism*' (1978) and '*Culture and Imperialism*' (1993). Culture and Imperialism was mainly to address the criticism leveled on his *magnum opus* work '*Orientalism*'. In his masterpiece of work '*Orientalism*', Said drew much of his inspiration from the work of Michel Foucault and Antonio Gramsci's idea of the relationship and close connection between knowledge and power.

---

119 Gayatri Chakravorty Spivak, *In Other Worlds: Essays in Cultural Politics* (New York: Routledge, 1988); Gayatri Chakravorty Spivak, *The Postcolonial Critic: Interviews, Strategies, Dialogues*, ed. Sarah Harasym (New York: Routledge, 1990); Gayatri Chakravorty Spivak, *Outside in the Teaching Machine* (New York: Routledge, 1993); Gayatri Chakravorty Spivak, *A Critique of Postcolonial Reason: Toward a History of the Vanishing Present* (Cambridge: Harvard University Press, 1999).

120 Bhabha, *The Location of Culture.*

121 David Huddart, *Homi K. Bhabha* (London and New York: Routledge, 2006), 150-151.

122 Stuart Sim, *The Routledge Critical Dictionary of Post Modern Thought* (New York: Routledge, 1999), 354.

b. Said and Orientalism[123]

'Orientalism' is a study of Western discourses[124] about the 'Orient'/East, i.e., western conceptions of the East. 'Orientalism' is one of the fundamental concepts of the postcolonial theory. As mentioned earlier, the chief argument of Said in his work 'Orientalism' is based on Foucault and Gramsci's views of the 'relationship between 'knowledge[125] and power'. For him, 'the relationship between the Occident and the Orient is that of power, dominion and of varying degrees of a complex hegemony'[126]. His argument is based on the stand that the West can discern the East/Orient, for which he made

---

123 The *Orientalists* are the Europeans who dominated the Eastern/Asian civilization and culture. They considered themselves as superior to Orientals. Though their interest was political, it was the culture that prompted them to act dynamically, i.e., culture along with political, economic and military rationales. *Orientalism* is a western approach for dominating, restructuring, and having authority over the Orient, i.e., the European knowledge about the western representations of the Orient, which was tactfully created to have power over them. They had control and dominated the Orient in all aspects, i.e., 'politically, socially, militarily, ideologically, logically, scientifically and imaginatively during the post-enlightenment period'. The power of knowledge was used to colonize the minds, bodies and space of the colonized. It is also a 'distribution of geopolitical awareness into aesthetic, scholarly, economic, sociological, historical, and philological texts'. Hence, it is a political and cultural truth. The word *Orient* is the peoples of the colonies where Europe dominated and had control for decades. It is the place of Europe's greatest and richest colonies and is an integral part of European material civilization and culture. Because of Orientalism, the Orients were marginalized, i.e., 'they never spoke of themselves and can never represent their emotions, presence or history'. The West determines what can be said about the Orient. They spoke and represented on their behalf. They considered the Orient as inferior. The relationships between the West and Orient were mainly of 'power, domination and hegemony'. The decades long material investment made them to have a strong hold upon the Orient (Said, *Orientalism*, 1-28).

124 Western or Orientalist discourses legitimize the colonial aggression, political and cultural supremacy of the Western world over the Eastern world.

125 Knowledge means 'surveying a civilization from its origins to its prime to its decline', i.e., their race, character, culture, society, traditions, history etc and having such knowledge indicates 'domination and authority'. Such knowledge gives power (Said, *Orientalism*, 32-42).

126 Edward W. Said, *Orientalism* (New York: Vintage Books, 1978), 5.

a stinging critique. The European's understanding of the Orient is not merely of knowledge about Orient, rather cultural and political. For him, the Orient/East is the self-evaluation of the Occident/West, i.e., the Orient is evaluated based on the viewpoint of Eurocentrism. The reason for such an evaluation is based on their thinking that the Orient cannot represent itself and hence they have to speak and act on their behalf. They portray the East as symbol of backwardness and profligacy.[127]

Said, in the first chapter of his book "Orientalism" states that there are two principal factors in the relation between the East/Orient and the West/Occident, which had been existing since the middle of the 18th century. They are

> Firstly, the growing systematic knowledge in Europe about the Orient, knowledge rein-forced by the colonial encounter as well as by the widespread interest in the alien and unusual, exploited by the developing sciences of ethnology, comparative anatomy, phi-lology, and history; furthermore, to this systematic knowledge was added a sizable body of literature produced by novelists, poets, translators, and gifted travelers. Secondly, the Europe was always in a position of strength....one between a strong and a weak partner.[128]

For Said, the expression 'Orientalism' is a mindset of the West which has two levels: manifest and latent. The former is a conscious act articulated based on the views and opinions concerning the East, and the latter is the unconscious act, i.e., an assumption of the West that the Easterners are backward and decadent.[129] Both in

---

127 Sobhanlal Datta Gupta, "Imperialism and Colonialism: Towards a Postcolonial Understanding " in *History of Science, Philosophy and Culture in Indian Civilization: Science, Technology, Imperialism and War*, ed. D. P. Chattopadhyaya (Delhi: Centre For Studies In Civlizations, 2007), 437. Said has written an extensive description on the relationship between Occident and Orient (Said, *Orientalism*, 1-28.)

128 Said, *Orientalism*, 39-40.

129 Bhabha, *The Location of Culture*, 71-72; Gupta, 437.

conscious and unconscious level, their perception about the East are profligacy.

c. Said's Contribution in Postcolonial studies

Positive Observations[130]

1. Said's contribution in the field of Postcolonialism is par excellence. His approach with regard to the Orient is beyond the traditional understanding of imperialism. For him the colonizers not merely dominated the Orient, but they were the subjects and agents of colonialism as understood traditionally. Furthermore, they had a hidden strategy which was both political and cultural.
2. The method used by the colonialists/subjects in the colonies like census, ethnography, land-settlement reports, development, etc., in the name of science and reason clearly reveals their agenda of having control and authority over the colonies.
3. The colonialists consciously/manifested and unconsciously/latently employed the Orient/East to authenticate their supremacy, in so doing projected the backwardness of the people of the colonies.
4. Said brought out the 'binary oppositions' of superiority and inferiority, solidarity and fragmentation, the rational and irrational, which is at the heart of colonial ideology. For him, Postcolonialism challenges to look at the text to unearth the silent spaces. (Said, 45, 73, and 201).
5. His writings point out a remarkable denunciation on Western racism and their misrepresentation and lack of knowledge towards the East/Orient.

Negative Observations

Though Said's work on Orientalism inaugurated the dawn of a thorough appraisal of colonialism, it also brought criticisms from within the postcolonial tradition itself.

130 Gupta.

The main criticism is that Said's text on 'Orientalism' had many weaknesses and contradictions.

Weaknesses[131]

1. Said brought out strong points to indicate the hidden agenda of the Colonists, but failed to project the resistance, struggles and the challenges of the colonized. He places too much emphasis on the passivity of the Orient but failed to address the response and resistance of the Orient towards Colonialism. The pertinent question here is: If there is no resistance from the side of the colonized, what is the outcome and how the colonized can be freed?
2. Said got inspired by two stalwarts, Gramsci and Foucault. The humanism aspect of Gramsci drove him to relate his own life as a Palestinian exile. This made him to focus on manifest Orientalism, which is a conscious aspect. Foucault's theory inspired him for latent Orientalism, which is an articulation of the idea of unconscious construction of the Orient, i.e., the people of the East are backward. The issue here is as to how we can take both stands as they are opposite trajectories. Said failed to address this issue, hence it is a methodological ambivalence.[132]

---

131 Ibid., 439. Though David Kopf acknowledges the work of Said, he attacks Said for 'adopting a method which is profoundly structural and synchronic and diametrically opposed to history. He strongly feels that Said's analysis is one-sided, as he fails to take into consideration the positive contribution of Oriental discourses such as starting schools, systematized languages, printing press, journals, newspapers and other media of communication. Kopf in his writings brought out the differentiation between modernization and westernization [C.f. Richard King, *Orientalism and the Myth of Modern Hinduism* (New Delhi: Critical Quest, 2008); David Kopf, "Hermeneutics Versus History," *Journal of Asian Studies* 39, no. 3 (1980).]

132 Said in his later work *Culture and Imperialism*, based on the critics of his methodological ambivalence, argues that earlier he was influenced by both Foucault and Gramcsi, but later he found Gramsci's idea more relevant especially in the area of resistance (Gupta, 439-440). Said in *Culture and Imperialism* projected and emphasized the 'alternative history to counterattack the history of the West, Nationalist resistance to recognize the suppressed and

Contradiction

On one hand, Said establishes that the western scholarship and Orientalism had largely facilitated the project of European expansion in the East resulting to progress and development. On the other hand, it is also argued that it is the European conquest of the East which, with the physical discovery of the Orient, generated the interest in Orientalism.[133]

(ii) Gayatri Chakravorty Spivak

Gayatri Chakravorty Spivak, the foremost feminist critics was born in Calcutta, West Bengal on 24 February 1942 during British Colonial rule, and was educated as an undergraduate from Presidency College of the University of Calcutta, as postgraduate at the University of Cornell in the United States and completed her doctoral dissertation on W. B. Yeats (Life and Poetry of Yeats). She has lectured both within and outside of the United States and as Professor of English and Comparative literature at Columbia University, New York.

Spivak's groundbreaking work is the English translation of the French Philosopher Jacques Derrida's *De la grammatologie* (*Of Grammatology*). Besides this, she published series of books and articles. She was critically engaged by the writings of Freud, Marx, Derrida and Foucault. Her work is a combination of Marxism, feminism and deconstruction. She has a command of philosophy, and she challenged the high ground of established philosophical discourse. She is well acquainted in Political Science, Economics and Social theory. [134]

---

marginalized and an indigenous nationalism separating from the fetters of West and their hegemony'.

133 Gupta, 439.

134 Gerald Maclean Donna Landry, ed., *Selected Works of Gayatri Chakravorty Spivak*, The Spivak Reader (New York and London: Routledge, 1996), 2-3. Spivak's work involves 'feminist perspective on deconstruction, the Marxist critique of capital and the international division of labor, the critique of imperialism and colonial discourse, and the critique of race in relation to nationality, ethnicity, the status of the migrant...'. She is well recognized for her stand on subaltern and their issues (c.f. Gerald Maclean, Donna Landry, 3).

Spivak was concerned about the individuals and the social groups (oppressed subject), who have been historically driven out and subjugated both by the colonial powers and the leaders of the anti-colonial national independence movements. To address the cause of these individuals and groups, she proposed the word 'subaltern' as it will accommodate their social identities and struggles.[135]

a. Spivak and Postcolonialism

Spivak,like other postcolonialists such as Edward Said and Homi Bhabha, challenged the Western academia who dominated the marginalized. She was concerned about the subaltern/Marginalia (the new immigrant, the working class, and women) and the international division of labor especially the third world female labor. She also questioned the notion developed by the western world that they are more civilized in comparison to the non-Western world. In her interview on the topic 'Subaltern Talk' (Can the Subaltern Speak?[136]), she strongly claims that the Subaltern can speak but unfortunately they are not heard and unnoticed by both the privileged group of First World and Third World. If they are allowed to speak, their status would change drastically and they would cease to be subalterns.[137] Unfortunately, the voice of the Subaltern is represented by the powerful groups/ representatives, who speak on behalf of the subaltern'.

---

135 Morton, 45-46.

136 In her article 'Can the Subaltern Speak?' Spivak brought out the history of a young, middle-class, Indian woman Bhubaneshwari Bhaduri, a member of a group involved in the armed struggle for Indian Independence. Bhubaneshwari was entrusted with a political assassination, for which she was unable to face. To avoid capture by the British Colonial rulers, she committed suicide in her father's apartment in 1926. Spivak argued that though she was involved as an anti-colonial freedom fighter, her name didn't figure out in the official, male-centered historical records. Bhubaneshwari's voice was unheard. Her struggle was untold and her historical role disenfranchised [Gayatri Chakravorty Spivak, "Can the Subaltern Speak?," in *Marxism and the Interpretation of Culture*, ed. Cary Nelson and Larry Grossberg (Urbana: University of Illinois Press, 1988), 307-308.]

137 Gerald Maclean, Donna Landry, ed., 5-6.

Spivak also criticized both the western feminists and the leaders of the anti-colonial resistance movement who fought for the independence in India. The Western feminists though claim that they speak for all women, but in reality they ignore the Asian and African Women. The leaders of the anti-colonial resistance movement fought against the colonial powers and the unbending class system established under the British Empire, but unnoticed the struggles of lower caste especially the subaltern women.[138]

Spivak strongly argues that the deconstruction is a vital tool for postcolonial studies and can be effectively employed in the milieu of postcolonial thought.

b. Spivak and Deconstruction

Spivak had a significant influence from Jacques Derrida's deconstruction approach. She employed deconstruction as a tool to speak and advocated for the subaltern/margins. For her, deconstruction is a 'powerful political and theoretical tool'.[139] She was both practical and political in her approach. She suggested that a change is possible by representing both politically and by participating. She adopted the two German words: *Vertretung* and *Darstellung*. The former is a political representation and the latter representing yourself/oneself ('proxy and portrait').[140]

Deconstruction does not claim that there was no subject, truth or history but rather questions the privileging of identity. It is persistently looking into how truths are formed. It advocated for examining the processes of truth, which would provide a new way of looking at things.[141] Spivak challenged the identity politics. She was not much convinced of identity or voice, rather interested in creating a space, as she strongly believed that identity or voice can create another form of colonialism and oppressive agent.

Spivak puts forward the feminist activity of the deconstruction of the opposition between the private/margin/outside and public/centre/inside sphere. The political, social, professional, economic

138 Morton, 39-40.

139 Ibid., 4.

140 Donna Landry, ed., 6.

141 Ibid., 6-11.

and intellectual arenas are public, whereas the emotional, sexual and domestic are private. Some practices of religion and arts, though belong to the public, also come under the private sphere. The feminists, since the European eighteenth century, suggest that the public sphere also operates emotionally and sexually. Hence, they advocate for a reversal of the public-private hierarchy.[142] For Spivak 'the deconstruction of the opposition between the private and public is implicit in all and explicit in some feminist activity'.[143] The opposition is not merely reversed, but displaced. Deconstruction questions 'all transcendental idealisms'.[144] Hence, for Spivak, the reverse-displacement binary oppositions are useful for a proper and meaningful reading, especially the feminist reading. This deconstructive point of view would reverse and displace the hierarchies. It will also reduce the gap between the public/centre and the private/margin.

c. Spivaks' contribution to Postcolonialism

Positive Observations

1. Spivak's deconstruction approach is more practical, where she advocates not merely for a reversal, rather to a reversal-displacement approach. This approach will provide a new way of looking at things. It will dismantle the western tradition that justifies their colonialism.
2. Spivak insists on the two fold representation, a political representation (aesthetic representation) and a practical representation (standing for others). She argues for interconnectedness/bonding. This strategy will help to respond and strengthen the subaltern women, whose voices are not heard or recognized within dominant political systems of representation.
3. Spivak, instead of stressing and arguing for identity and voice, prefers for creating a space.

142 Ibid., 30. The public/centre sector is considered masculine and more important than private/margin sector. The feminist movement emphasizes and argues for a reversal. They insist that sexuality and emotion are much more important (30).

143 Ibid.

144 Ibid.

4. Spivak differs from Said and Bhabha by challenging their gender blindness. She gives attention to the lives and struggles of the 'Third World' women.
5. Spivak questions the western feminist movement and stresses that all women are same/equal and due respect must be given irrespective of her race, class, religion and culture.

Negative Observation

Spivak argues that the subaltern cannot speak or resist. She makes her argument based on her stand that the subaltern cannot be heard by the privileged group. If heard, her status as subaltern will cease. It is dangerous to make it as a universal one. There are signs of resistance in the side of the subaltern, though not always. One of the best examples in Indian history and politics is of Bandit queen Phoolan Devi.

Some of her critics are Benita Parry, Bart Moore-Gilbert. Parry argues that Spivak's approach will further silence the disempowered women, as it restricts the space in which the colonized can be written back into history.[145] Moore-Gilbert argues that there are ample evidences in the histories recorded in the colonial discourse, where the subaltern women resisted.[146]

(iii) Homi K. Bhabha

Homi K. Bhabha[147], a cultural theorist and one of the prominent figures in present-day Postcolonial studies was born in 1949 in

---

145 Benita Parry, "Problems in Current Theories of Colonial Discourse," *Oxford Literary Review* 9, no. 1-2 (1987): 39.

146 Bart Moore-Gilbert, *Post-Colonial Theory: Contexts, Practices, Politics* (London: Verso, 1997), 107.

147 Bhabha was greatly influenced by two stalwarts and thinkers. They are Jacques Derrida and Michel Foucault. The core of his reading methods are 'iteration' a term derived by Derrida and 'the statement' from Foucault. Iteration means 'any mark, idea or statement repeated'. If it occurs once, it is meaningless and hollow. It is the processes from which the meaning is derived. It must reappear not only in one particular context and a particular time frame and space, but rather in different contexts, time and space. He locates Derrida's idea of 'iteration' in line with the term 'statement'. For him, meaning of the

Mumbai (formerly known as Bombay) in India. Bhabha in his writings introduced and developed challenging concepts that are vital to postcolonial studies. They are hybridity, mimicry, difference and ambivalence. Broadly, these concepts explain the ways in which the colonized resisted the colonizer.[148]

a. Bhabha and Postcolonialism

Bhabha's thinking and approach differs from other postcolonialists like Said and Spivak. He not only examines colonial history and the role of the colonizer, dominating the colonized but also takes seriously the colonized and their response, and how the colonialism of the past be related to the present situation. He strongly argues that the colonialism is not locked in the history and is still in existence.

Bhabha is interested in Psycho analysis approach[149] and he is an anti-essentialist. He questions and argues against the so-called

---

statement is subjected to change. It can be changed according to the context or based on its function. The statement expressed now can lead to the emergence of a new statement, the other day. Bhabha is not interested to adopt a fixed, pre-arranged and pre-determined position, rather advocates for 'process', i.e., 'ambivalence of the process'. His thinking is both challenging and productive; as he strongly feels that the statement can be transformed or translated, when it is driven into a new context (Bhabha, *Location of Culture*, 22; David Huddart, *Homi K. Bhabha*, 15-18).

148 Huddart, 1. Huddart described briefly on two areas: The 'Stereotype' and 'Mimicry'. The colonizer in stereotype style (i.e. anxious knowledge) projects the laziness or stupidity of the colonized population. Some of the stereotype ways are racist jokes, cinematic images. The problem of stereotype is the presumption of the colonizer to understand and judge the colonized group or individual based on prior knowledge, which is defective. The colonized group retaliates or resists through mimicry. Mimicry is 'an exaggerated copying of language, culture, manners and ideas of the colonizer'. It is 'a form of mockery', which is both 'a resemblance and menace to the colonizer,' thus undermining colonialism and their domination. Hence, mimicry is a strategy of resistance to make the colonizer aware that there is 'no fixed, final, foundational/absolute pre-existent identity' (Huddart, 35-75). C.f. Bhabha, 85-92.

149 Psychoanalysis is the analysis of individuals and this analysis suggests that all identities whether individual or collective are incomplete. It is not possible to have a full or complete identity. Bhabha advocates that the incompleteness is not a problem to be solved and it must be acknowledged (David Huddart, *Homi K. Bhabha*, 9).

traditional philosophy of truth, meaning, self or identity. For him there is no absolute truth and identity, as they all are subjected for a change. He questions the 'unitary identity'. Based on this argument, he brought out the concept 'hybridity'[150], which is 'an anti-monolithic model of cultural exchange which negates the polarity of binary models of culture with elements that are, 'neither the one, nor the *other*'. This concept contrasts the terms and territories of both the colonized and the colonizer.[151] He also directs us not merely to pure cultural interaction, but rather to the borderlines of cultures, which he terms it as *liminal*'[152].

In connection to the relationship of the 'colonizer and colonized', he found Said's argument of 'Orientalism' very helpful, but goes further by pointing out that the distinctive features of 'Colonial/ Western discourse'[153] is 'Colonial mimicry' induced in the mind of the colonized to imitate the Colonizer. The Colonized are placed in the position of Colonizer but with no freedom.This function of

150 Bhabha in his writings *The Location of Culture* (1994) deals clearly on culture and hybridity. Culture/s are not in isolation, rather they are in contact with each other, thus leading to cultural mixedness. Like many literary writers, he is not merely insisting on hybridity, rather on hybridization. For him cultural interaction and identities are not fixed. It is in continual process. For further reading refer David Huddart, *Homi K. Bhabha*, 4-7.

151 Stuart Sim, "Homi K. Bhabha," in *The Routledge Critical Dictionary of Postmodern Thought*, ed. Stuart Sim (New York Routledge, 1999), 201.

152 This term means border or threshold. It brings our attention to in-between cultures or identities, i.e., 'self' and 'other'. For him, this development is central as it brings out the creation of new cultural meaning and also marks the constant process of creating new identities. Both the space and time are involved in the process (David Huddart, *Homi K. Bhabha*, 7). C.f. Bhabha, *Location of Culture*, 44-45.

153 Colonial discourse gives more weightage to colonial power and is dependent on 'the concept of 'fixity' in the ideological construction of otherness' (Bhabha, 66). This discourse divides the world into 'self' and the 'other'. The main reason for such a division is to justify that they are superior both in culture and economic. This discourse fixes individuals or a group in one place, i.e., fixes identity without giving any room for change. Bhabha opposes to fixed identity and realism. There is a sense of ambivalence in colonial discourse. On one hand, the colonizer expresses aggressive form of domination, and on the other hand, they are anxious about the self, which troubles their authority resulting to a split (Huddart, *Homi K. Bhabha*, 36-43). C.f. Bhabha, 70-74.

ambivalence is one of the most discursive and psychical strategies of the colonizer. Despite the visible domination and discriminative power of the colonizer, the colonized hang on to their power to do something.[154] He further suggests that the Colonial discourse only seems to be successful in the domination of the Colonizer over the colonized. The domination is based on the assertion of 'difference', i.e., the Colonizers are superior and the Colonized inferior. However, the Colonizer unconsciously knows that this imaginary difference is destabilized by the real identicalness of the colonized. The unconscious knowledge is disavowed and the identicalness is concurrently accepted and refused. The tension between conscious and unconscious knowledge leads to anxiety.[155] Hence, the colonizer never achieves stability, which becomes advantage to the colonized. Though the Colonizer tries to dominate, in reality, the resistance of the colonized ultimately makes the colonizer anxious and ultimately plagues them to attain the goal of mastery.

b. Bhabha's contribution to Postcolonialism

Positive Observations

1. Bhabha brings out a strong point in favor of colonized people. Though the colonizers dominate the colonized, there is anxiety within them. The reason for anxiety is because of the resistance by the colonized groups. The colonized groups are using the colonizer's conceptions. This writings on 'anxiety' alter the white traditional colonial studies.
2. He brought out the notion of 'hybridity' which strongly points forward that the colonial discourse are intensely ambivalent.
3. There is an interaction between the colonizer and the colonized in the area of cultural identity. He emphasizes on hybridity of cultures, as there is no fixed identity, and he strongly feels that no culture is pure. It is in progress and subjected to change.

154 Bhabha, *The Location of Culture*, 67; Sim, "Homi K. Bhabha," 201.

155 Huddart, 4-6.

4. There is also economic identity, where both groups are depending on each other.

Negative Observations

1. Bhabha unlike Said claims that there was resistance from the colonized population. The pertinent questions then to be addressed are: What was the proportion of resistance? If the resistance is equivalent or near to the amount of domination, then what is the role of a postcolonialist to analyze the colonial discourse or why do we need to have a postcolonial approach?
2. Aijaz Ahmad, a Marxist literary critic known for his criticism on postcolonialism raises a question 'if hybridizing process characterizes or defines postcolonialism... then postcolonialism itself does not really exist since oppositions and restraints continue to govern people's lives'.[156]
3. Bhabha asserts strongly that there is no fixed identity and pure culture as both changes in time and space. But there are understandings that culture/cultures are justifiable and firm. So, the question is how can we make a standard rule to judge a culture? What is the role or importance of context? What is the inner connection between culture and context? Is it possible to bifurcate culture and context?

Summary

The Postcolonial triads have done a major contribution in the field of hermeneutics. Each has played a dominant role. Said's Orientalism, Bhabha's mimicry, resistance and hybridity, and Spivaks's deconstruction, representation and creating space created a new way of looking at history. Each person though had different stands, complemented each other in the issue of 'centre' and 'margin'. Their approach especially resistance and deconstruction can be used as a foundation to read and interpret biblical texts.

---

156 Ibid., 152-153.

Postcolonial and Biblical Studies

The pertinent question needs to be addressed is: What Postcolonial has to do with Biblical Studies?

As mentioned earlier, Postcolonialism[157] is a heterogeneous concept and has a multiplicity of meanings. Hence, it is impossible to describe satisfactorily what its study might entail. It is a paradigm that involves many different disciplines. It has emerged as a critique of and a revolt against the age old dominance of imperialism[158] which had its political and cultural manifestations in history in the form of conquest and colonialism. Postcolonialism is a domineering tool which refuses to take the dominant reading as an uncomplicated representation of the past and advocates for an alternative reading.

157 Colonialism can be understood in a wider way. In general term, it means having domination and hegemony both in the form of political rule and economic control over other nation/s, which also includes cultural supremacy. However, it is not merely something that happens from outside a country; rather it can operate within the collusion of forces inside. It can be duplicated from within. Postcolonialism challenges and revises the dominant by definition of race, culture, language and class in the process of making their voices heard. It engages in few areas, i.e., how it articulates experience, how ideology works, how human subjectivism is formed, and what we might mean by culture. C.f. Nicholas Dirks, "Colonialism," in *New Keywords: A Revised Vocabulary of Culture and Society*, ed. Lawrence Grossberg Tony Bennett, and Meaghan Morris (UK/ USA/ Australia: Blackwell Publishing, 2005), 42; Loomba, 16.

158 Imperialism is sometimes used interchangeably for colonialism. Though it focuses mainly on the economic aspects, i.e., capitalist, however, it also imposes its languages, trade, religions, democracy, and its political rule on foreign nations and lands. The role of the imperialist/colonizers is to erase the memory of its subject/colonized by negating their culture and marginalizing those who sought to participate in and keep alive its traditions. The colonized were marginalized, and those who wished to escape life on the margins and to obtain some advancement in the new world of the foreign empire had to embrace the ideals, values and worldview of the imperialists/conqueror and to repudiate their own culture, languages, values and beliefs [Leo C. Perdue, *Reconstructing Old Testament Theology: After the Collapse of History* (Minneapolis: Fortress Press, 2005), 283.] C.f. Loomba, 16ff., Edward W. Said, *Culture and Imperialism* (New York: Alfred A. Knopf, 1993), 8-14.

It allows silenced and often marginalized people to find their own voices when they are at loggerheads with the dominant readings.[159] The Biblical texts in general, and laws in particular, were misused by a dominant group. The powerful group ill treats the 'others' by justifying their stand. To withstand that oppressive power, many communities of faith used decolonization (Deconstruction[160]) as the tool to dismantle colonist view. It will cross-examine biblical narrative which legitimizes colonial tendencies. Hence, Post colonialism is a process of unmasking and dismantling colonialist power in all its forms, as it brought into being an unequal power structure, especially racial and cultural supremacy.

Postcolonial method can historically analyze historical events and its interpretations using the methodology of either oppositional reading or re-reading, whichever is applicable in a particular situation.[161] So, the post-colonial reading of the Bible is a new way of reading scripture. Its emergence outclassed the imperialistic colonial exegesis.[162]

Postcolonialism is one of the possible approaches for reading the Biblical text in Indian context, as we too were governed and dominated by the colonial powers of the West. This approach will encourage and uplift the sentiments and experiences of the exploited ones. It will decolonize or deconstruct the colonial tendencies in the Bible that have been knowingly or unknowingly used to support colonialism. In the context of the Indian Church in general, and North Indian Church in particular, as she faced many forms of oppression both inside and outside the Church, this approach will play as a powerful instrument for liberating herself from the existing colonial structure. Moreover, this approach has a support of other approaches such as Dalit and subaltern reading. Good number of Postcolonial scholars such as R. S. Sugirtharajah, Simon Samuel and David Joy and Postcolonial feminist scholars such as Musa W.

---

159 Sugirtharajah, 3.

160 Deconstruction tool has been used by several postcolonial writers to develop new understanding of old texts.

161 V. V. Thomas, "Research Methodology: History of Christianity," in *DTh Methodology Seminar* (Bangalore: SATHRI, 2008), 9.

162 Joy: 20.

Dube, Jeffrey L. Staley, and Kwok Pui-lan, supports the postcolonial hermeneutics as it serves, and it is a good method to understand the Asian realities.

Uniqueness of Postcolonial Criticism[163]

1. It challenges the universalizing forms of western interpretation, revealing its co-optation by imperial interests and destabilizing its frames of meaning.
2. It challenges their dominant stand by unveiling the neglected voices and characters in the Bible.
3. It places the Bible within the multi-faith context of Asian world.
4. It provides spaces to those groups who are marginalized by the dominant voices for ages particularly Dalit, women etc.
5. It seeks to examine how the colonizer constructs and justifies the domination of other in various places and periods of history.
6. It advocates knowing and reading the experiences of the exploiter and the exploited, oppressor and the oppressed, and the centers and the margins/periphery politically, economically and culturally.
7. It takes the help of other approaches which stand for the cause of the marginalized group.
8. It gives importance to the problem of identity.

In short, this method will help us to use one's experiences and insights and also includes the experiences and insights of all other peoples to achieve new possibilities for life. It will also bring together, i.e., the culture of the oppressed and liberation, which is possible through dialogue.

163 Kwok Pui-lan, *Introducing Asian Feminist Theology* (Sheffield: Sheffield Academic Press, 2000), 46.

Postcolonial Womanist Reading

The postcolonial womanist approach, though has some common elements like language of gender with womanist approach, it is different from womanist[164] approach.

According to Kwok Pui-lan, the colonizers were often portrayed as the active and masculine while the colonized were seen as passive and feminine.[165] The critics who follow the Postcolonial womanist approach consider themselves not as passive, rather as active and step forward to project new vision of their identities and new methods of reading and interpretation. They use women's marginality as a deconstructive starting point.

The womanist criticism has contributed to reveal the problems arising from language that refers to sexual violence, humiliation against women etc.[166] The failure to respect difference and the constant incorporation of the 'other' into one's own perspective are deeply rooted in the social and cultural matrix of colonialism. Womanism deconstructs the patriarchal approach of male dominance over female; however, they miserably failed to provide tools to examine colonialism, cultural imperialism, religious pluralism and the horizontal violence of women against women.[167]

The postcolonial womanist approach attempts to deconstruct those tendencies created by the womanist and their theologies, as they

---

164 C.f. 34-36. Bell hooks puts forth a demarcation between the women at the center (feminists) and those in margins (Womanists). Feminism emerged from privileged women who love to be at the center and also live at the center, whose perspectives on reality rarely include the knowledge and awareness of the lives of women and men who live in margin. The women of third world were considered by them as mere chattel, a thing or an animal. This led the Third-world women to raise voices against sexism, racism, classism and casteism. Womanism is not limited to the effects of sexism on women but also considered much of racism, ethnic prejudice, economic classes and the exploitation of human and non-human natures (bell hooks, *Feminist Theology from Margin to Center* (Boston: South End Press, 1984), 41.

165 Pui-lan, 17.

166 Jean K. Kim, "Uncovering Her Wickedness: An Inter (Con) Textual Reading of Revelation 17 from a Postcolonial Feminist Perspective," *JSNT* 73 (1999): 61-62.

167 Pui-lan, 30.

realize that they cannot be gentle and passive, but rather to challenge the past to envision a new future. Moreover, the postcolonial womanist criticism realized that all feminist or womanist interpretation is context bound and hence not applicable to all contexts. This made them to have their own ideology.

Postcolonial womanist approach questions the narratives which present the history of the colonized. They not only question the male supremacy but also the diversity among women created by class, ethnicity, region and cultures. They re-examine the colonial and patriarchal interpretations of the Bible and search for liberating elements for their struggles.[168] They realize that both colonizing power and decolonizing power are male, and the strife between the two powers is waged over the territory of the female.[169]

Postcolonial Womanism and its Approaches

Rebecca Chopp[170] distinguishes two approaches based on women's experiences: standpoint theory and social constructionist approach.

Standpoint Theory

This theory argues that women's knowing is ontologically different from men's. People who have suffered due to colonialism will see immediately the fallacy of this romantic view of women's nature because their colonizers have been both male and female.

The Social Constructionist Approach

This approach refuses to universalize women's experience and stresses instead the diversity of experiences as they are shaped by a complex interaction of factors such as class, race, colonialism and sexual orientation. So, a woman's situation in which she lives and her perspective matters. This approach will examine the oppression that exists in political, economic, social and cultural realms.

---

168 Ibid., 38.

169 Kim: 62.

170 Rebecca Chopp, "Eve's Knowing: Feminist's Theology's Resistance to Malestream Epistemological Frameworks," in *Concilium 1996/1: Feminist Theologies in Different Contexts*, ed. Elisabeth Schussler Fiorenza and Mary Shawn Copeland (New York: Orbis Books, 1996), 116-123.

Postcolonial Womanism and Models of Power

Rita Nakashima Brock and Rebera distinguish two major models of power: Power-over-others and Power-with-others. Power-over-others is the power of domination and control which is a colonist color, and power-with-others is based on the inter-connection that exists between all who share in a community. The latter can lead to a partnership within the community of faith.[171] The former can lead to imbalance and the latter will allow freedom for all which will lead to a just society.

Uniqueness of Postcolonial Womanist Approach[172]

1. It examines the Bible from the position of women who are oppressed due to race, class and colonialism and discern the strategies of resistance that have been used in reading colonizing and patriarchalizing text and translations.
2. It examines 'issue of subjectivities and scattered hegemonies composed in and through patriarchies, nations, states, empires, political economy, and (neo) colonialism'.[173]
3. It challenges, dislodges and unravels any simple dualistic picture of the power dynamics behind domination/submission, insider/outsider, powerful/powerless and colonizer/colonized.
4. It investigates how marginalized women are rendered unseen, consigned to signify the 'Other' and denied a voice of their own due to androcentric politics.

---

171 Rita Nakashima Brock and Rebera cited by Pui-lan, 106.

172 Musa W. Dube, *Other Ways of Reading: African Women and the Bible* (Atlanta: Society of Biblical Literature, 2001), 7, 17; Pui-lan, 46, 62; Musa W. Dube and Jeffrey L. Staley, "Descending from and Ascending into Heaven: A Postcolonial Analysis of Travel. Space, and Power in John," in *John and Postcolonialism: Travel, Space and Power* ed. Musa W. Dube and Jeffrey L. Staley (Sheffield: Sheffield Academic Press, 2002), 3.

173 Hyun Sook Kim, "The Politics of Border Crossings: Black, Postcolonial, and Transnational Feminist Perspectives," in *Handbook of Feminist Research: Theory and Praxis,* ed. Sharlene Nagy Hesse-Biber (New Delhi/London: SAGE Publications/Thousand Oaks, 2007), 112.

5. It reconstructs those marginalized women and plots a subversive womanist discourse based on fragments and traces that are still left in the biblical tradition.
6. It seeks to illuminate the everyday lives of ordinary women by challenging the gendered colonialisms.
7. It will help us in developing a fair, gender-neutral and decolonizing reading.
8. It seeks to create a space in which women are empowered against the shackles of patriarchy and imperial oppression at various levels and various forms, and thereby can be involved in creating a world of liberating interdependence, a world of balanced co-existence where all is good, and where none is involved in the exploitation or suppression of others.

Hence, a postcolonial womanist reading insists that the woman should not be treated as inferior because of her gender, as she is also shaped by every credentials which her male counterpart has. She must not be considered as a means for productivity either as a means to boost economy or as a property to meet the selfish ends of men. She must be treated as co-partner in building up the family, society, nation and cosmos. This perspective will help us in providing life-enhancing values and activities which will bring dignity to all human beings. This will open a new window and a 'third eye'[174] for looking at a text as it will unmask the Biblical text from their Colonial ideologies.

174 This term was used by Uma Chakravarti, Feminist Historian, University of Delhi in a key note address in the National conference of "Indian Feminism: Towards New Frontiers" held on 26th August 2010 at Asian Centre for Cross-Cultural Studies, Chennai. For Chakravarti, 'Unless we open our third eye, we cannot see the other two eyes'. The 'third eye' will strip the so-called ideology of Patriarchy, which is an extremely violent structure. For her, 'without looking at class and caste, it's impossible to look at Gender issues'. Hence, dislodging the so-called norms is essential.

Limitations of Postcolonial Reading

Though postcolonial reading is one of the major critical discourses in the field of humanities, it has certain limitations[175]. Some of the limitations are:

a. It lacks a coherent methodology, as there are little consensus regarding its scope, content and relevance. The very word 'post' is defined in different ways. For some it means decolonizing, whereas for others it is 'after colonialism'.
b. Within the postcolonial studies, there are fragments, for which a synthesis is essential. Some of the fragments are poststructuralism, Marxism, indigenous and feminism.
c. Postcolonialism is trapped between the politics of structure and totality on the one hand, and the politics of fragments on the other.
d. There are margins both in the state that faced colonialism and the states not under colonialism.

The postcolonial reading has to address these issues. If not, it will become another method and theory.

Though Postcolonialism has few limitations, still it is one of the best approaches as it addresses the plight and struggles of a major group of people living in the world today. It is an open approach as it accommodates the feminist, womanist and subaltern approach.

A Methodological Proposal

"Every act of Interpretation of the past text should take a lead from and towards the contemporary politico-historical and socio-cultural contexts"[176]

"If scriptural texts have served not only noble causes but also to legitimate war, to nurture anti-Judaism and Misogynism, to justify the exploitation of slavery and to promote colonial dehumanization,

175 C.f. Leela Gandhi, *Postcolonial Theory: A Critical Introduction* (Delhi: Oxford University Press, 1999), 1-7, 167-176.

176 A. Maria Arul Raja, "Dalit Layers of Consciousness in Dialogue with Biblical World," in *Dalit-Tribal Theological Interface: Current Trends in Subaltern Theologies*, ed. James Massey and Shimreingam Shimray (Jorhat, New Delhi: TSC and CDS, 2007), 199.

then Biblical scholarship must take the responsibility not only to interpret Biblical texts in their historical contexts but also to evaluate the construction of their historical worlds and symbolic universes in terms of a religious scale of values"[177]

The author will employ Postcolonial Womanist approach in his research, which is a fusion of Postcolonial and Womanist approach.

We have to pose the following questions in our research. What Postcolonialism has to do with Israelite Law system, i.e., how this method will help in reading the Israelite law System? Is the Israelite Legal Code distributed unevenly between the powerful and the powerless (free and slave, male and female) and between the colonized and the colonizer? Had the Israelite Law system in the locale of colonial powers like Egypt, Assyria and Babylon undergone great socio-political changes which had its influence in her religion which includes her culture and practices? Was the newly created nation Israel influenced by AWA or was forced to adopt their Law system? Was the subjugation of women in Israelite Law system related to land and economy? Was the Israelite law system pro-colonial, anti-colonial or ambivalent in approach?

The following chapters will investigate the Laws in Ancient West Asia and Israel especially women and specifically the role played by dominant cultures and groups (within Israel and outside Israel). An exegetical study would be made on selected passages to explore the position of women. The author would seek to unmask the Biblical text from their patriarchal and Colonial ideologies using inter-textual and deconstruction methods.

177 Elisabeth Schussler Fiorenza, "The Ethics of Biblical Interpretation: De-Centering Biblical Scholarship," *JBL* 107 (1988): 15.

Chapter 2

Status of Women in the Ancient West Asian Laws

Introduction

There are a few countries known as Super powers. They are more powerful than others. They often impose restrictions on developing and underdeveloped nations. As a result, the second and third world nations are forced to support the policies of the super power nations. The United Nation council too is handled and governed by those super nations. Similarly during the time of Old Testament, there were a few nations which were considered powerful nations. They are Egypt, Assyrians, and Babylon. They often made pact or treaty with the weaker nations. The purpose of such treaty was not merely to help and defend the weaker nations in case of war, rather to control and have an upper hand over their functioning. The weaker nations gradually in their course of history got influenced or were forced by the cultures and practices of the powerful nations. Probably Israel, surrounded by these powers was influenced or perhaps mimiticized the cultures and practices of her surrounding nations in order to compete with other nations and to show herself that they too were equally capable and potential.

The culture and practices of Israel were not unique, rather had similarities with her neighboring nations. The laws of Israel are those which have similarities with few differences. Many of the laws of Israel especially the Book of the Covenant Code is similar to the laws of Babylonia, Assyria and Hittites. There are many laws in Exodus 20-23 which are similar to the Code of Hammurabi, Laws of Eshnunna, the Middle Assyrian laws and the Nuzi text.

Importance of Ancient West Asian Laws

Is a study on Ancient West Asian laws imperative? Traditionally, Israelite law[178] is believed to have been spoken directly from God, but the similarities in style and nature make one to rethink whether Israelite law is unique or one within a larger framework.

Modern scholars in general agree that the whole of Ancient West Asian laws including the Israelite law got changed with the passage of time.[179] For W. G. Lambert, "The Old Testament is a collection of diverse texts assembled by a religious community… and laws in general are copied from the earlier into the later. The length of the codes increased with a passage of time. Besides these, the kings also promulgated legal decrees for economic purposes'.[180] The Biblical law can be known in a meaningful way through a thorough reading of non-Israelite laws. Samuel Greengus feels that "many legal practices and problems described in the Bible appear in the non-biblical AWA[181] traditions. While there are, to be sure, cultural differences between these ancient societies, there are also similarities".[182] Based

---

178 Does the law mean the first five book of Moses, Decalogue or the law codes? It appears that the law given by God to Moses was the Decalogue. The law codes as such were an outgrowth, which came to its final shape during Israel's proximity with her neighboring nations (8th-6th century BCE).

179 Refer Introduction chapter.

180 W. G. Lambert, "Ancient near Eastern Studies: Mesopotamia," in *The Oxford Handbook of Biblical Studies*, ed. J. W. Rogerson and Judith M. Lieu (Oxford: Oxford University Press, 2006), 82.

181 Greengus uses 'ANE' instead of 'AWA'.

182 Greengus, 243.

on these opinions, it appears that the law collections in general went for an inner change and appear as a secondary inclusion within larger literary frameworks.

The above view leads us to a possible conclusion that the whole of Ancient West Asian laws including the Israelite ones were not a complete codes of law and were not in isolation, rather were taken or influenced by the earlier laws. The laws in general were not merely a religious one; rather they were created due to socio-economic and political factors.

The Empires and their Supremacy: A Brief History

Assyria and Babylonia, who were the members of the Semitic racial group collectively, encompass Mesopotamia.[183] They were originally comprised of a single group called Akkadians. Akkadian is the language spoken both by Assyria and Babylonia.[184]

The Assyrian and Babylonian empire, which had been shaped and influenced by the fusion of two distinct cultures Semitic[185] and Sumerian culture[186] (particularly from *circa* 2000-612 BCE) made a great impact on the culture of the whole of West Asia in its political, social and religious aspects. Throughout these centuries, there was a period of conflict and also a time of friendship between these two empires. They acquired their dominance by fighting for their own security and well being. The victory over their enemies conferred on them the right to rule over the defeated enemies. The

183 In classical times, Babylon was the southern part and Assyria the northern half of the country. C.f. John C. Miles G. R. Driver, *The Babylonian Laws*, vol. I (Oxford: Clarendon Press, 1960), 1-4.

184 Georges Contenau, *Everyday Life in Babylon and Assyria* (London: Edward Arnold Publishers Ltd, 1955), 3-7.

185 Semitic was patriarchal in nature. The position of women was inferior to man. The woman was considered as the helper and shadow of man. The inferior stage was applied even to the goddess (Rollin Chambliss, *Social Thought: From Hammurabi to Comte* (New York: The Dryden Press, 1954), 35-36.

186 The Sumerian culture was matriarchal in nature, where women were given respectable position and fully recognized. C.f. Ibid., 36-37; S. H. Hooke, *Babylonian and Assyrian Religion* (London: Hutchinson's University Library, 1953), 21.

victory eventually not only gained them security but also profit and prestige.

Imperial Egypt and her Supremacy

The civilization of Egypt was much older than Babylonia and other Ancient West Asian nation. They were in peak stage in the area of art, literature, religion, etc., during Eighteenth dynasty (circa 1546-1319 BCE). During this period, the Egypt rose as a dominant empire extending from upper Nile to the upper Euphrates. This period was known as her golden age. The trade in Asia which was controlled by Babylon was diverted to Egypt. Assyria was in infant stage and Babylonia had no longer any political influence in the West.[187] The Egyptian power started declining after 1150 BCE. The empire which stood tall broke up into small principalities.[188]

The successful rulers during this period were Queen Hatshepsut (circa. 1504-1482 BCE), Thutmose III[189] (circa. 1482-1450 BCE), and Amenhotep III (circa. 1412-1375 BCE).

Egypt,unlike Assyria and Babylon, had no fixed legal codes. The Egyptian king was considered as both god and man. He was conceived of as a divine being actually descending from the gods. Although, he was living among mortals, he remained as an important part of the divine world. When he is dead, he again becomes god. He alone was entitled to communicate with the gods. The king was truly the sole source of authority. All official actions, both in the secular and in the religious sphere were controlled and authorized by the king.[190] Hence, the king was supreme and what he declared was considered as laws. The people were expected to obey the word of the king.

187 Chambliss, 42, 46. During this period the royal coffers were filled with tribute and the rulers exercised power throughout the vast empire which they had conquered.

188 Ibid., 46.

189 Thutmoses III was known as the 'Naploean of Ancient Egypt'.

190 Siegfried Morenz, *Egyptian Religion*, trans. Ann E Keep (London: Methuen & Company Ltd, 1973), 37-40.

Imperial Babylon and her Supremacy

The first dynasty of Babylon was from 1894-1595 BCE. The founder of this dynasty was Sumu-abum from a West Semitic origin. In his fourteen years of rule, he was engaged in strengthening Babylon by fortifications and subjugating neighboring nations through diplomatic or military means.[191]

The successful king among the Babylon was Hammurabi (1792-1750 BCE). He became the sole ruler of Babylonia in 1763 BCE. During his reign, the state was expanded to the Persian Gulf and Elam. The reason behind his success other than his military achievement was his administrative and diplomatic skills. His administrative achievements matched with his military success. He turned many city state including Sumer and Akkad into one kingdom, a centre of an empire. The whole land had one language for administration and business, and one legal system. The policy laid down by Hammurabi with regard to land was practiced throughout the history of Babylonia. His achievements could be seen in the collection of laws (Hammurabi Laws) promulgated by him.[192]

After the reign of Hammurabi, the Babylonian dynasty became weak. The rulers who succeeded Hammurabi were Hammurabi's son Samsu-iluna (1749-1712 BCE), Abi-Eshuh (1711-1684 BCE), Ammi-ditana (1683-1647 BCE), Ammisaduqa (1646-1626 BCE) and Samsu-ditana (1625-1595 BCE). Unlike Hammurabi, these kings were engaged in small scale border campaigns and were more defensive.[193]

---

191 H. W. F. Saggs, *The Greatness That Was Babylon* (New York and Toronto: The New American Library, 1962), 80.

192 Ibid., 81, 86-87. It was even argued that it was king Hammurabi who gave to Babylonia one pantheon, with Marduk, the god of the city of Babylon, as it's head. Though Hammurabi received the credit for unifying the kingdom and brought out the collection of laws, in reality he set out not a new law, rather picked up the laws from the earlier common collection of laws. For instance, the language of laws seen in Code of Hammurabi resembles with the laws written down by Bilalama, king of Eshnunna and Sumerian Laws (G. R. Driver, 6-11, 12-13.)

193 Saggs, 87-88.

Comparing all other legal codes, the code of Hammurabi stands tall as it covers a good number of areas. The policy and legislation laid down and executed by Hammurabi had a lasting influence not only in Babylonia but also throughout Ancient West Asia. For instance, the Hammurabi Code had striking parallels with the Laws of the Old Testament, which will be discussed in the following chapters.

Imperial Assyria and her Supremacy

Assyria made a great impact throughout Ancient West Asia from 1365 BCE when Ashur-uballit I (1365-1330 BCE) came to the throne. The Assyrian dominance over others including Babylonia could be seen under the leadership of Enlil-nirari (1329-1320 BCE), Arik-den-ilu (1319-1308 BCE), Adad-nirari I (1307-1275 BCE), Shalmaneser I (1274-1245 BCE), Tukuti-Ninurta I (1244-1208 BCE), Kashtiliash IV (1242-1235 BCE), Tiglath-Pileser I (1115/1114-1077/1076 BCE), Adad-nirari II (911-891 BCE), Tukulti-Ninurta II (890-884 BCE), Ashur-nasir-pal II (883-859 BCE), Shalmaneser III (858-824 BCE), Shamshi-Adad V (823-811 BCE), Adad- nirari III (810-783 BCE), Shalmaneser IV (782-772 BCE), Ashur-dan III (771-754 BCE), Tiglath-Pileser III (753/744-727 BCE), Sargon II (722/721-705 BCE), Sennacherib (705/704-681 BCE), Esarhaddon (681/680-669 BCE), and Ashurbanipal (669/668-626 BCE). The above mentioned kings not only extended and strengthened their control over the region of Assyria but also went farther into Asia Minor. All the principal trade routes were in Assyrian hands.[194]

The Assyrian empire unlike other nations was known for her military strategy. The king was the supreme head and chief commander. Every male member was obliged to actively involve in military activities. The strategy adopted was threefold: siege warfare, pitched battles, and psychological warfare. The first two requires energy, time and manpower. The third one was more effective and consumed less time. For this, the empire conquered a particular region and allowed the inhabitants to surrender. If they failed to do so, the next step was to surround the capital city and once again offered for surrender. If still they failed to do so, the city would be captured and the Assyrians would do extreme act of cruelty such as

194 Ibid., 96-141.

burning houses, rape, mutilation, slavery etc. This act would be a warning to the inhabitants of other region. If the captured people failed to pay tribute, they were even taken far away from their land in order to lose their identity.[195] This would not only strengthen their colonies but also the economic resources.

Besides political factor, ideological and religious factor motivated the Assyrian king to capture other regions. Being a king and commander of the army, he made an annual military expedition to extend further his regions than those of the king's predecessors. King being the vice-regent of the state god Asshur, carried out his expedition on behalf of the god. And when he conquered a new territory, he projected as if he conquered with the support of the god Asshur.[196]

Hence, the Assyrian empire adopted military strategy over other territories and their key factors, besides political factors, appear as an ideological and religious one.

Summary

The Babylonian and Assyrian supremacy in particular for centuries with few exceptions (threat from Aramean and Uratu) indicates the influence of their culture and religion upon other nations. In order to have control, probably legislations and policies were introduced where vassals were expected to obey. The vassals were compelled to recognize the sovereignty of Assyria. The Assyrian colonists and administrators were placed in each vassal state to execute the policies. Economic and military expansion was the major development during the rule of Assyria.

The interest to dominate surrounding nations was manifold. Greed for flourishing trade was one of the main interests. The wealth acquired from trade placed them in a very strong position. The Assyrian ruler in particular made a successful raid. The culture and politics of domination over 'other' found in each state was a product of powerful empire of each period.

---

195 A Kirk Grayson, "Assyrian Rule of Conquered Territory in Ancient Western Asia," in *Civilizations of the Ancient near East*, ed. Jack M Sasson (Massachusetts: Hendrickson Publishers, 1995), 959-961.

196 Ibid., 962. Refer also pages 963-967.

The Laws in Ancient West Asia

Law played a crucial and key role throughout Ancient West Asia. Throughout Mesopotamia, in case of family, the father and in case of nation/society the male members made all the important decisions. Women were classified lower to man. Each had a different standing in Laws. The man was vested with authority and the woman with purity. The women were supposed to stay at home to take care of children and household activities. They were having the additional responsibility to pray for their family. The wealthy family sent one daughter to a cloister to pray on behalf of the other members of the household. She could marry but could not bear children. She was having the option to give her sister to provide offspring [197]

The rights of woman were nowhere near to man. It was not so in the early Neolithic period. Women had freedom in the early Neolithic period. On one side, law projected protection of women from Patriarchal abuse but on the other side, women were categorized as moveable property. The laws on the one hand restricted the husband on the use of dowries/bride price, on the other hand in case of divorce they were sent back with bride's price with no additional compensation. If husband was found guilty, he had to pay back the bride price, and if wife, either her position as wife would be relegated as a maid servant or drowned (CH §141-§143). In this respect, women were treated similarly to slaves, where they had no voice. The following sections will deal briefly on the position of women in Ancient West Asia, i.e., position of women in their stages of life.

Women and Family in the Ancient West Asia

The family in Ancient West Asia (Assyria, Babylon and Israel) was patriarchal in nature[198]. As the kings ruled the state, so the father

---

197 Marten Stol, "Private Life in Ancient Mesopotamia," in *Civilizations of the Ancient near East*, ed. Jack M. Sasson (Massachusetts: Hendrickson Publishers, 1995), 490-491.

198 The Sumerian had rich culture and language. They instigated a wealth of cultural advances. They invented writing and produced literatures that included law codes. After 2400 BCE, the Akkadians led by Sargon established a Semitic empire. The Semites started migrating to the land of the Sumerians. Gradually, the Semitic culture and language dominated the Sumerians. With every

dominated the household. The father was addressed as the owner of his wife/wives and children. In some state, particularly in Assyria and Palestine, the father was given absolute authority and legal rights. This freedom and rights paved way to treat wives and children as he wished. However, in state like Babylonia, the father had power but within a certain limit.[199] The female folk were treated as property to bear children, and they had to take care of household activities.

The hierarchical order could be seen throughout Ancient West Asia, where the rulers were at the top who dictated the day to day affair of the empire. In family, the male members had authority over his household members. In this hierarchical order, the voice and rights of women were almost minimal. In order to make the hierarchical system more strong, perhaps the legislations were introduced. The legislation to a large extent supported the hierarchical system. Though in superficial readings, the laws might soundlike protecting the weaker sections of the society from the powerful, in reality they were treated as property to be controlled and utilized both in the area of politics and economic boost.

Unfortunately, as mentioned earlier, the whole of Ancient West Asian laws that are available to us are not a complete one and are in fragments. The following sections are based on the available laws, and moreover, only those areas which are useful for the research are addressed here.

---

passing year, the Sumerians were subjected and the Semitic culture became stronger and stronger both ethnically and linguistically. The rich culture and language of the Sumerian slowly deciphered and died out. The Sumerian culture was favorable to all including women. The Semitic culture was headed by the male members of the society. This could be seen throughout their life patterns. The father of the household was the decision maker [Jean Bottero, "The First Semitic Empire," in *Delacorte World History- the near East: The Early Civilizations*, ed. and Elena Cassin Jean Bottero, and Jean Vercoutter (New York: Delacorte Press, 1967), 91-132; Dietz Otto Edzard, "The Early Dynastic Period," in *Delacorte World History-the near East: The Early Civilizations*, ed. Elena Cassin Jean Bottero, and Jean Vercoutter (New York: Delacorte Press, 1967), 52-90.]

199 I. Mendelsohn, "The Family in the Ancient near East," *The Biblical Archaeologist* 11, no. 2 (1948): 24.

The Nuzi Text

Marriage and Dowry

The marriage in Nuzi had contracts known as *tuppi riksi*. The dowry is called as *tirhatu*. It is known as 'marriage by price'. The bride's father declared that he received from his son-in-law bride price amounting to thirty shekels of silver. He also declared 'I have received, I am paid'.[200] This statement clearly indicates that the bride was considered as property to be sold by male members of the society.

The Lipit-Ishtar Law Code

Lipit-Ishtar (1934-1924 BCE) was the fifth ruler of the Dynasty of Isin and the last king of the house of Ishbi-Erra. He was known for his legal enactments. He was referred to as the guardian of the law with the phrase 'when he had established justice in Sumer and Akkad'.[201] The Lipit-Ishtar code begins with a statement that the Sumero-Babylonian deities Anu and Enlil had asked him to bring justice to the Sumerian and the Akkadians. He even mentioned some of his achievements with regard to the welfare of his people. Unfortunately, the available legal text is only 38 laws and that too wholly or in part.[202]

Form and Structure

The laws are casuistic in style (*if* style). It is made up of a collection of legal rules preceded by a prologue and followed by an epilogue,

200 Ibid.: 26-27.

201 Dietz Otto Edzard, "The Third Dynasty of Ur: Its Empire and Its Successor States," in *The Delacorte World History-the near East: The Early Civilizations*, ed. Elena Cassin Jean Bottero, and Jean Vercoutter (New York: Delacorte Press, 1967), 138. It was king Ur-Nammu, who invented a new title 'king of Sumer and Akkad' for his new empire. This expression was coined by him to bring the composite nationality of Babylonia under one single state (c.f. Dietz Otto Edzard, 137).

202 S. N. Kramer, "Lipit-Ishtar Lawcode," in *Ancient near Eastern Texts Relating to the Old Testament*, ed. James B. Pritchard (Princeton: Princeton University Press, 1950), 159.

a structure similar to the Code of Ur-Nammu[203] and the Code of Hammurabi. The text deals with hiring of boats (§§4-5), real estate and orchard (§§7-11), slave (§§12-17), non-payment of taxes (§§18-19), inheritance and marriage (§§20-33), and rented oxen (§§34-37).

Inheritance and Marriage

The laws on inheritance and marriage[204] are comparatively large. It gives due respect to all whether free or slave. The daughters whether priestess or a hierodule shall be treated like an heir (§22). The first wife and her children are given more legal rights than second wife or harlot (§§24, 26, and 28). The children born through second wife like first wife shall divide equally the property of their father (§24). The children born through harlot should be treated as the heir and harlot shall be provided the daily needs (§27).

Women and Dowry

The marriage price was paid by the bridegroom or his father to meet the expenses of the wedding feast known as *ni-mi-usa*. It is an integral part of a legally contracted marriage. This form of practice is different from the Akkadian practice of *terḫatum*. *Terḫatum* is a price paid by the bridegroom for the bride, which is marriage by price.[205]

Based on these laws, we can arrive at a possible conclusion that the law codes of Lipit-Ishtar, the last Sumerian Code unlike the Akkadian code (Code of Hammurabi and Middle Assyrian laws) rightly executed justice to all sections of the society. Women and her children were treated well. The Sumerian Code unlike the Akkadian Code is humane in nature. The judgment for the accused is fines instead of punishment like talion and capital punishment.

---

203 The Code of Ur-Nammu is in fragments. It has prologues, text and epilogue. The texts are in the form of conditional sentences (If......he shall....). The prologue highlights the praise of king for his concern towards justice in the land, which reappears in the Code of Lipit-eshtar, the Code of Hammurabi and other Codes.

204 The laws on inheritance and marriage though comparatively large, has incomplete sentences (§§19, 20, 21, 23, 26, 30, 31, 32, 33).

205 Dietz Otto Edzard, 170

The Laws of Eshnunna

The Laws of Eshnunna, an Akkadian Code dated around 1790 BCE, appeared a century after the Code of Lipit- Ishtar, a Sumerian law. It falls in the period between the fall of the Third dynasty of Ur and the time when it was conquered by Hammurabi, the king of Babylon. It consists of sixtyone laws.[206] In the domain of family laws, it deals with bride price, betrothal, marriage, divorce and slave laws.

The Laws of Eshnunna distinguish three social classes which are similar in line with the Code of Hammurabi: the *awilu* (this group enjoys freedom and full rights both politically and socially); the *mushkenu* (though they are free but subjected to certain limitations) and the *wardu* (they are slaves).[207]

Form and Structure

The Laws are casuistic in style (*If* style). The laws are sixty one in number in which the last two laws are badly mutilated. It deals with the price of daily commodities (§§1-2), hire and wages (§§3-11), thefts (§§12-13), commercial transactions (§§14-16), marriage and dowry (§§ 17-18), loans (§§19-21), slave laws (§§ 22-24), marriage and related laws (§§25-35), property and business (§§ 36-41), assault and theft (§§ 42-50), slave (§§51-52), cattle (§§ 53-57), negligence on the part of the owner (§ 58), and divorce (§59).

Women and Marriage

The law indicates that a man unlike other AWA laws could marry a girl without the consent of her parents, but she would not be considered as a legal wife (§27).[208] However, if he marries with a formal marriage contract, she would be considered as a legal wife (§ 28).

206 Leon Epsztein, *Social Justice in the Ancient near East and the People of the Bible* (London: SCM Press Ltd, 1986), 7-8.

207 Ibid., 8.

208 Hennie J. Marsman, *Women in Ugarit and Israel: Their Social and Religious Position in the Context of the Ancient near East* (Leiden: Brill, 2003), 53.

The Code of Hammurabi

Hammurabi, the king of Babylon was the sixth king of the first dynasty of Babylon who probably would have reigned at the close of the 18th century and the beginning of the 17thcentury BCE (approx. 1792-1750 BCE).[209] The Hammurabi code belongs to the last years of his reign and may be dated around 1690 BCE.[210] It is the best known, most complete, the oldest known code of laws in the world and one of the great classics of Babylonian literature. Hammurabi had not composed an entirely new set of laws, rather would have collected from his predecessors and revised.[211] It contains prologue, epilogue and two hundred and eighty two laws with few incomplete laws (§§65-100). It has striking parallels to the Biblical Laws especially the Book of the Covenant Code (Exodus 21-23).

There are two opinions[212] concerning the origin of the code:

1. The king would have stood before the god *Shamash* (sun god) and received the code from the hands of the deity.
2. The king himself enacted the laws. He turned to the gods only to ask them to give a good reward to those who keep the law and punish those who transgress the law.

If we agree the first opinion, then the code represents a ritual ceremony and was religious, and if second opinion, it inclines more of secular. However, from the introduction and concluding words of the code, it appears that the law did not spring from gods; rather it was Hammurabi who enacted the laws. Perhaps the intention to project him as receiving from the sun god was to make known to the people that the law is divine and he represents god and is ruling by divine right. A careful reading shows that the whole law is conceivably neutral to rituals or religious matter, and is secular in content.

209 The date of the reign of King Hammurabi varies. There are three opinions: 1848-1806, 1792-1750, and 1728-1686 BCE. The general agreement is in favor of 1792-1750 BCE (Refer Epsztein, 9; Chambliss, 19.).

210 Cassuto, 258. The Code of Hammurabi was written in Semitic Babylonian language. Prior to the time of Hammurabi, it was written in Sumerian.

211 Epsztein, 9.

212 Cassuto, 260.

The Hammurabi Law protects the rights of the Babylonian society, especially the free men (*awelum)*, the semi-free men (*mushkenum*), and to some extent the slaves (*wardu*). It deals with property, marriage, inheritance, prescribes fines and penalties for damage.[213] Though at one look, it conveys justice to all, a closer reading reveals that the law prefers the privileged group. The best example is the famous *lex talionis*[214]. If damage was done against the freemen, the punishment for the accused was *lex talionis*, whereas for others (semi-freeman and slaves), the accused had to pay a fine, proportional to the damage. The law made a distinction depending on the position or rank of the individual.

Form and Structure

The Hammurabi Code is casuistic in style, i.e., *if,* followed by a suppositious offence in third person, which is followed by the action/penalty. The style in Hammurabi Code is strictly impersonal. [215] The same form is seen in the Covenant code.

The Hammurabi code like the Code of Ur-Nammu and Lipit-Ishtar code has prologue and epilogue with a series of laws in between. It has a multitier social system in which the citizens were judged as per their status.

The Prologue and Epilogue

The prologue and epilogue is written in the first person, which clearly shows that it was promulgated by King Hammurabi. The

213 G. T. Manley, *The Book of the Law: Studies in the Date of Deuteronomy* (London: The Tyndale Press, 1957), 67.

214 CH §§196-199, §§200-201, and §§203-204: If a man destroys the eye of a man, they shall destroy his eye. If one breaks a man's bone, they shall break his bone. If one destroys the eye of a freeman or break the bone of a freeman, he shall pay one mina of silver. If one destroys the eye of a man's slave, or break a bone of a man's slave, he shall pay one half his prices. If a man knocks out a tooth of a man of his own rank, they shall knock out his tooth. If one knocks out the tooth of a freeman, he shall pay one-third mina of silver. If a man strikes another man of his own rank, he shall pay one mina of silver. If a freeman strikes a freeman, he shall pay 10 shekels of silver (c.f. Exod 21:23f; Lev. 24:20; Deut 19:21) See Percy Handcock, *The Code of Hammurabi* (London: Society for Promoting Christian Knowledge, 1932), 33.

215 Manley, *The Book of the Law: Studies in the Date of Deuteronomy*, 68-69.

prologue begins with the exaltation of Marduk. It also appoints King Hammurabi as a shepherd who will bring justice to the people and the land. In the epilogue, Hammurabi calls god and goddesses to curse those who break the laws.[216]

Both the prologue and epilogue has its own significance. The king when occupies the throne is expected to declare *mēšarum* in the first year of his reign. It was to establish his royal authority over the people and land, to ordain justice and to project himself as an efficient ruler. It is addressed to *Shamash* to demonstrate that the law is divine and the word which he declares is from God and hence to be practiced for successive generation.[217]

This act was not new or unique to Babylonia, rather was practiced in Sumerian culture. This was operative in the earlier law codes of Ur-Nammu and Lipit-Ishtar. The Hebrew kings too practiced during their reigns. If a Hebrew king had executed law and order, he would have been pronounced as the one who has done justice (*hayyāšār*) in the eyes of God, and if not, would be addressed as the one who acted 'in his own eyes'.[218]

This clearly shows that the *mēšarum* act of Babylonia and *yāšār* was not a distinct one, rather an act performed from the earlier period. Each succeeding kings demonstrated it from the previous practices of the kings. Hammurabi took it from the Sumerian practices, and kings of Israel like Asa, Jehoshaphat, and other kings borrowed it from their neighbouring cultures.

Classification of the Laws

The Code of Hammurabi deals with various issues related to individual, women, marriage, family, property, inheritance and society. It deals with cases concerning witches (§§1-2); false witness (§§3-4); reversing a judicial decision(§5); theft (§§6-13); stealing children and slaves (§§14-19); housebreaking and brigandage (§§21-24); stealing a house where fire occurred (§25); duties and privileges of soldiers, constables, and tax-collectors (§§26-

---

216 Michael D. Coogan, *The Old Testament: A Historical and Literary Introduction to the Hebrew Scriptures* (New York/Oxford: Oxford University Press: 2006), 121.

217 D. J. Wiseman, "The Laws of Hammurabi Again," *JSS* 7 (1962): 163, 166.

218 Ibid.: 167.

42); agriculture (§§42-58); horticultural laws (§§59-66); agents and merchants (§§100-107); wine merchants (§§108-111); deposits and distraints (§§112-116); debts (§§117-119); storage of grain (§§120-121); deposits and losses (§§122-126); slandering women (§127); chastity, marriage and divorce (§§128-161); inheritance (§§162-184); adoption (§§185-191); renunciation of sonship (§§192-193); foster-mothers (§194); assault and battery (§§195-214); physicians (§§215-225); branding (§§226-227); responsibility of house-buildings (§§228-233); responsibility of boatman (§§234-239); the collision of ships (§240); cattle (§§241-256); wages of laborers (§§257-258); stealing farming tools (§§259-260); shepherds (§§261-267); wages of animals and men (§§268-277); sales of slaves if void (§§278-281); and renouncing a master (§282).

The Position of Women

The foundation of life was in the family and in the clan with the father as the head. The women were always under the control of male members of the society and they were considered as property. The father determined whom she should be given for marriage. The daughter could be given not only in marriage, but also could be dedicated to some god or given as a concubine. She had no choice. If father dies, her brother/s had the rights to take decision.

Within women, there were different categories. A woman had the highest marital status if she was a wife. She was referred to as first-ranking wife to differentiate her from the handmaid with whom her husband could have children. The wife was followed by concubine who falls in between the maid servant and a wife. Since the concubine was not legally married, her rights were lesser than the wife. The children born out of a concubinage relationship were not considered as legitimate heirs. The status of slave woman was further lower. She was the possession of either her master or her mistress. The sons born from her could be acknowledged and become heirs. If not acknowledged, after the death of father, she and her children should be released (CH §§170-171).[219]

219 Marsman, 123-124. CH §§170-171: If a man's wife bears him children and his maid servant bears him children, and the father during his life time says to

Women and Marriage

The laws regarding marriage is stated in detail (§§127- 184). It deals with the constitution of the marriage, betrothal gift (*biblum*), bride-price (*tirḫâtum*) and dowry (*šeriktum*), matrimonial offences, dissolution of marriage etc.

Though the Babylonian family is basically monogamous in character, there is provisions for a man to have a second wife or concubine while his first wife is still alive (§141, §§144-146, §148).[220] Other than these provisions, he can have slave concubines (§§ 170-171).[221]

---

the children which the maid servant bore him 'my children', and reckon them with the children of his wife, after the father dies the children of the wife and the children of the maid servant shall divide the goods of the father's house equally. The child of the wife shall have the right of choice at the division. But if the father during his lifetime had not said to the children which the maid servant had borne him 'my children', after the father dies, the children of the maid servant shall not share in the goods of the father's house with the children of the wife. The maid servant and her children shall be given their freedom... (c.f. Gen 15:15, 21: 10, 25:6, 27:37, 31:16; Exod 21:10f; Deut 21:16f) See Handcock, 28.

220 CH §141: If the wife of a man who is living in his house sets her face to go out and plays the part of a fool, neglects her house, belittles her husband, they shall call her to account; if her husband says 'I have put her away', he shall let her go. On her departure nothing shall be given to her for her divorce. If her husband says 'I have not put her away', her husband may take another woman. The first woman shall dwell in the house of her husband as a maid servant; CH §§144-146, § 148: If a man takes a wife and that wife gives a maid servant to her husband and she bears children, (after that) if that man sets his face to take a concubine, they shall not allow him. He may not take a concubine. If a man takes a wife and she does not present him with children and he sets his face to take a concubine, that man may take a concubine and take her into his house. That concubine shall not rank with his wife. If a man takes a wife and she gives a maid servant to her husband and that maid servant bears children and afterward would take rank with her mistress, because she has borne children, her mistress may not sell her for money, but she may reduce her to bondage and count her among the maid servants. If a man takes a wife and she becomes afflicted with disease, and if he sets his face to take another, he may marry her. His wife, who is afflicted with disease, he shall not put away... (see Handcock, 24-25.)

221 Mendelsohn: 24.

Marriage was based on a written contract where both bride and bridegroom parties were expected to adhere to the stipulations written down in the contract. The contract was much of a civil affair, where religious sanction was not given importance. A marriage without contract was considered as invalid. The contract has clauses such as the name of the parties, declaration of marriage, *tirḫâtum/ mohar*[222], settlement in case of divorce, oath, name of the witnesses and date.[223]

The decision regarding marriage was taken between the father of the bride and bridegroom. The bride was bought by the bridegroom by giving an amount (*tirḫatum/mohar*)[224] to her father. Other than this, it was customary for the bridegroom to send a betrothal gift (*biblum*) to the bride's father. If the bridegroom changes his mind, he loses the gift and on the other hand, if bride's father changes his mind, he has to pay double the amount (CH §159-§161).[225] In either

222 The amount given as bride price or purchase price is known as *tirhatu* in Babylonia, Assyria and Nuzi. In Old Testament, it is known as *mohar*.

223 Mendelsohn: 25-26.

224 *Tiraḫatum/ mohar* were practiced throughout Ancient West Asia including Israel (Gen 34:12; I Sam 18:25; Exod 22: 5-16). In certain cases, the husband works in his in-Law's house as a price for the girl (Gen 29; Exod 2:21). Sometimes the heroic deeds of a person entitle him to receive the daughter of a king as an award (Josh 15:16; I Sam 18:25). In all these cases, the women were equated with property to be sold or to be owned.

225 Mendelsohn: 28. CH §§159-161: If a man, who has brought a present to the house of his father-in-law and has given the marriage settlement, changes his plans for another woman and says to his father-in-law, 'I will not take your daughter', the father of the daughter shall take to himself whatever was brought to him. If a man brings a present to the house of his father-in-law and gives a marriage settlement, and the father of the daughter says, 'I will not give you my daughter', the father-in-law shall pay back double the amount which was brought to him. If a man brings a present to the house of his father-in-law and gives a marriage settlement, and his friend slanders him; and if his father-in-law says to the claimant of the wife, 'my daughter you shall not have', the father-in-law shall return double the amount which was brought to him, but his friend may not have his wife (Handcock, 26.). In certain cases, the wealthy parents give their daughters with a dowry and female slave/s. The female slaves serve as personal maids to the married woman. In case, the woman fails to bear child, she can have child through her maid. This practice can be seen in the Old Testament (Sarah, Leah, Rachel, and Rebecca).

case, the decision makers are the male and the bride has no right whatsoever. The male members have absolute discretion whether to make or refuse. The bride was placed in between. She was purchased or sold by a price. If groom party fails to stick on to the contract, he loses only the amount he had paid, but if the bride party fails, her father has to pay double the amount. The bride was equated with the purchase of goods.

When the betrothal gift and the bridal gift is received by the bride's father from groom's father[226], both the bride and the bridegroom are inchoately married but reside in her father's house until the marriage is completed. The time when the gift is offered to the time when the bride joins her husband, she remains as inchoate and bridegroom is addressed as 'the owner of the wife' (*bêl aššatim*). The marriage will be considered as complete after marital intercourse takes place. The marital intercourse is regarded as essential to a complete marriage.[227]

After the completion of the marriage, the father of the bride hands over a part of his property to her, this is called 'dowry' (*šeriktum*). She has the right over this property. After her death, it passes over to her sons, and if she has no sons, it will be returned to her father's house. In case of divorce for not having son, she takes *šeriktum* with her. But during her stay with her husband, he will handle the *šeriktum* (§§159-161, §§ 163-164, §167). She has no rights to sell it to others.[228] Though wife had the rights to keep *šeriktum* with her, but it was handled by her husband and later by

226 There is difference of opinion within the Babylonian law. According to §166, the groom's father gives the betrothal gift and the bridal gift to bride's father, whereas in §§159-161, the bridegroom himself offers the betrothal gift and the bridal gift to his future father-in-law (refer G. R. Driver, 249.). The possibility is that in the former case, the groom was a minor and in the latter case he is matured enough to handle his case. In either case the decision makers are male and bride is a property to be transacted.

227 Ibid., 249-250, 322-323. Other than this usual form of marriage, there was a practice where the bridegroom's father gives *tirḫâtum* to intended bride's father and bride being a minor was placed under his control either as a daughter or servant of the house. This type of marriage is called *kallâtu* (daughter-in-law or bride) [see G. R. Driver, 251-252].

228 Ibid., 271-273.

her sons. After her death, it passes to her sons and not to daughters, which shows a clear demarcation between male and female members of a family and society.

Marriage was monogamous for women, whereas men were free to take a secondary wife and concubines and could have children even through slaves. This was legally accepted.[229] A wife though considered higher in position comparing to her son or daughter, her sexuality belonged exclusively to her husband. The society took pride in having a large number of progeny to carry on their family line and also to progress economically. In short, wife was subjected to her husband and society.

The wife was treated as husband's property. He could sell her or force her to work. If the wife transgressed, he could send her away.[230]

In short, women were considered as a property and were purchased[231] by the male members of the society to bear children for her husband which increased his economic position. If a woman fails to produce son, her husband can marry a second time to have a son. In case his wife dies without providing him a son, the amount received by him as a bridal gift can be deducted (§§163-164). It brings out a clear picture that he has deducted the amount based on the expenses of keeping her. Had she provided a son, he would have compensated the amount spent for her. The law of marriage can be seen as a law of sale, where everything depends on profit and performance.

---

229 Alfred Jeremias, *The Old Testament in the Light of the Ancient East: Manual of Biblical Archaeology*, ed. Canon C. H. W. Johns, Theological Translation Library, vol. II (New York: William & Norgate, 1911), 109.

230 Ibid.

231 The word 'purchase' or 'bought' can be seen even in the Old Testament. For instance, Rachel and Leah complained of his father Laban saying 'Is there any portion or inheritance left to us in our father's house?...For he has **sold** us, and he has been using up the money given for us' (Gen 31: 14-15). Similarly prophet Hosea uses the phrase 'I **bought** her for 15 shekels of silver and a homer of barley and a measure of wine' (Hos 3:2). Also refer Ruth 4:10 ('I have also **acquired/purchased** Ruth the Moabite...').

Women and Progeny

Childlessness was considered as a serious problem. All blame for not having children comes upon the woman. If a wife failed to bear children, her husband was permitted to divorce her or else she had to give her maidservant to her husband.[232] The child through her was counted as the wife's child. If the maid servant failed to bear children, the husband was allowed to marry, but the second wife would not have the same status of the first wife. And if the first wife became sick and acquired long-term illness, her husband could take a second wife but he must take care of his first wife. If she refused she could take her dowry and return to her father's house.[233]

Women and Adultery

Adultery was defined as a sexual relationship between a betrothed or married woman and a man not her husband. If a woman were caught because of alleged sexual relationship with a man other than her husband, it is adultery. The punishment for such an act could be even death. But if a man had sexual relationship with a woman other than her wife, he was not termed as adulterer. He would face punishment only if he had relation with a married woman, as the married woman is the husband's property.[234] It clearly shows that there was a dissymmetry in the legal judgment.

According to the Hammurabi code, a woman caught in adultery was tied with her lover and thrown into the water. However, if her husband wants, he can save her life. In such case, the king will save his subject 'the male offender'.[235] It is strange to note that the king spares the life of the adulterer and not the husband. The law clearly discourages for any sort of clemency. In normal case, the aggrieved

232 If she fails to provide her husband a maidservant, the husband can take a concubine. The first wife will have no power over the concubine and the children through her are legitimate. She could be divorced on the same conditions as a wife. Refer Chambliss, 36.

233 CH §§144-149.

234 Marsman, 169-171; Mendelsohn: 33.

235 CH §129: If the wife of a man be taken in lying with another man, they shall bind them and throw them into the water. If the husband of the woman wishes to spare his wife, then the king in turn may spare his subject (Handcock, 22.)

husband will prefer to punish the man, but since he saves his wife, the king in turn will save the offender. The husband has only two options, either to face same penalty or have same clemency.

If a woman's husband accuses her she may swear to her innocence before god and can then return to her home. If someone else other than her husband accuses her of adultery, she has to swear before God and then jump into the river. If she is innocent, god will save her, and if drowned she is guilty of her act.[236]

Woman and Assault against her during Pregnancy

The Code of Hammurabi deals briefly concerning the assault on pregnant woman (§§209-214)[237]. The judgment/penalty depends on the status of the women in the society. It deals about the three classes of women: *mârat awīlim* (free woman), *mârat muškênim* (commoner), and female slave. If the assault is done against a free woman, the offender has to pay ten shekels of silver in case of marriage, and the principle of talion (death for death) will be applied in case she dies. It is strange to note that in case of death, instead of offender, his daughter will be punished. The innocent daughter has to face the judgment. If the assault is committed against a commoner, the offender has to pay 5 shekels of silver in case of miscarriage and one-half mina of silver in case of death. And if assault has taken place to a female slave, the penalty for miscarriage is two shekels of silver and

236 CH §§131-132: If a man accuses his wife and she has not been taken in lying with another man, she shall take an oath in the name of the god and she shall return to her house. If the fingers have been pointed at the wife of a man because of another man, and she would have not been taken in lying with another man, for her husband's sake she shall throw herself into the river (Ibid.)

237 CH §§209-214: If a man would strike another man's daughter and would have caused her to have a miscarriage, he shall pay ten shekels of silver for her foetus. If that woman has died, they shall put his daughter to death. If by blow he has caused a commoner's daughter to have a miscarriage, he shall pay five shekels of silver. If that woman has died, he shall pay one-half mina of silver. If he would strike a man's female slave and would have caused to have a miscarriage, he shall pay two shekels of silver. If that female slave has died, he shall pay one-third mina of silver (Theophile J. Meek, "The Code of Hammurabi," in *Ancient near Eastern Texts,* ed. James B. Pritchard (New Jersey: Princeton University Press, 1955), 175.)

one-third mina of silver if she dies. The law does not state to whom the penalty is to be paid. Most probably, it will be paid to husband in first two cases and to master in the third case.

Woman and Divorce

The right of divorce was granted only to the male members of the community. A man could divorce his wife virtually on any grounds: Childlessness, adultery and even poor household managements, sometimes even without stating any reason.[238] However, if he has children with her, some conditions are laid down. For instance, he has to give her children, dowry and half of the field in order that she may rear her children.[239] If the woman wishes for separation, a separate yardstick is adopted. The matter will be brought before the court. If she is proved innocent, she will receive back her dowry. If it is established in favor of man, nothing is given to her as her divorce-settlement upon her departure. He can marry another woman, and she can live as a servant[240]. If the woman hates her husband, the matter must be reported to the court for investigation. If she is found guilty, she should be thrown into the water and drowned. And if the husband is at fault and has been going out and disparaging her greatly, he has to return back her dowry.[241] The code is in favor of husband. If a wife is found guilty, her husband could degrade her to the position of a slave or drowned. And if her husband is found guilty for his cruelty, he can receive back her dowry. There is no other punishment.

---

238 CH §§148-149 (See foot note 195); Jeremias, 109-110.; Jessica Bieda, "Women in Ancient Mesopotamia", *http://www.assyrian voice.net/forum/index.php? topic=16767.5*, 2.

239 CH §§137-138: If a man sets his face to put away a concubine who has borne him children, or a wife who has presented him with children, he shall return to that woman her dowry and shall give to her the income of the field, garden, and goods, and she shall bring up her children….. If a man would put away his wife who has not borne him children, he shall give her money to the amount of her marriage settlement, and he shall make good to her the dowry which she brought from her father's house and then he may put her away (Handcock, 23.)

240 CH §141.

241 CH §§141-143.

In short, a husband could divorce at will, whereas a woman wanting divorce will be scrutinized. If found guilty she will lose both dowry and status, and if not can retain dowry.

Egypt

The monarch/king played a key role in all matters particularly political and religious areas. He was active both in the administrative and religious affairs. The monarch/king was considered not merely as mortal but as divine being/god. In principle, the whole of the land belonged to Pharaoh and the people were allowed to use his lands. He was free to impose tax. Being a god-king, he was the law giver and justice was one of his divine attributes. What he declared was considered as the law. The will of the king was considered as supreme and binding to all.[242]

Social Classes

There were three classes of people: The upper class, the middle class, and the lower class. The upper class was the higher officials of the kings and the temples. The middle class comprised of minor officials, merchants, foremen, artisans and the upper peasants. The bottom/lower class was the poor laborers. One of the ways to climb the social ladder was by gaining wisdom.[243] The best example is Joseph who was sold to Potiphar, but his wisdom elevated him second to Pharaoh. In order to be honored and to gain social recognition, acquiring knowledge was essential.

The Position of Women

The culture of Egypt unlike Babylon and Assyria was matriarchal in nature. The family system was matriarchal and unlike other nations the genealogy was traced through the mother. The best example is Moses where he was addressed through his mother and sister (Exod 2). Unlike other nations where father was given importance in genealogy, in Egyptian genealogy the name of the father was often omitted. The inheritance of a family property was divided among the

242 Chambliss, 49-53. Unlike Babylonian and Assyrian laws, the Egyptian law has not survived.

243 Ibid., 55-56.

daughters rather than the son. The husband enjoyed the property as long as his wife lived. After her death, his daughter had rights on the property.[244] It makes very clear that legally, women had a high status. It was not limited to women of noble class but also to all sections of women.

Unlike other Ancient West Asian culture, women occupied a dignified status in society. They were given freedom to go to market and have trade. They were economically independent. Though they held reputable position, but it was not a female domination over male.[245]

Women and Marriage

According to the Egyptian custom, marriage was a private contract. The written document was not a requirement. Mutual agreement between two parties was required. If any party withdraws, they can do it. The law does not specify any penalty in case of divorce.[246]

Monogamy was a normal practice for almost all people. The Pharaohs had more than one wife other than large harems. The princess had many handmaidens.[247]

The Middle Assyrian Laws

The Middle Assyrian period is from 1365-1057 BCE. By the 14th century BCE, they ruled Northern Mesopotamia and gradually the whole of Mesopotamia came under their control. During this period they had friendly relations with those states which agreed their terms and conditions. Those who rebelled and refused to be their vassal and refused to pay tribute were punished by war. The war captives were deported to distant parts of empire far away from their homeland. They were provided food, shelter and wives. One of the main reasons for the provisions was to provide labor for the empire.[248]

---

244 Ibid., 60.

245 Ibid., 61, 63-64.

246 Ibid., 62.

247 Ibid.

248 Elisabeth Meier Tetlow, *Women, Crime and Punishment in Ancient Law and Society*, The Ancient near East, vol. 1 (New York: Continuum, 2004), 125-126.

The Middle Assyrian kings wrote laws. They sent out the jurists to collect the laws of Assyria. The laws collected were amended and added to their laws by the legal scholars and Jurist. The law was finally promulgated by the king. The final laws were a mixed collection of Old Babylonian laws, Amorite customary law and the decrees of the Assyrian kings.[249]

The Middle Assyrian law codes are found in two tablets. The available codes are small in content about a quarter of the code of Hammurabi and one-third the length of the Hittite Code.[250] The laws inscribed in the tablet are broken and fragmentary. Therefore, it has many lacunae in the text. Among the tablets found in the excavations of ancient Asshur, tablet A is the longest and best preserved. The Laws in this tablet mainly deals with issues related to women such as marriage, divorce and inheritance. It also deals with crimes committed by women and crimes in which women were victims.[251]

Form and Structure

The laws are casuistic in style. The casuistic laws deal with variety of topics such as theft, personal injury, sexual aspect, inheritance, marriage etc. As mentioned earlier, the Middle Assyrian laws are found in two tablets. Tablet A deals extensively on women (§§1-59) and Tablet B deals with real estate (§§1-21). Comparing Middle Assyrian law codes with other AWA Codes, the laws related to women are much more in length. The treatment towards women is harsh. The laws on adultery and rape are similar to the Babylonian law. Unlike Eshnunna and Hammurabi code, the Middle Assyrian laws include no prologue or epilogue, and is not orderly structured.

The Position of Women

The Middle Assyrian Laws further limit the rights of women. The position of women comparing to the earlier civilizations of Sumer and Babylonia was considerably lower than male. They

249 Ibid., 126.

250 George A. Barton, *Archaeology and the Bible* (Philadelphia: American Sunday School Union, 1916; reprint, 1941), 427.

251 Tetlow, 126.

were controlled by men first by her father and after marriage by her husband. If she commits crime, her husband will decide the punishment (MAL A § 59). Her position was worse than that of a beast used for carrying burden.[252]

The primary role of women was a private sphere, to get married and bear children. The marriage was initiated by the father of the groom and bride. The marriage price was negotiated during the gathering. Once the bridal price was finalized, the couple was betrothed followed by a feast. Once she enters the house of her husband, she becomes the legal property of her husband.[253] Hence, before marriage she was the property of her father and after finance negotiation and marriage she becomes her husband's property. The opinion of the girl was not given importance.

The Assyrian woman was accountable for the crime or misdeeds committed by her husband. For instance, if a man strikes another man's wife resulting into miscarriage, his wife will be treated in the same manner (MAL A § 50). The wife and the unborn child have to face the consequence, which clearly indicates that the woman is the property. If a married man seduces a virgin, his wife will be treated in the same way (MAL A § 55).[254]

In short, the women's rights and freedom are much harsher in Assyrian laws comparing to the Babylonian laws. The reason is probably due to the militaristic policy. The Assyrian empire encouraged for a high birth rate as it needed soldiers. Women who bore sons were honored and the others especially who miscarried were impaled on a stake.[255]

Women and Marriage

The marriage in Assyria though monogamous in principle was basically polygamous. A man has one chief/veiled wife but he can also have as many freeborn concubines regardless of whether he had

252 Mendelsohn: 36.

253 Tetlow, 127.

254 Mendelsohn: 36-37.

255 Jessica Bieda, 3.

children by his chief wife.[256] The primary reason for polygamy was because of the importance of male heir. The first wife has superior status and the second wife will be treated as concubine.[257]

Marriage in Assyria was of two types: Patriarchal type where the woman left her own family to enter the house of her husband; and *Erebu* type, where married woman stays in her father's house and her husband visits her. The former one is a normal practice and the latter is rare case.[258]

In either case, marriage was considered to be an agreement between the bride and bridegroom's house. Girls were married during their teen age.[259] The gifts and related matters are discussed. The bride groom's father pays the bride price. The bride family also pays a part of his inheritance to groom's father with an understanding that the groom will take care of his wife. In normal case, it is the father of the groom who decides for the knot. The groom's decision can be overruled by his father. If a man took the virgin by force and had sexual intercourse, he was obliged to marry her, unless the father of the girl refuses for it (MAL A §55).[260] In either case, she has no freedom of choice. Either she has to silently accept the decision of her father or be a victim.

Marriage in Assyria like Babylonia was more of a civil affair where religious sanctions had not much importance. The valid

---

256 Mendelsohn: 24. Both Canaanite and Israelite practiced polygamy (Deut 21:15; II Chron 11:18-21; 13:21). The Assyrian man is allowed to take a second wife, if the first did not bear children. The position of the second wife was that of a slave girl in respect to the first wife. However, her social position was protected (Stol, 489.)

257 Samuel Greengus, "Legal and Social Institutions of Ancient Mesopotamia," in *Civilizations of the Ancient near East*, ed. Jack M. Sasson (Massachusetts: Hendrickson Publishers, 1995), 478-479.

258 Mendelsohn: 25. G. R. Driver and J. C. Miles, however argue that the mere presence of a married woman staying in her father's house cannot be categorized as a type of marriage. The argument raised makes sense, because a periodical visit of husband or staying in in-law's house is illogic.

259 Stol, 488. The Assyrian texts speak of brides having height about three feet, which shows how young they are. Husbands generally are ten years older at first marriage.

260 Marsman, 51-52.

marriage must have a written contract, if not, marriage would be considered as invalid.

Other than these, the Middle Assyrian Laws also support Levirate marriage. The practice of Levirate was applied if husband died after the betrothal ceremony. The bride groom's father had the right to either give the girl to one of his son or he could marry her, as he bought her with a price (MAL A § 38).[261]

Women and Dowry

The Assyrian bridegroom like Babylonian practice sent gifts to the bride's father. If marriage would not take place, the gift would be returned to the bridegroom (MAL A §§30-31). The bride received dowry from her father, which was her property. It was inherited by her sons after her death (MAL A § 29).

Woman and Assault against her during Pregnancy

Unlike the Code of Hammurabi, the law in Middle Assyria differentiates between a daughter (*mârat awīli*) and wife (*aššat awīli*). In the former case, the penalty for the offender was two talents thirty minas of lead and flogging him fifty times and making him to do the work of the king for one full month (MAL A §21). In the latter case, the penalty was in a form of talion in case of miscarriage and in case she died, the man who assaulted would be put to death. If the woman's husband had no son, and miscarriage took place, the offender would be put to death, and even if her foetus was a girl, the offender should compensate with a life (MAL A §§50-51).

Woman and Divorce

If a husband wants to divorce his wife, he has to give her a bill of divorce (MAL A §§30, 38). Unlike the Babylonian rule, where the husband has to pay a fine if he divorces (MALA §38), the Assyrian law absolves him of any responsibility. The man has freedom either to give her amount as per his wishes or sends forth her empty handed

261 Mendelsohn: 30.:30 The Levirate marriage is also practiced in the Old Testament (Gen 38; Deut 25:5-10)

(MAL A § 37).[262] Unlike the Babylonian law, the Assyrian woman has no right to divorce her husband.[263]

The penalty in case of *aššat awīli* is harsh than *mârat awīli*. The laws do not state about the commoner and the female slave.

Women and Adultery

An Assyrian woman caught in adultery is put to death. If the woman is married, the one who has relation with her will face the same fate (MAL A §13). If the man was unaware about her status, he shall go free and the husband can treat her as he sees fit (MAL A §14). If the husband finds his wife committing adultery, he can put both his wife and the man to death instantly, but if he fails and wants the court to decide, the court will investigate. The punishment upon the man will be same as that of the woman (MAL A§§15, 24). In all of these cases, the wife was treated as husband's property.

Women and Other Laws

Some of the laws related to women are severe. For instance MAL § 8: If a woman has crushed a member's testicle in a brawl, they shall cut off one finger of hers, and if the other testicle has become affected along with it by catching the infection even though a physician has bound (it) up, or she has crushed the other testicle in a brawl, they shall tear out both her [eyes].[264] The law specifies two cases. The consequences are based on the harms. If it affects one testicle, the punishment for her is: a finger will be cut off. This is in parallel with Deuteronomy 25:11. The law in Deuteronomy is much more severe, as her hands will be cut off. In the second case, the woman will lose

262 For Paul Heger, 'It is possible that Israelite custom allowed the divorcing man the choice of whether to grant his ex-wife any payment similar to the MAL rule (A §37). Refer Paul Heger, "Source of Law in the Biblical and Mesopotamian Law Collections," *Biblica* 86, no. 3 (2005): 328.

263 Mendelsohn: 32. The Hebrew man like in Assyria could divorce his wife and was not obliged to make any provisions (Hos 2:2), though there are references to pay a fine if not justified (Deut 22:9; 24:1 cf Isa 50:1; Jer 3:8).

264 Theophile J. Meek, "The Middle Assyrian Laws," in *Ancient near Eastern Texts: Relating to the Old Testament*, ed. James B. Pritchard (Princeton: Princeton University Press, 1969), 181.

both her eyes/ nipples?[265] In the first case, the woman will lose part of her organ, i.e., finger which comes closer to the part of the organ damaged. In the second case, the principle of talion is exercised. The law does not specify the reason behind the brawl, i.e., whether it occurred on the part of a woman as a defense or a purposeful act.

The Hittite Laws

In the period 1650-1200 BCE, Hittite was one of the most powerful states. The Hittites controlled many smaller states. These smaller states were forced to serve them as vassals. The Hittite rulers made treaty with these smaller states which carried a set of rules the vassal had to do.[266] A large part of Hittite laws are dated from the 14th century or fifteenth century BCE. The Hittite laws are found at Hittite city (Boghaz Koi). It came into force during the great Hittite dynasty. It is a collection of two hundred paragraphs. There are both old Hittite (1650 BCE) and New Hittite laws (1350-1200 BCE). The people who are responsible to administer and enforce the laws are king, dignitary, slave owners and the magistrates[267].

Other than laws, Hittite treaty can be seen, whose structure and nature is in line with the covenant passage of Exodus. The treaty form is of five parts: The first part is an introduction citing the name of the Hittite king and the favor done by the king to his vassal; the second part is a command expecting the duties vassal has to do which includes loyalty to the king and his state and following the instructions laid down by the king; the third part carries an order about the treaty, which are placed in the temple of the vassal's god and are sometimes read out in public; the fourth part is witnesses of a long list of gods; and the last part has curses and blessings, curses to those who break the treaty and blessings for those who keep it. The Book of the Covenant Code is similar in line with the Hittite treaty [Introduction-Exodus 20:1-2; Commands and instructions- Exodus

---

265 Meek refers it as 'eyes', whereas R. Yaron refers it as 'nipples'. See R.Yaron, "The Middle Assyrian Laws and the Bible," *Biblica* 51 (1970): 552.

266 John H. Dobson, *A Guide to the Book of Exodus* (London: SPCK, 1977), 114.

267 Harry A Hoffner, "Legal and Social Institutions of Hittite Anatolia," in *Civilizations of the Ancient near East*, ed. Jack M. Sasson (Massachusetts: Hendrickson Publishers, 1995), 555,561.

20:3-17, 21-23 and 25-31; Orders- Exodus 25:16; 34:1, 28-29; Witnesses- Exodus 24:4 ; and Blessings and Curses- Exodus19:5-6 and 20:5-7].[268]

Form and Structure

The Hittite form can be classified into two different forms- a) Direct commands and b) Conditional form 'If'.[269] The Covenant Code is similar in form and style to the Hittites treaties as it also has both the direct commands and conditional laws.

The Hittite laws deals with cases concerning assault and battery (§§1-18); slaves (§§19-24); using another's cooking utensils (§25); marriage (§§26-36); bandits (§§37-38); leased land and feudal holdings (§§39-41); losses and damages (§§42-45); land (§§46-49); classes exempt from military service (§§50-56); stealing and killing domestic animals (§§57-59); taking stray cattle and horses (§§60-92); theft (§§93-97); fires (§§98-100); horticulture (§§101-118); theft (§§119-133; §§142-144); fixing the amount of damages (§§145-149); fixing wages (§§150-152); rental of various objects (§§157-162); responsibility of a shepherd (163); ritual laws (§§164-169); witch law (§170); regulating prices (§§172-186); unnatural sins (§§187-188; §§199-200); Incest (§§189-190); adultery and fornication (§191); killing a man's wife (§192); levirate law (§193); adultery and rape (§§194-195); and various kinds of disorder (§§196-198).

The Position of Women

The activities of women are limited. Their primary responsibility was to take care of household activities and fulfill the role of daughter, wife, mother and widow. Her power was depended on her husband. Outside home, there are some areas in which they can contribute, for instance, manual works, serving in palace and temple. The wages paid to women was half to men. If married, they have to bear offspring or provide a slave woman to her husband to have offspring.[270]

268 Dobson, 116.

269 Ibid., 118.

270 Hoffner, 566-567.

Women and Marriage

In Hittite culture like Assyria and Babylon, Polygamy and Levirate marriage was practiced. The marriage was arranged by legal contract, where in normal case the groom's parent approached the bride's parents with a proposal and gift. If both the parties agree, the next step was official betrothal where the groom's side would pay the bride price. If the bride party changes their mind, they have to pay double compensation and if the groom's party changes their position, they would lose the bride-price (HL §§28-30).[271] The law was lenient towards the groom as he would lose only the bride price, whereas the bride had to pay double the amount.

Once the bride price (*kusata*) is paid, her position will be almost similar to that of a married woman (HL §28) and to acquire marriage contract, she has to bring dowry (*iwaru*), a practice seen throughout Ancient West Asia. During marriage, a contract will be written which contains clauses of obligation on both sides supported by witnesses and a seal.[272] The women's will for marriage is not specified in the laws. It was purely the rights of the parents.

The law also deals in detail about the marriages between members of different economic or social classes (HL §§31-36).

Women and Assault against her during Pregnancy

The laws for assault during pregnancy are short and precise. Like Babylonian and Assyria, the penalty for the offender varies with the position of the victim in a society. The distinction is drawn between a free woman and a slave woman. It also specifies the period of the growth of the unborn child in case of a free woman. The penalty for the offender during the tenth month of a free woman and a slave woman are 10 shekels (20 shekels- later version) and 5 shekels (10 shekels) of silver respectively. If it happens in the 5th month to a free woman, the offender has to pay 5 shekels of silver (HL Tab I §§17-18).

---

271 Ibid., 558.

272 Fiorella Imparati, "Private Life among the Hittites," in *Civilizations of the Ancient near East*, ed. Jack M. Sasson (Massachusetts: Hendrickson Publishers, 1995), 573.

Women and Divorce

The law on divorce is difficult to comprehend (HL §§26, 31). The divorce between free persons is not clearly specified (HL §26) as the text is in a fragmentary state. However, there are references regarding the dissolution of mixed marriages, i.e., between one who is free and one who is not free. In the latter case, the divisions of goods and the ownership of children are specified. The woman will receive only one child and the rest will go to the man (HL §31).[273] Here, the woman is in economic disadvantage position, as she receives only child. In ancient times, the number of children determines the economic position.

Women and Adultery

The woman consented for sexual relation to another man in public place was punished by death (HL §§197-198). If a man sleeps with mother, daughter or step mother, it was considered as adultery (HL §§189-190). However, if he sleeps with his sister or mother staying in different region and are ignorant of his blood relation, it shall not be considered as adultery (HL §§191, 194). He was permitted to sleep with his step mother of his deceased father (HL §190), sister of a deceased wife (HL §192), or with woman related to his father, brother or son (HL §194). The law like Middle Assyrian and Biblical laws supports for Levirate marriage (HL §193, MAL §33; Deut 25:5-10; Gen 38; Ruth)[274].

Family and Sex Laws in Ancient West Asia: A Unified reading

In the earlier section, the laws related to women were briefly dealt with. A closer reading reveals that there are a number of family and sex laws in Ancient West Asia, which are similar to the Biblical laws. This section will deal briefly on the family and sex laws in Ancient West Asia.

---

273 Ibid., 574.

274 Hoffner, 557-558. Also refer Imparati, 574, 576-577.

Laws regarding rape and Seduction[275]

Like the Israelite Legal system, the Ancient West Asia has three categories of free women- married women, betrothed, and virgins.

1. Married women: If a man has sexual relations with a married woman, it is a capital offence
   a. If the woman is raped, the rapist is to be executed (MAL §12, §23b; HL §197a)
   b. If a woman commits adultery, both of them are to die (EL §28; CH §129, §143; MAL A §§13- 15, §§22-23; HL §197b).
   c. If a woman seduces a man, and the man is unaware of her marital status, she alone is to be punished by death (Laws of Ur-Nummu, section 4[1.222-231]; MAL §16).
2. Betrothed woman: The legal position of a betrothed woman was same as that of a married woman (EL §26; CH §130).
3. Virgins: The legal position of unbetrothed woman was different from married or betrothed woman. The offence in case of rape or seduction is not death, rather monetary payment (MAL A §26, §55). The virgin's father receives compensation from the rapist or seducer for the loss of his bride-price. The father has the right to decide about her daughter. He can give her to the one who deflowered her or can give to another person with a reduced price, or with no bride-price.

The legal position of virgin differs from that of the betrothed and married woman. In case of the former, she is the property of her father and receives compensation. In the latter case, the woman becomes the property of her husband, and to commit crime against her is to commit crime against her husband. In either case, the compensation was paid to the male members and women whatsoever has no voice and rights to express.

---

275 Alexander Rofe, *Deuteronomy: Issues and Interpretation*, ed. David J. Reimer, Old Testament Studies (London: T&T Clark, 2002), 175-176.

Laws regarding Adultery

In the Ancient West Asian legal codes, the adultery was considered a tort in private law. The injured party was allowed to come to a decision about the execution of the punishment. In the Code of Hammurabi, a husband may pardon his adulterous wife, if so, the king may pardon his wife (CH §129). In the Middle Assyrian Law, the punishment decided by the husband was binding to her lover as well (MAL A §14-§15). In the Hittite Law, the husband has the right to determine whether to pardon his wife and her lover, with the king having the right to grant mercy (HL §§197-198).[276] Here too, the decision to punish or save was in the hand of the husband. In Israelite law, adultery with a married woman is considered as a serious crime demanding death penalty for both offenders (Lev 20:10), as it is the matter of external threat to man's honor and authority. However, as mentioned earlier, if it is committed with a virgin, the accused has to marry her by paying the bride price to her father and he is not free to divorce her all his days (Deut 22:28-29).

Laws regarding Divorce

The right to divorce was only to the male members of the society. This was found common throughout Ancient West Asia. In Babylonian Law, a man could divorce his wife on any ground. In the Middle Assyrian Laws, a husband could divorce his wife and unlike Babylonian law it was not necessary for him to pay fine or compensation. In Israel, a woman could be divorced if her husband did not favor or had discovered some 'indecency'. In short, the man had every right to divorce his wife, and woman did not have a right to rid herself from her husband even if she discovered 'indecency' in her husband's life. For Carmody, 'the women's being is pushed out and pulled back by husbands who kept changing their minds and she is disposable.'[277]

---

276 Ibid., 181-182.

277 Carmody, 23.

Laws regarding Slavery

Slavery was widespread throughout Ancient West Asia (CH §§114-119; MAL A §48). The basic supply source was the freeborn native defaulting debtor. The defaulting debtor was forced to do compulsory service. The debtor in such situation not only enslaved himself, but also his slave, concubine, wife and children. The owner kept them in bondage until the debt was cleared off. Hence, they remained as the possession of the owner.[278]

In the Ancient West Asian legal codes, there are mainly two different types of slaves: Debt slaves and Chattel slaves. The Debt slaves were released after six years and were not regarded as property whereas the chattel slaves were always the property of their owner. Concerning the debt slaves, the creditor/owner has only purchased the service of the slave to receive back the amount paid for his debt and not the person.[279] The chattel slave was the property of the owner where he has the right to extract work from him and to keep him forever.

Laws of Hammurabi Code

1. If an obligation came due against a man and he sold (the services of) his wife, his son, or his daughter, or he has been bound over to service, they shall work (in) the house of their purchaser or oblige for three years, with their freedom re-established in the fourth year (CH § 117).
2. When a male slave or a female slave has been bound over to service, if the merchant foreclosed[280] , he may sell (him), with no possibility of his being reclaimed (CH §118).
3. If an obligation came due against a man and he has accordingly sold (the services of) his female slave who bore him children, the owner of the female slave may repay the

278 Jacob Milgrom, "Leviticus 23-27," in *The Anchor Bible*, ed. William Foxwell Albright and David Noel Freedman (London: Yale University Press, 2001), 2213.

279 Ibid.The Pentateuch slave laws unlike Ancient West Asian codes do not distinguish between the debt and chattel slave.

280 Lit. 'he caused (the time-limit) to expire'.

money which the merchant paid out and thus redeem his female slave (CH §119).

These laws (CH §§117-119) are quite similar to that of the Covenant Code (Exod 21:2-11) and Deuteronomic Code (Deut 15:12-18) with few differences. The major two differences are:

1. In Biblical law, the man sells himself, whereas in Code of Hammurabi, the man can sell his wife, son or daughter.
2. In Biblical law, the time period to be a slave is 6 years[281], whereas in Code of Hammurabi 3 years.

Ancient West Asian Law and Israelite Law: Similarities and differences

Similarities[282]

1. Both contain a significant amount of criminal law for instance murder, adultery, theft etc.
2. Both are similar in content and form.

Differences[283]

1. Ancient West Asian laws focus much on civil law (marriage, inheritance, property, slaves etc). Biblical law though has civil law, emphasizes more on cultic law (types of sacrifices, purification rites, modes of worship etc).
2. Israelite law transformed the Ancient West Asian laws with its religious application. In Mesopotamia, law was primarily for the good of the society and offense was viewed against the well being of the society. Israelite laws consider the offence were against God and society.

281 There is a difference within the Biblical law. In Exodus, the reason for six years of slavery is not specified, whereas Deuteronomy 15: 18 clearly states that the slave has served 'doubles the hire of a hireling'. It brings out a point that normal slavery was of three years.

282 Bill T. Arnold and Byran E. Beyer, ed., *Readings from the Ancient near East* (Grand Rapids, Michigan: Baker Academic, 2002), 104.

283 Ibid.

3. The Biblical law is traditionally understood as revelatory, since it is given by God to the people. The Mesopotamian laws though approved and sanctioned by the gods, describe how a well-ordered society should be like.

Summary

Women had a higher standing in the early Neolithic and earlier Mesopotamian periods. Thereafter, the position of women came under the domain of the male members of the society. The privacy of women was connected to the social status. The higher the status, the more they were secluded. They were confined in the house to bear children, take care of the children and manage the household affairs. The husband was regarded as the lord of the house and had power over his wife. The role of the male member of the society was mainly in the public sphere, whereas the role of the woman was in private sphere. Even in the private sphere the male had control over the female. These forms of discrimination were seen throughout the Ancient West Asian laws, where women were under the control of male members of the society and male decision makers. For instance, in AWA society other than the practice of monogamous (marriage), there was the practice of bigamyand polygamy. The polygamy was practiced among the elites whereas bigamy was a common practice. The male members of the society probably married more than one wife to have more children and also to display their wealth. This practice could be seen more among the wealthy groups of people. The women had no right whatsoever to defend their case.

Is this form of discrimination present in Israelite law system[284]? The following chapters will investigate the position of women in Pentateuchal law codes.

284 As mentioned in the 'Introductory' chapter, the Israelite Law system covers all the three legal codes of the Pentateuch namely Covenant Code, Deuteronomic Code, and the Holiness Code. Since this work gives more importance to the Covenant Code due to its indifference towards women, and the other two codes are fairly more sympathetic to women, the author will deal first with the Deuteronomic and Holiness Code. This is done mainly to investigate how the Covenant Code differs from the other two codes.

Chapter 3

The Status of Women in the Deuteronomic Code

The Israelite Law

Law played a key role in the life of Israel. It provides the framework for legal decisions. Though it is not a complete law, it enables the executors to govern the daily life of Israel.

Laws in the Pentateuch

The laws in the Pentateuch are connected to the concept of the Covenant, made between Yahweh and His people. The biblical covenants were modeled after the formal agreements or treaties that existed between the monarchs and their vassals in the political sphere of the world.[285] The Covenant has important theological ideas, i.e., the divine authority; the obligation of Israel to obey; reward and punishment for keeping or disobeying the laws etc. Now, the difference

285 Greengus, "Law," 245. The biblical covenant treaty form has similarity with the Hittite treaty form. Scholars such as G. E. Mendenhall, Gerhard von Rad, Martin Noth and others support this view.

between AWA treaties and that of Israelite law is that, the AWA treaties were rooted in political contexts and not to the population in general[286]. In the Pentateuchal laws and commandments, the Covenant is central, whereas the Ancient West Asian treaties deal with political matters of loyalty, dealing with hostile powers, military activity and support, extradition of fugitives, etc., with no place for divine activity as seen in Israelite law. [287]

The Israelite legal traditions have various genres (*Gattungen*). The predominant laws in the Pentateuch fall in two major categories/genres: apodictic and casuistic. Albrecht Alt separated the laws according to the form.

The Apodictic Laws

Apodictic is derived from a Greek word (ἀπο-from and δεὶκνυμι-to show). It is uttered in a single-sentence formula.[288] It is in imperative form 'you shall not…' In general, its style is unique and it appears predominantly in second person, where לא is placed with an imperfect verb, for instance מְכַשֵּׁפָה לֹא תְחַיֶּה (you shall not allow a sorceress to live [Exod 22:17]). A. Alt describes it as categorical, unconditional formulations of laws, including those presented in the imperative form, i.e., words and commandments spoken by God in direct address to the Israelites. It is usually introduced in singular form and occasionally in plural form. It is formulated in metrical-rhythmical language and it is often found in series. The apodictically formulated laws relate to religious as well as secular realms of life. It has its closest parallel in the Suzerainty treaties. Alt observes it as uniquely Israelite in origin, and represents Israel's own peculiar contribution. [289] Though he claims that the apodictic laws are unique

286 Ibid.

287 Ibid.

288 Rao, 23.

289 A Alt, "Die Ursprunge Des Israelitischen Rechts," *BSAW* 86, no. 1 (1934): 101-171. C.f. John Bright, "Modern Study of the Old Testament Literature," in *The Bible and the Ancient near East*, ed. G. E. Wright (Indiana: Winona Lake, 1961), 23; John Bright, *A History of Israel* (London: SCM Press, 1980), 172; Martin Noth, *The Laws in the Pentateuch and Other Studies* (Edinburgh: Oliver & Boyd, 1966), 7-8.Thomas B. Dozeman, *Commentary on Exodus*, ed.

in Israel, the similar form of laws[290] are found in the Eshnunna[291], the Hammurabi[292], the Middle Assyrian[293] and the Hittite laws[294], though comparatively lesser to Casuistic laws.

In the Apodictic laws on the one hand, there is no introductory conditional clause, and it gives a precise statement of the facts in the case. While on the other hand, the apodictice law, either always states the same punishment, i.e., exclusion from the community by curse, excommunication, or death, or like the Decalogue, says nothing about legal consequences.[295]

Concerning apodictic law, McCarthy opines that the second person imperative statements occasionally also appear in the Hittite vassal treaties alongside of the more common casuistically formulated ones. There are non-casuistic formulations to be found even in casuistically styled AWA Law collections.[296] So, his approach is that apodictic statements are not unique to ancient Israel.

Though apodictic laws are found in some of the neighboring nations, unlike Casuistic laws, the apodictic laws are unique to Israel.

The Casuistic Laws

Casuistic law, the oldest known law collection throughout Ancient West Asia comes from the Latin word *casus* meaning 'case'. It is in case form, i.e., conditional in structure. It consists of protasis and apodosis. Protasis is a conditional clause stating an action or a state

David Noel Freedman, The Eerdmans Critical Commentary (Cambridge: William B. Eerdmans Publishing Company, 2009), 7-8.

290 In Israelite law apodictic laws are in second person 'you', which is not the case in AWA (See foot note 276, 277 and 278) [C.f. Rao, 26].

291 §§10-11, 15-16, 51-52.

292 §§36, 38-40.

293 §§ A 40, 57-59.

294 §§ 48, 50-52, 54-56.

295 Schmidt, 127.

296 D. J. McCarthy, "Treaty and Covenant," *AnBib* 21 (1963): 47.

of affairs (*If when*) and apodosis is a clause that designates the legal consequences of the case described in the protasis.[297]

A. Alt observes casuistic law or case law, as part of common heritage shared with the Canaanites and other West Asian peoples/ ancient codes. These laws were taken over by Israel after her settlement in Palestine.[298] Both in form and content it is widely paralleled, and by no means distinctly Israelite.

Casuistic law describes a legal situation in all its detail and also determines the penalty. This type of law has three characteristics: a) conditional; b) couched in impersonal and general terms (third person); and has link with the Ancient West Asian background. A conditional clause, usually introduced by כִּי, *if, when* gives the facts of the case in the first part of the sentence, called protasis; further conditional clauses, usually introduced by אִם, *if then* may specify the facts even further. The principal clause, which follows, known as apodosis, states the legal consequences.

The Deuteronomic Code

As mentioned earlier, this research is a Postcolonial Womanist Reading of the Israelite law (Pentateuchal laws) with special reference to the Book of the Covenant Code. Though chronologically, the Book of the Covenant Code is understood to have been formulated as the first and foremost law code followed by the Deuteronomic and Holiness Code, the author purposefully placed Covenant Code at the end to make out how the Covenant Code differs from the other two codes pertaining to women.[299]

Historical Background

It is generally agreed that the Deuteronomic Code (12-26), though widely regarded as the 'original' Deuteronomy and the oldest part of the book of Deuteronomy, is a product of Josiah's reform (Martin

297 Assnat Bartor, "The Representation of Speech in the Casuistic Laws of the Pentateuch: The Phenomenon of Combined Discourse," *JBL* 126, no. 2 (2007): 233.

298 Bright, "Modern Study of the Old Testament Literature," 23.

299 The order of exegesis (DC, HC and BC) as such is notdue to the redaction history of the Book of the Covenant or the Deuteronomic revision of the Book of the Covenant.

Noth and others). If we agree this view, the political changes occurred during that era has much significance. The law and the reformation had a strong bearing on the weakening and collapse of the Assyrian control over Judah. For a century, Assyria had control over Judah (736/733 BCE- 630/622 BCE). The Assyrian dominance upon Judah can be seen from the Syro-Ephramite war (736-733 BCE) to Josiah's reform (622 BCE). By the time Josiah came to the throne, the power of Assyria declined, which probably was a major reason for reformation in Judah (cf. II Kings 22-23). This development also paid the way for Judah to control her sister kingdom Israel. The destruction of the sanctuary at Bethel and the suppression of its priesthood (II Kings 23:15-20) is a clear reference. The rapid decay of the Assyrian world empire must have encouraged Josiah to throw off his vassalage, abandon the agreement made between him and the Assyrian king. Thus, Josiah took full advantage of the weakness of the Assyrian empire and brought oneness in Israel by attaining separate identity and freedom from external political, social and religious interference. This oneness aspect can be seen in the book of Deuteronomy. In the light of this political development we can better understand the laws of Deuteronomy. The laws of Deuteronomy unlike other law codes are highly moral and humanitarian. The laws are very deeply concerned with the idea of Israel as the nation chosen and redeemed expecting the same attitude towards fellow human beings. The laws unlike the other parallel codes give more importance to the overall social and cultural development of Israel.[300]

The section Deut.12-26 is the detailed law of the covenant. It deals with the religious life (unity and purity of Israel's worship, sporadic obligations and institutions), political life (the responsibility of the officials of theocratic state towards their nation and vice versa), and social life (respect of individuals particularly in the context of family relationships, humanitarian behavior, first fruits and tithe etc).

300 The law deals with the fundamental aspects of family life such as release of both male and female slaves at the end of every seven years (Deut 15:12-18), prohibition against selling a wife, who had been chosen from among captives (Deut 21:14), protection of women in marriage (Deut 22:19). C.f. R. E. Clements, "Deuteronomy," in *Old Testament Guides*, ed. R. N. Whybray (Sheffield: JSOT Press, 1989), 85-93.

Based on the correspondence between some of the laws, for instance Decalogue and slavery, it is proposed and argued by some scholars that Deuteronomic Code is a modification of Exodus Code while others argue that the Deuteronomic Code harmonizes the legislation of Covenant Code and Holiness Code. The author's interest is not to have a detailed study on these issues, rather to read the text with a Postcolonial Womanist approach, as it deals with a revolution of freedom to all members of the society irrespective of their class and gender.

Form/Structure/Setting

The main legislative section of Deuteronomy compromising of chapters 12-26 is generally known as the Deuteronomic Code. It opens and ends with a call to observe and keep the laws and ordinances (11:32-12:1; 26:16). In between this call it carries a series of laws such as cultic laws, laws against idolatry, laws on war, family and sex laws, laws for kindness towards the oppressed etc. Julius Wellhausen considered these chapters as the original book, which was written shortly before 621 BCE and discovered, by accident or design, by Hilkiah in the Temple.[301] Moreover, all considers this portion as the kernel of the book in its earliest forms.

Many of the laws are ancient, going back to the beginning of Israel's existence as a nation. It is widely known and recognized that the laws and exhortations of Deuteronomy were once delivered orally (Moses or Samuel, or a group of Levites). The oratorical style of the book, the introduction of time and place, the appeals to memory of the past and to the present conditions, all presume that Moses is the speaker and the tribes on the banks of Jordan the people addressed.[302] The section 12-26 is set before the people at the end of

301 Manley, *The Book of the Law*, 65. Some scholars argue that these laws were the product of Josiah's reform, but majority opines that they were contained in the law book found in the temple. Cf. Anthony Philips, *Deuteronomy*, ed. A. R. C. Leaney, P. R. Ackroyd, J. W. Packer, The Cambridge Bible Commentary (Cambridge: University Press, 1973), 82. Gerhard von Rad though admits Deuteronomy as a literary work but argues that it has a cultic form [Gerhard von Rad, *Studies in Deuteronomy* (London: SCM Press Ltd, 1953), 14-15.] The dating of the codes is mentioned in first chapter.

302 Manley, *The Book of the Law*, 70.

the wilderness wanderings (11:31, 32), and is introduced as 'statutes and judgments' (12:1), to which in 26:17 the word 'commandments is added'.

The Deuteronomic laws are not being considered as a fully comprehensive law code dealing with all aspects of Israelite life at the time of Josiah. The laws are nowhere concerned with civil wrongs leading to actions for damages as found in the Book of the Covenant (Ex 21:18-22:17). The main and overall concern of deuteronomic law is to ensure Israel's exclusive allegiance to God, and thereby to maintain the covenant relationship.[303]

With regard to the setting, though it is generally expressed that chapters 12-26 are the original, and the kernel of the book, a closer study reveals that chapter 11 has something to do with chapter 12. The reference in 11:21 to length of days in the land is echoed in 12:1; the promise to drive out the demons in 11:23 is echoed in the command to destroy their shrines in 12:2; 'you shall Passover Jordan' in 11:31 is followed by 'when you go over Jordan' in 12:10; and the command in 11:32 to observe to do the 'statutes and Judgments' immediately introduces 12:1, 'These are the statutes and judgments, which ye shall observe to do'.[304] So, a connection can be viewed between Chapter 11 and 12. Now, if we notice chapter 27: 1, it seems that it begins the story where chapter 11 leaves it. Compare 11:29 with 27: 4 (Ebal and Gerazim are still in view), 11:31 with 27:3 (Jordan), 4:44, 11:32 with 27:2-4 (the laws, which has been 'set before' the people must soon be inscribed on the stones).[305] Now, the question arises, whether chapters 5-11 has connection with chapters12-26 (the Deuteronomic Code) or with chapter 27. It seems that 12-26 was the original text, and later both the text (5-11 and 27) was inserted with some editorial work, so as to maintain the unity and continuity of the book.

303 Philips, 82.

304 Manley, *The Book of the Law*, 71.

305 Ibid. Walter C. Kaiser considers that the entire discourse of Deut 5-26 is a single literary unit [Walter C. Kaiser, *Towards Old Testament Ethics* (Grand Rapids, Michigan: Zondervan Publishing House, 1983), 129.]

Deuteronomy 15:12-18 (The Liberation of the Hebrew Slaves)

Translation/Textual Comments

12 If your brother[306] Hebrew man or a Hebrew woman is sold to
you[307], he shall serve you six years and in the seventh year you shall let
him go free[308] from you. 13 And when you send him free from you,
you shall not send him out empty-handed[309]; 14 You shall provide
him liberally[310] out of your flock, out of your threshing floor[311], and
out of your wine press; You shall give to him as[312] Yahweh your God[313]
has blessed you. 15 You shall remember that you were a slave in the
land of Egypt, and the Lord your God[314] redeemed you; therefore I
command you this word today.[315] 16 But if he says to you, "I will not
go out from you" because he loves you and your household, since
he is well off with you, 17 then you shall take an awl, and thrust it
through his ear[316] into the door, and he shall be your slave forever.

306 The slave (man or a woman) is considered as a member of the community (Israelite).

307 Few Versions like NEB prefer 'sells himself or herself to you' (hithpael) instead of 'sold to you' (Niphal). Grammatically both translations are possible. It is interesting to note that the law completely avoids the term 'owner', which clearly shows the brotherly act of responsibility and generosity.

308 It is a technical term for a special social status, i.e., 'freedman'.

309 Cf. Gen. 31:42; Exod 3:21.

310 Lit., put upon the neck. The purpose behind this generosity is to break the cycle of servitude.

311 Few Hebrew manuscripts and Targum codex manuscripts read without *waw* conjunction.

312 The Samaritan Hebrew Pentateuch and few other versions read כַּאֲשֶׁר (cf.16:10). MT lost a כ(k) possibly by haplography, as the preceding word ends with a כ.

313 A reading of Hebrew manuscripts from Qumran (I Q Deut) read אדני (Lord) instead of יהוה (Yahweh).

314 Septuagint adds an adverb *ἐκεῖθεν* 'from there' [*ἐλυτρώσατό σε κύριος ὁ θεός σου ἐκεῖθεν* 'Lord your God redeemed from there'].

315 MT adds 'today' but this word is absent in LXX. The IQ Deut, Targum Pseudo Jonathan and Septuagint supplement the word 'to do' after 'commanding you'.

316 Thrusting the awl through the servant's ear has a symbolic significance such as obligation to obey, attached to the owner's house [Refer Duane L. Christensen,

You shall do the thus (same) likewise to your female slave. 18 It[317] shall not seem hardship to you (your eye)[318] when you send them out from you free, because for six years he has served you worth the wages[319] of hired servant[320]; and the Lord your God will bless you in all that you do.

Form and Structure

The slave law 15:12-18 is casuistic in style[321] and is of two sections (vv.12-15a and vv.16-18). Verse 15 b stands as the centre of the literary unit emphasizing the reason to redeem the indentured

---

"Deuteronomy 1:1-21:9," in *Word Biblical Commentary*, ed. John D. W. Watts (Nashville: Thomas Nelson Publishers, 2001), 320-321.]

317 Few manuscripts Samaritan Hebrew Pentateuch, Septuagint, Latin and Syriac add *waw* conjunction at the beginning of the negative particle לא

318 Septuagint reads preposition with genitive ἐναντίον σου 'before you'. It has been proposed as 'in your eyes'.

319 It can be translated as 'twice', 'double' or equivalent. The Septuagint translates this verse as 'ὅτι ἐφέτιον μισθὸν τοῦ μισθωτοῦ ἐδούλευσέν σοι ἓξ ἔτη' (because he has served you six years for the *annual* wage of a hired man laborer). For more reading on this difficult text refer Christensen, 321; James M. Lindenberger, "How Much for a Hebrew Slave? The Meaning of Misneh in Deut 15:18- Critical Notes," *JBL* 110, no. 3 (1991): 479-498.

320 AV and KJV reads '...his service has been worth *twice* as much as that of a hired servant'. RSV reads it as 'half'. NRSV reads it as '...worth the wages of hired laborers'. For von Rad and Thompson, the word *misneh* is probably a technical term meaning 'equivalent to' [See Gerhard von Rad, *Deuteronomy* (London: SCM Press Ltd, 1966), 108; J. A. Thompson, *Deuteronomy: An Introduction and Commentary*, ed. D. J. Wiseman, The Tyndale Old Testament Commentaries (England: Inter-Varsity Press, 1974), 191.] For Philips, the Hebrew is uncertain. If twice, then the normal three year contract of hire is being contrasted with six year of slavery. The 19th century BCE Babylonian code of Lipit-Ishtar provides the release of a debtor once he had given services equivalent to twice the amount of his debt. The Code of Hammurabi granted release after three years [see Philips, 106-107.Peter C. Craige, *The Book of Deuteronomy* (Grand Rapids, Michigan: William B. Eerdmans Publishing Company, 1976), 238-239.]

321 Unlike the impersonal style, which is a typical form in Casuistic style, here it is in second person singular form.

servant. Each of these sections has a law in casuistic form followed by an exhortation (v.15 and v.18).[322]

The law in Deuteronomy advocates for the release of all Israel's slaves after a period of six years. Moreover, at the time of release, the owner must not send him with empty hand, rather must provide him a generous provision. The people should show empathy to those who have been forced into servitude due to difficult circumstances.[323] However, in spite of this provision, the slaves are free to remain with their masters for life. It totally contradicts the law of release in the Book of the Covenant (Exod 21:2-11). The comparison between the law codes will be explored in the following section.

Comments and Explanation

This law provides remission to those who have lost their freedom because of debt and poverty. This law refers to debt slaves and not foreign slaves. The Hebrew man or woman after serving as slave for six years must be freed on the seventh year and the owner are expected to provide them liberally so that they may start a new and independent life. As saving and sacrificial love of Lord God was bestowed upon the people of Israel in Egypt, when they were weak and enslaved, hence they are expected to do so with their fellow brethren.

Verse 12

אָחִיךָ הָעִבְרִי אוֹ הָעִבְרִיָּה (*a fellow Hebrew man or Hebrew woman*)- Unlike the Covenant Code, the uniqueness of Deuteronomic Code is not just the word 'Hebrew', rather the word 'brother'. The additional word 'brother' marks a radical and significant difference from the parallel law codes especially the Covenant Code. Women are also given equal privilege with men in the release (v.12 and 17). These additions mark a significant step from the Covenant Code. The Deuteronomic Code supersedes the Covenant code by granting

---

322 A. D. H. Mayes, "Deuteronomy," in *New Century Bible Commentary*, ed. Ronald E. Clements (Grand Rapids, Michigan: Wm. B. Eerdmans Publishing Company, 1979), 252.

323 Christensen, 318. Also refer Victor H Matthews, *Manners and Customs in the Bible* (Massachusetts: Hendrickson Publishers, 1991), 136-138.

equal treatment to female.[324] The position of equality clearly shows that the Deuteronomic Law springs from a more advanced stage of society where the power of a father over his daughter was no longer supreme.[325] The one whom you are obliged to free is your fellow brother or sister, which pictures a strong humanitarian concept, where there is no room for 'power over others'. This humanitarian approach is missing in Exodus 21:2-11. In Exodus, the female slave is given a lower status and is in a different footing. For Thompson, the woman is a concubine probably a slave. What is implicit in Covenant Code becomes explicit in Deuteronomic Code.[326]

הָעִבְרִי – Originally this term was widely used in Ancient West Asia as people who occupied a particular social status. The term is used in varied ways in Old Testament. More frequently, this term was used for Israelites in a foreign nation, when they were in a position of slaves (Exod 2:6, 11, 13; 3:18; 5:3; 7:16; 9:1; I Sam 4:6; 13:3; 14:11 etc).[327] However, there are occasions where it was used as a synonym

---

324 Jeffrey H. Tigay, "Deuteronomy," in *The Jewish Publication Society Torah Commentary*, ed. Nahum M. Sarna (Jerusalem: The Jewish Publication Society, 1996), 148.

325 S. R. Driver, "Deuteronomy: A Critical and Exegetical Commentary," in *The International Critical Commentary*, ed. A. Plummer and C. A. Briggs S. R. Driver (Edinburgh: T&T Clark, 1996), 182-183.

326 Thompson, 189. Also see S. R. Driver, *A Critical and Exegetical Commentary on Deuteronomy* (Edinburgh: T&T Clark, 1902), 182; Meredith G. Kline, *Treaty of the Great King* (Grand Rapids, Michigan: William B. Eerdmans Publishing Company, 1963), 90. For S. R. Driver, The law of Deuteronomy comes from a more advanced society than the law of Exodus.

327 Thompson, 189-190. Christopher Wright feels that the word 'Hebrew' has a socioeconomic meaning rather than merely an ethical one [Christopher J. H. Wright, "Deuteronomy," in *New International Biblical Commentary*, ed. Robert K. Johnston Robert L. Hubbard Jr. (USA: Paternoster Press, 1996), 192.] For Jeffrey H. Tigay, the word 'Hebrew' refers to a social class of rootless, subservient individuals (Tigay, 148.) Many other scholars argue that the word 'Hebrew' is derived from the verb ***'abar*** meaning 'to cross' , thus designating as those who have crossed into Western Palestine from Jordan or semi nomadic group who frequently crosses from one region to another region [Ian Cairns, "Word and Presence: A Commentary on the Book of Deuteronomy," in *International Theological Commentary*, ed. Fredrick Carlson Holmgren and George A. F. Knight (Edinburgh: The Handsel Press Ltd, 1992), 149.] For

word for Israelite (Jonah 1:9). Is the word 'Hebrew' referring to Israelite or a foreigner? For Anthony Philips, the word 'Hebrew' refers to Israelites and not to foreigners as the latter have no right of release[328]. In our observation also, it refers to the Israelite.

חָפְשִׁי - It is a legal term which refers specifically to the status of a released slave or the one who has discharged his or her obligations. Lemche reads this word as an individual having a particular social status, subordinate to a free citizen but above a slave. This understanding can be seen in Ancient West Asian laws.[329]

If a member of your community is sold to you is in the context of vv. 1-11, the reason for the sale would be due to the default in the repayment of debt. The way to substitute the debt is by servitude. He or she shall serve you six years. These are not the six years of the sabbatical cycle, rather six years following the sale. In the seventh year, they are declared as free.

You shall let him go free- This command is in line with the phrase 'Let my people go' (Exod.5:1). This expression is a humanistic approach. In Exodus the command stated is 'he shall go out free' (v.2), whereas here the owner is indebted to release his slave (cf. v.18).[330]

Verses 13-14

הַעֲנֵיק תַּעֲנִיק - Literally it means 'garland him'. The owner is asked to garland the slave, i.e., a necklace of flocks, grain and wine in abundance.[331] The understanding here is to bestow generously.

---

more details on the word 'Hebrew' see Exodus 21:2 (Chapter 5-exegetical study).

328 Philips, 106. Gerhard von Rad too supports for Israelites. For him, the slave was an Israelite who was free once but now sold himself into slavery [Rad, *Deuteronomy*, 107.]

329 N. P. Lemche, "The Hebrew Slave: Comments on the Slave Law Exodus 21:2-11," *Vetus Testamentum* 25 (1975): 140ff.

330 Moshe Weinfeld, *Deuteronomy and the Deuteronomic School* (Oxford: Clarendon Press, 1972), 282-283.

331 Wright, 192-193.

The Deuteronomic Code goes beyond the provision of Exodus 21:2-11[332]. The obligation aspect is missing in the Covenant Code. Here, the owner's responsibility towards the slave is highlighted. The slave would not begin his state of new freedom in destitution, a state of indigent insecurity, rather must enjoy himself or herself as a full and independent member of the society. The strong humanitarian spirit and concern for the weak and the oppressed can be seen clearly. A remarkable advance of social thinking is shown in this text. The principle of love, for God and for fellow man, is vital to the covenant community,[333] and it is strongly demonstrated in this text, but Exodus 21:2-11 makes no provision for the released slaves.

Verse 15

עַל־כֵּן אָנֹכִי מְצַוְּךָ אֶת־הַדָּבָר הַזֶּה הַיּוֹם (*therefore I command you this word today*)- The word 'today' is unique in the command of freeing the indentured servants. It stands exactly at the centre of the literary unit (between two sub units: vv. 12-15a and 16-18).[334]

Here, the call to remember was not merely a means to evoke sympathy or compassion for the slave, which would lead to generosity, rather to realize their past, when they were slaves under Egypt (Deut 5:15, 16:12, 24:18, 22). The freedom from the bondage in Egypt was not their merit, rather the love of God towards them. The love of God is shown both by delivering them from the hands of Egypt and also by providing ample provisions (cf. Exod 3:21-22 [you will not go empty-handed], 11:2, 12:25-27).[335] In return, they

---

332 For Driver, the regulation of slave respecting the wife and family of a slave (21:3-4) is disregarded in Deuteronomy and is replaced by the provision aspect (See Driver, *A Critical and Exegetical Commentary on Deuteronomy*, 183.). For Christenson, in the Exodus narrative, the people received gifts of silver and gold objects from their former masters in Egypt (Refer Christensen, 318.)

333 Craige, 238; Thompson, 190. For Philips, the deuteronomic code actively encourages the slave to claim freedom, and the master has no longer any control over the slave's private life (See Philips, 106.) For Wright, the command of generosity is a sign of honor (Wright, 192.)

334 Christensen, 319.

335 Refer Eugene H. Merrill, "Deuteronomy," in *The New American Commentary*, ed. E.Ray Clendenen (USA: Broadman & Holman Publishers, 1994), 245-246.

should do no less to the manumitted slaves in the seventh year. A powerful motivating force is indicated. As per our study, comparing this passage with other codes, the proper love and concern of God towards the poor are expressed here. In Exodus, the taste of injustice is seen, especially towards the female slave. Here, the liberation of the male and the female slave is an act of love, whereas in Exodus, the act of cruelty. The total justice is seen, when a person set free has some hope of success ahead. And if it is not achieved, it is nothing other than leading them to further slavery.

Verses 16-17

The law intends that freedom be given to all. But, if a slave, in spite of receiving freedom, decides to stay with the owner, he shall be categorized as *perpetual slave* עֶבֶד עוֹלָם[336] v. 17). The regulation and exhortation contained in vv.12-17 are applied equally to male and female slaves (v. 17b), which are missing totally in Exodus 21. In Exodus passage, the slaves are brought to God (household gods before whom the ceremony was performed), but Deuteronomy is not mentioning it. The reason for it is that, it had been rendered illegal objects under Josiah's reform (II Kings 23:24).[337] The pierced ears indicate to the general public about the slave's legal position. It also symbolizes his/her obligation to hear the owner's order. It also served as a slave mark.

וְאַף לַאֲמָתְךָ תַּעֲשֶׂה־כֵּן (*You shall do thus (same) likewise to your female slave*) – The law purposefully adds this sentence as they also could be sold for family debts (cf. II Kings 8:3).[338] The Deuteronomic code

336 The Hebrew phrase *'ebed 'olam* is a technical term who is accorded a preferential status over the other slaves [see Mayes, 252.] In such case, the slave had an important place in his/her master's house (Genesis 24:2ff), as it refers to one who remains permanently rather than temporarily (Tigay, 150.)

337 The Deuteronomic legislator avoids the word 'God' rather prefers the word 'door' to highlight the 'single sanctuary' practice and consider the household gods as illegal objects under Josiah's reform. Also see Cairns, 150; Philips, 107.

338 Richard D. Nelson, "Deuteronomy: A Commentary," in *The Old Testament Library* ed. Carol A Newsom and David L Petersen James L Mays (London: Westminster John Knox Press, 2004), 198.

'demands that maidservants also be given freedom in the seventh year like male slaves.' [339]

Verse 18

Had the slaves been of free service for six years, there would have been every possibility of selfishness and greed on the side of owner? So, here the law clearly indicates that, the six years of service is worth the wages of hired laborers. The slaves had worked for no pay, and the wages that would have been paid to an employee for the same labor were to be considered as full repayment for the debt that had caused the slavery in the first instance.[340] The law here again cautions the owner of the slaves, which had served under them due to the debt. So, do not consider it as hardship, rather free them with total willingness. The result will be blessing from God. This concept is totally absent in the Exodus passage.

Hence, the law of slavery in Deuteronomy is sound both theologically and economically. The economic feasibility to have a new and fresh beginning of life, i.e., a historical and economic redemption (Exod 12:33-36) is given much emphasis. It recognizes and respects the private life of the slave. The Law regards him as a brother, who sells himself/herself his/her service, and not his/her person. Unlike Exodus, there is no mention of the hidden agenda of the owner to increase his slaveholdings by giving the slave a wife and at the end of six years keeping back the wife and children. The slave has a voice in the community, and as a citizen he enjoys the same rights as his master. He has not only the rights of freedom but also can stay with his family (In the Covenant Code, the slave has to decide whether he needs freedom or family and in Holiness code, children can go with him, but the freedom of wife is not mentioned). The Deuteronomic Code does not view male and female slave as chattel under owner's control, rather as 'brother'/fellow Israelite. The justice and compassion to the weak and powerless members of the community are well addressed in this law.

---

339 Tikva Frymer-Kensky, "Deuteronomy," in *Women's Bible Commentary*, eds. Carol A. Newsom and Sharon H. Ringe (Kentucky: John Knox Press, 1998), 59.

340 Craige, 239.

Deuteronomy 16:11-14 (The Festival Reviewed)

Translation/Textual Comments

11 And rejoice before the Lord your God, you and your son and
your daughter, and your manservant[341] and your maidservant, and
the Levite who is within your towns, and the sojourner, and the
fatherless and the widow who are among you at the place that the
Lord your God will choose to dwell (as a dwelling) for his name. 12
You shall remember that you were a slave in Egypt[342] ; and you shall
be careful to observe these decrees. 13 You shall keep the feast of
booths (tabernacles) seven days, when you have gathered from your
threshing floor and from your wine press; 14 you shall rejoice in your
feast, you and your son and your daughter, and your manservant and
your maidservant, the Levite, and the sojourner, and the fatherless
and the widow who is within your towns.

Form and Structure

Deuteronomy 16:1-17 deals with the three feasts of Israel. Within the series of festival, vv.1-8 (the feast of Passover) is much discussed as verse 3 contradicts with verse 8. It is generally argued among the scholars that the two feasts, Passover and unleavened bread have been combined.[343] This chapter consists of the Passover with unleavened bread (vv.1-8), the feast of weeks (9-12), the feasts of booths (13-15) followed by a summary (16-17).The expectation of Yahweh in all these feasts to the people of Israel is to remember the faithfulness of God in their lives, to observe the feasts from generation to generation by involving all members of the society (vv. 11, 14).

---

341 The Samaritan Hebrew Pentateuch, Septuagint (ὁ παῖς σου) and Vulgate miss out the *vav* conjunction.

342 Some Hebrew manuscripts like Samaritan Hebrew Pentateuch (בארץ מצרים), Septuagint (ἐν γῇ Αἰγύπτῳ) read 'in the land of Egypt' cf. 5:15. In MT here and in 24:18 במצרים (in Egypt) is used.

343 Mayes, 254-256. For Christopher Wright, Deuteronomist has woven together Israel's two great feasts with a purpose. It looks back their past and points to the future. The Passover is primarily the celebration of the exodus and the feast of unleavened bread though rooted in Exodus could only be celebrated in the context of land (Wright, 198.). The Deuteronomist makes the three feasts as two with the word 'rejoice' in both of these sections (v. 11 and v. 14).

This passage is a deuteronomic version as it gives more importance to worship (the word 'rejoice' is unique in Deuteronomy). The three feasts with the exception of Passover have an agricultural setting and belong to the period of settlement.[344]

Comments and Explanation

The heart of the festival is not merely to remember the salvific act of God and His blessing, but to have a fellowship meal involving all members of the community regardless of their socio-economic status. The law here motivates the owner to extend the celebration to servants and other members connected to his family.

Verses 11-14

Deuteronomy 16:9-17 deals about the feast of weeks and the feast of booths. Unlike the parallel passages in Exodus (23:14ff. and 34:18ff) and Leviticus (23:15-22, 33-44), Deuteronomic passage has a difference. Neither of the two feasts in Deuteronomy is connected with salvation history (cf. Exod. 23:15; 34: 18; Lev. 23:42-43). In the Book of Leviticus, the dwelling in booths is projected to remind the people of Israel of their wandering in the desert. In the Book of the Covenant the feast of weeks is called as the feast of harvest (23:16).[345] In the Deuteronomic Code, the striking significance is not merely her history, rather the involvement of each member of the society ('Rejoice ...you and your sons and your daughters, your male and female slaves, the Levites, the strangers, the orphans and widows- vv.11 and 14). In the parallel passages only the male members were given the privilege as they were considered as the members of the covenant community. For the Deuteronomist, the dependent members are given the privilege, as Israelite too was once in a similar dependent social position (cf. 15:15).[346] Verse 12 is the reason for such stipulation 'Remember that you were a slave in Egypt'. For Deuteronomy, the reason for celebration is not merely

344 H. Cunliffe-Jones, "Deuteronomy," in *Torch Bible Commentaries*, ed. Alan Richardson John Marsh, R. Gregor Smith (London: SCM Press Ltd, 1951), 101.

345 Rad, *Deuteronomy*, 110-113.

346 Merrill, 254; Philips, 113-114.

to know how they came out of Egypt, i.e., exodus experience, rather how their lives were when they lived in Egypt, i.e., their servitude (Exod. 23:14; Lev. 23:43; Deut 16:12).[347] Since in Egypt all faced the same experience and got deliverance, hence the participation of feast was not limited to male members of the society, rather to all.[348] Each member of the community had access and rights to enjoy the feast. For the Deuteronomist, the festivals were a time of rejoicing for all members of the community. He creates empathy for the weak and marginalized and creates a sense of feelings among them that they too are given rest to celebrate the redemptive act of God. Hence, the celebration unlike other codes gives a new meaning to the community emphasizing the significance of each member irrespective of their social standing. This change is vital as it brings social bonding and renewal, and a deep conviction that they are part of the community of God.

Deuteronomy 20:10-14 (Law to Offer Peace to a Besieged City)

Translation/Textual Comments

10 When you draw near into[349] a city[350] to fight against it, offer (terms of) peace to it. 11 If it accepts your terms of peace and surrenders to you, then all the people in it shall do forced labor for you and they shall serve you. 12 But if it does not make peace with you, but makes/engages war against you, then you shall besiege it. 13 And when the Lord your God gives it into your hand[351] then you shall

347 For Mayes, the reference to Egypt in the context of this festival is of deuteronomic origin…(Mayes, 260).

348 In our observation, along with God, there were human agents for the deliverance of Israel. The human agents were not merely the male members of the society, rather people irrespective of sex. Hence, the rights of rejoicing are for all. Surprisingly, the other parallel codes center around the male members of the society. Possibly, the Deuteronomist had that in mind while giving away this particular legislation.

349 The MT reads אל whereas the Samaritan Hebrew Pentateuch reads על 'to'.

350 Though the text is not clear in stating whether it is the city in the land or outside the land, but verse 1 makes it clear that the city is outside the land.

351 Few manuscripts like Septuagint (τὰς χεῖράς σου) and Syriac read as plural 'into your hands'.

strike all of its male to the sword[352], 14 only the women and the little ones, the cattle and all that is in the city, all of its plunder[353], you shall take for you as booty, and you shall enjoy[354] the plunder of your enemies, which the Lord your God has given you.

Form and Structure

Deuteronomic code, of all the books of the Old Testament lays considerable stress on laws concerning warfare (20; 21:10-14; 23:9-14; 24:5; 25:17-19). The form is of formal regulations.[355] The style of the law is introduced by כִּי 'when' and formulated in second person singular form (20:1, 10, 19). The laws of war in chapter 20 are concerned with the proclamation before the battle (vv.1-9), the siege of the city (vv.10-18) and the handling of the trees (vv.19-20). The laws in vv, 10-18 are unimaginable before the period of the monarchy, as it is heavily politics in nature and strategically based. This form of law is possible only when Israel had become active factor on the great political scene.[356]

Comments and Explanation

The law deals about the city that agrees for peace and cities that resist/reject peace. The law is not merely of war but of peace. The enemies are offered peace, if they surrender. It is a merciful and redemptive act. However, if they reject the offer the male members will be executed but the innocent women and children will be spared.

Verses 10-14

וְקָרָאתָ אֵלֶיהָ לְשָׁלוֹם - The term peace in this context means vassal treaty in which the defeated party would become subject (Josh 9:15; Judg 4:17; I Sam 7:14; I Kings 5:12; Isa. 27:5). The possible translation

352 Lit., 'to the mouth of the sword'.

353 Many manuscripts of Septuagint and Syriac add *waw* conjunction to כל i.e., 'and all'.

354 Lit., eat, consume, devour or feed (to make use of it).

355 J. A. Thompson, "Deuteronomy," in *The Tyndale Old Testament Commentaries*, ed. D. J. Wiseman (England: Inter-Varsity Press, 1976), 218-219.

356 Rad, *Deuteronomy*, 132-133. Also see Philips, 135.

of this phrase is 'and you shall call for treaty'.[357] The verb also means surrender or submission.

מַס – The Hebrew word מַס is not an abstract concept, but a collective noun (common masculine singular absolute) denoting those people who are reduced to forced labour or a group of forced labourers working for the state .[358]

The law in vv.10-14 is humanitarian in nature though conditional. They are asked to make an offer of peace.[359] In normal case, when the city was prepared to enter into a treaty, the inhabitants especially the male members are put to death. But, here they are offered to be a vassal and to put under forced labor.[360] The Israelites are not to engage in bloodshed in first sight, rather offer an opportunity to the enemy for surrender. If they surrender, then the lives of the inhabitants are to be spared. If not, then all the males are slain with the sword. All the rest can be plundered and enjoyed by the Israelites in any way.

Deuteronomy 21:10-14 (Marrying a Captive Woman)

Translation/Textual Comments

10 When you go forth to the war against your enemies[361], and the Lord your God gives them into your hands[362] and you take them captive, 11 and you see among the captives a beautiful woman[363],

357 Thompson, "Deuteronomy," 222. C.f. Christensen, 444-447; Merrill, 285; Wright, 229-230.

358 Mayes, 294; Tigay, 189.

359 The same idiom is found in the Akkadian letter from Mari, 'When he had besieged the city, he offered it terms of submission'. In an Egyptian inscription, the prostrate princess of Canaan says 'shalom' when submitting to Pharaoh (Tigay, 188-189.)

360 Thompson, "Deuteronomy," 222. See Deut. 7:22ff; Josh 9:11-23.

361 One Hebrew manuscript (*varia lectio codicis kennicott* 69) and Cairo Geniza fragments read אֹיבְךָ 'your enemy' instead of MT אֹיְבֶיךָ 'your enemies'.

362 Few Hebrew manuscripts, Cairo Geniza fragments, Syriac and Targum Pseudo Jonathan read בידיך 'into your hands' instead of MT בְּיָדֶךָ 'into your hand'.

363 Samaritan Hebrew Pentateuch and Syriac read בשביו אשה 'among his captives a woman' whereas MT reads בַּשִּׁבְיָה אֵשֶׁת 'among the (female) captives a woman'.

and you have desire for her and would take her[364] for wife, 12 then you shall bring her home to your house, and she shall shave her head[365] and pare her nails[366]. 13 and she shall put off[367] her captive's garb[368], and shall remain in your house and mourn for her father and her mother a full month[369], after that you may go in to her and you may marry her and she shall be your wife[370]. 14 But if you are not satisfied with her, you shall let her go free[371] where she wants[372] and not sell[373] her for money, you shall not treat her as a slave[374], since you have dishonored[375] her.

---

364 One Hebrew manuscript (*varia lectio codicis kennicott* 1), Septuagint, The Samaritan Hebrew Pentateuch, Syriac and Targum read וּלְקַחְתָּהּ 'and you shall take her'. The suffix is missing in MT. MT reads it as וְלָקַחְתָּ 'and you shall take'.

365 In Septuagint, verse 12 a-a reads 2 sg. 'καὶ ξυρήσεις τὴν κεφαλὴν αὐτῆς καὶ περιονυχιεῖς' i.e., 'you shall shave …and you do/pare…'instead of MT וְעָשְׂתָה אֶת־רֹאשָׁהּ 'and she shall shave… and she shall do/pare'. This ritual is a symbol of accepting her as a member of the covenant community (cf. Lev.14:8; Num 8:7).

366 Cf. II Sam 19:25.

367 Septuagint reads the verb in 2 sg περιελεῖς 'you shall put off' whereas MT read it in 3 sg. וְהֵסִירָה 'she shall put off'

368 The clothes she was wearing when taken as a captive.

369 Mourning period (Deut. 34:8; Num.20:29). There are OT passages referring for 7 days of mourning (Gen.50:10; I Sam. 31:13; I chron.10:12). There are other possible interpretations: a) change of status from a foreigner to a member of the covenant community, 2) The one month period provides her the time to have her menstrual period and a proof that she is not pregnant by any other man (Nelson, 259.)

370 The freedom to take the captive as a wife contradicts with Deut 7:3.

371 The verb used here points in two different ways: 1) Freeing her as a slave is freed (Deut.15:12) and 2) The piel form of the verb may refer to divorce (Deut.22:19, 29). Since verse 13 indicates marriage, the possibility is divorce.

372 Lit., 'according to her desire'.

373 Septuagint reads πραθήσεται 'she shall be sold'.

374 Septuagint reads ἀθετήσεις 'you shall treat ..'. The verb denotes one's power of commercial disposal. The piel verb עִנִּיתָהּ is connected to the preceding verb which means 'had sex with' usually indicates humiliation through forced sex (Nelson, 254.)

375 The understanding here is either 'I find no delight in her' or 'the emotional strain to which she has been subjected' (Cairns, 190.)

Form and Structure

The law concerning the marriage of an Israelite with a captive woman is in its form a homogeneous whole[376] and comes under Deuteronomic law related to warfare. The style of this text is in the same form (כִּי with second person singular form) as in Deut. 20:1-20. The main case (vv.10-13) is followed by a sub case (v.14). The sub case contains double prohibition. It is placed between two family laws (vv.1-9 and vv.15ff). The opening words are exactly the same (*when you go forth to war against your enemies*). However, in 20:10-18, women are listed among the spoils.

Comments and Explanation

The law deals with marriage to a woman captured in war. It focuses not only on marriage but also some of the rituals to be done prior to marriage. The law also presents the treatment to be taken after marriage (marital relations). For Christensen, the focus of the literary unit is the actual treatment the prospective bride is to be given.[377]

Verses 10-14

וְגִלְּחָה אֶת־רֹאשָׁהּ וְעָשְׂתָה אֶת־צִפָּרְנֶיהָ וְהֵסִירָה אֶת־שִׂמְלַת שִׁבְיָהּ מֵעָלֶיהָ (...*shave her head and pare her nails...put off her captive's garb)* – These activities are usually done as mourning rites. Do these actions denote mourning rites? The text is not clear. If it is so, it points to an inhumane act, as the text does not mention about the death of her near and dear ones (cf. Deut. 14:1). In the present context, this is not a mourning rite. It perhaps symbolizes the act of complete renunciation of her country of origin, a change of life and status. It is with new hair, nail and clothes that she starts a new phase of life as a married woman in Israel.[378]

---

376 Rad, *Deuteronomy*, 137.

377 Duane L. Christensen, "Deuteronomy 21:10-34:12," in *Word Biblical Commentary*, ed. John D. W. Watts (Nashville: Thomas Nelson Publishers, 2002), 473.

378 Philips, 140. The shaving of the head and putting of the garments is referred in the Mari texts as getting rid of everything that would remind the captive of her hometown dating to the 18th century BCE (C.f. Christensen, "Deuteronomy 21:10-34:12," 473-475; Mayes, 303; Thompson, "Deuteronomy," 228.)

Unlike other Deuteronomic passage, the captive women are placed under a series of rites and regulations such as shaving head, paring nails, putting off her captive's garb, remaining in the house and mourning for her parents for a month. Why do they have such a ritual regulation? Does it symbolize her change of status? The family was considered to be the real mainstay of the religion of Yahweh. The family could be infected by a foreign religion through a woman.[379] The text is not forbidding an Israelite marrying a foreign woman,[380] rather placed lot of rules to be adopted.The humanitarian approach can be seen where she is given a month to remember the loss of her near and dear ones. The significant aspect of this law is that it gives due respect to the personhood of the enslaved woman. Whether this development takes place in the late seventh century BCE especially during King Manasseh's period. There is a possibility.

וְאַחַר כֵּן תָּבוֹא אֵלֶיהָ וּבְעַלְתָּהּ וְהָיְתָה לְךָ לְאִשָּׁה (*and after that you may go in to her and you may marry her and she shall be your wife*) - After a full month's mourning she could become the wife of an Israelite citizen.The law demands that she must be regarded as a full member of the household guaranteeing her full measure of freedom like any other Israelite women.[381] The rights of becoming an Israelite wife cannot be demeaned as a slave even if he changes his mind. This clearly presents the positive approach towards the women and a full recognition of her status in society.

וְהָיָה אִם־לֹא חָפַצְתָּ בָּהּ וְשִׁלַּחְתָּהּ לְנַפְשָׁהּ (*but if you are not satisfied with her, you shall let her go free*) - Since the captive woman after performing the said rites is legally a wife, she cannot be treated as a chattel. She has every right of freedom like any free Israelite woman. Her husband has no right to sell her for money or treat her as slave. In Exodus 21:7-11, the same regulations can be seen but with a difference. Verse 8 says, "If she does not satisfy her master…then

379 Rad, *Deuteronomy*, 137. For more reading refer Merrill, 291; Tigay, 194.

380 A kindly consideration is given to a captive woman, which sharply contrasts with the cruel treatment meted out to the women captured in war (Deut 7:1-4). C.f. Thompson, "Deuteronomy," 228. The passage 7:1-7 falls outside the Deuteronomic Code (12-26).

381 Ronald E. Clements, "The Book of Deuteronomy," in *The New Interpreter's Bible*, ed. Leander E. Keck (Nashville: Abingdon Press, 1998), 445.

he shall let her be redeemed; he shall have no right to sell her to a *foreign people,* since he has dealt unfairly with her." The regulation stated in Exodus is for the Israelite concubine. The laws for a captive girl are different. In Deuteronomy, though she is a foreign captive woman, the approach taken against her is a positive tone. Though she has lost her original identity by entering a new life as a married woman in Israel, yet she has the right to leave her husband, which is a distinctive deuteronomic humanitarian viewpoint. The woman's social status must not to be damaged. The regulation points to a clear message that even the prisoners of war are persons and not things. A strong humanitarian approach, where there is space for people irrespective of class and gender. The law here gives upper hand to the female captive[382] and puts restriction on the person who took her as a captive.

לֹא־תִתְעַמֵּר בָּהּ (*not treat her as a slave*) - The verb תִתְעַמֵּר is found here and in 24:7. Its meaning is uncertain. Possibly it designates the action of one who has limitless power over others.[383]

Deuteronomy 22:13-21 (Laws of the Loss of Virginity Prior to Marriage)

Translation/Textual Comments

13 If a man takes a wife and goes into her, and then dislikes her[384],
14 and makes up charges against her[385], slandering her[386] and gives to her bad name, saying, "I took this woman, but when I came near her, I did not find proof of her virginity", 15 then the father of the young

---

382 She is given the status of a wife, given time to remember those whom she had left, not to disturb her in any way during the period of 30 days and if he is not satisfied with her, he must give her freedom (not to be sold as a slave) [refer Wright, 234.]

383 Mayes, 303-304.

384 Hate her or turn against her after his carnal desires have been satisfied (see Driver, *A Critical and Exegetical Commentary on Deuteronomy*, 254.) For Cairns, the man has leveled 'wantonness of words' and the charges are destructive (Cairns, 197.)

385 Lit. meaning 'accuse her of…things', i.e., misconduct.

386 Lit. meaning 'puts out a bad name…'

woman[387] and her mother shall take and bring out the proof of her virginity[388] to the elders of the city[389] at the gate[390]; 16 then the father of the young woman shall say to the elders, " I gave my daughter[391] to this man to be a wife but he dislikes her; 17 and now he has made up[392] shameful charges[393] saying , I did not find proof of virginity in your daughter', but these are the proofs of my daughter's virginity". Then they shall spread out[394] the cloth[395] before the elders of the city. 18 Then the elders of that city shall take the man[396] and punish him; 19 and they shall fine him a hundred shekels of silver and they shall give to the father of the young woman because he has brought a bad name to a virgin of Israel; and she shall continue to be his wife; he must not send her away[397] all of his days. 20 but if the charge is true, that[398] the proof of the virginity of the young woman were not found, 21 then they shall bring out the girl to the door of her father's

---

387 Many Hebrew manuscripts, Cairo Geniza, Samaritan Hebrew Pentateuch, and the Qere, נַעַר is stated as נַעֲרָה (throughout vv.15-29).

388 The 'proof of virginity' is usually taken to be the bloodstained sheet from the bridal bed resulting from first sexual union. The other argument is the proofs of menstruation, showing that the woman was not pregnant at the time of her marriage (Clements, "The Book of Deuteronomy," 455.). It can also refer to the inner garment stained with menstrual blood.

389 Septuagint reads γερουσίαν 'elders' instead of ἡ γερουσία τῆς πόλεως 'elders of the city'. In MT verse 16 reads 'elders' (also Septuagint γερουσίᾳ) instead of 'elders of the city' (vv.15, 17 and 18).

390 Refer 21:19.

391 Septuagint adds ταύτην 'this'.

392 One Hebrew manuscript (*varia lectio codicis kennicott* 69), few Hebrew manuscripts Cairo Geniza, Septuagint, Syriac and Vulgate adds לָהּ 'to her'.

393 Few manuscripts Syriac, Samaritan, Vulgate, Targum supplements 'against her' (cf. v. 14).

394 Samaritan Pentateuch read וּפָרַשׂ (3sg.) instead of MT וּפָרְשׂוּ (3 pl.).

395 It refers to the outer garment used as a cover while sleeping.

396 One Hebrew manuscript, Samaritan Hebrew Pentateuch, Septuagint and Syriac add הַהוּא 'that'.

397 One Hebrew manuscripts, Samaritan Hebrew Pentateuch read שַׁלְּחָהּ. It does not have the preposition as prefix found in MT לְשַׁלְּחָהּ 'to send her away'.

398 One Hebrew manuscript (*varia lectio codicis kennicott* 69) and Septuagint omits הַזֶּה 'this'.

house, and the men of her city[399] shall stone her to death, because she has done a disgraceful act in Israel by prostituting[400] herself in her father's house. So you shall purge the evil from the midst of you[401].

Form and Structure

This law comes under family law and is casuistic in form, i.e., conditional law with judicial language. It has subordinate cases, which begin with וְאִם.It is in two parts: 1) vv. 13-19 and 2) vv. 20-21. Both of these parts are written in a completely different style (כִּיand אִם) and at the end add a basis explaining the judgment. The first part (13-19) is a long description of the case where both parties are expressing their claims. The second part (20-21) is short and goes straight to the legal decision and the reason behind it, and also has an addition, which has a change in style, found also in 22b and 24b (*so you shall purge the evil from the midst of you*). This law unlike other laws has three parts: a) the legal case, where a man brings charges against his wife that she had lost her virginity by the time she married him (13-15), b) the process, where the legal defense is undertaken by her parents (16-17), and c) the verdict (18-19). Verses 20-21 is the other possibility in the case, where the accusation made by the man is truth and its verdict [402]

Comments and Explanation

The law describes briefly on the case of a false accusation and the case of a correct accusation, and its consequences. It protects the woman from slander and financial loss, if found innocent.

---

399 Many Hebrew manuscripts Cairo Geniza fragments, Targum add כל 'all' (all the men of her city). אַנְשֵׁי עִירָהּ is omitted in Septuagint (codex Vaticanus).

400 The Samaritan Hebrew Pentateuch and Septuagint read לְהַזְנוֹת instead of MT לִזְנוֹת. MT read as Qal form (Commit adultery). The Samaritan and Septuagint read in Hiphil form, where the father's house is taken as direct object which means prostituting her father's house.

401 Septuagint, Syriac, Targum Pseudo Jonathan read 2pl. Codex manuscripts of Vulgate reads מקרב ישראל 'in the midst of Israel'.

402 Rad, *Deuteronomy*, 142. C.f. Rofe, 173.

Verses 13-15

כִּי־יִקַּח אִישׁ אִשָּׁה (If a man takes a woman)- The Verb יִקַּח has multiple meaning such as marry, lay hold of, seize, acquire, snatch etc.

וְלָקַח אֲבִי הַנַּעַר הָנַּעֲרָהוְאִמָּהּ וְהוֹצִיאוּ אֶת־בְּתוּלֵי הַנַּעַר הָנַּעֲרָה (*then the father of the young woman and her mother shall take and bring out the proof of her virginity*) - The verb בתולים is usually referred as the bloodstains resulted from first sexual union. In this text, the parents are expected to produce before the elders with the matrimonial bed sheet stained with their daughter's blood to defend her daughter and defeat the claim of their son-in-law. This act is an evidence to prove their daughter's virginity.[403] This form of practice is common in Middle East and is practised among various Jewish and Arab communities. The parents would keep this garment to safeguard their reputation and the bride-price they receive, all depend on it.[404] The parents have the right to protect their daughter in front of their son-in-law.

---

403 Philips, 148. There are few other interpretations for the words 'the proof of her virginity'. Some argue that the girl's hymen was broken down when she was given for marriage. It is also argued that the word בְּתוּלִים is of a form which is often used for certain abstract nouns denoting age-groups, which could refer to 'female adolescence' as well as 'virginity'. Hence, it refers to proofs of menstruation immediately before marriage, as a sign that the woman was not pregnant at the time of her marriage and was menstruating regularly. It is a possibility, but what if she had sexual relation after the period of menstruation and before marriage. Now, if it is interpreted as the bloodstains of first sexual union after marriage, the problem is what if husband makes a foul play by destroying the evidence. The other interpretation is contrary to menstrual clothes or bed sheet. It refers to an apparel signifying virginity, which is worn by a young woman to signify respectability and eligibility for marriage. When a woman got married, this garment was put aside or torn (Driver, *A Critical and Exegetical Commentary on Deuteronomy*, 255; Mayes, 310; Thompson, "Deuteronomy," 236; Robert I. Vasholz, "A Legal 'Brief' on Deuteronomy 22: 13-21," *Presbyterion* 17, no. 1 (1991): 62; Bruce Wells, "Sex, Lies, and Virginal Rape: The Slandered Bride and False Accusation in Deuteronomy," *JBL* 124, no. 1 (2005): 41-72.)

404 Tigay, 205. C.f. Christensen, "Deuteronomy 21:10-34:12," 519-520.

Verse 18

וְיִסְּרוּ אֹתוֹ (*and they shall punish him*)- It has different meanings like discipline, admonish, chasten or instruct. It also indicates the infliction of corporal punishment (cf. 21:18-21).[405]

Verse 19

וְעָנְשׁוּ אֹתוֹ מֵאָה כֶסֶף (*they shall fine him a hundred shekels of silver*) - The fine is imposed for the damages he had done by falsely accusing her character. The fine is double the amount of the bride-price. The average bride-price is 50 shekels of silver (22:29). He is being punished for the breach of trust, which would have even forced the bride's father to return the bride-price.

וְנָתְנוּ לַאֲבִי הַנַּעֲרָה (*and shall give them to the girl's father*)- The fine is paid to the girl's father, as it is he who paid the bride-price (cf. v. 29) and moreover, based on verse 21, the father's reputation was at stake, where he was accused of not having an eye upon her daughter and acted deceitfully under false pretences by giving away her for marriage.

Verses 20-21[406]

If the accusation made by her husband turns out to be true, then she must be brought out of her father's house and she will be stoned to death. The law here not ends with a divorce, rather equated with adultery, which is a capital punishment.[407]

אֶל־פֶּתַח בֵּית־אָבִיהָ (*to the door of her father's house*) - If the claim of the man against his wife is proved, she will be stoned to death. She is not merely treated as an adulterous woman and stoned to death, but this act will take place to the door of her father's house as a sign of displeasure over her father's deceit and for failing to keep an

405 Philips, 148-149. For Mayes, the intention is not corporal punishment as different verb is used for it (25:1-3) [Mayes, 310.]

406 These verses are considered as a subsequent addition to the law (c.f. Mayes, 311.). Alexander Rofe argues that this law is in conflict with the other biblical sex laws (Rofe, 178.)

407 Frank Crusemann, *The Torah: Theology and Social History of Old Testament Law*, trans. Allan W. Mahnke (Edinburgh: T&T Clark, 1996), 255.

eye upon his daughter, as his daughter had committed fornication in his house.[408] The judgment taken against woman is more severe than that of the man (cf. Hos 2:2; Jer 3:8). For woman, if found guilty, the sentence is to stone her to death, and if the accuser is wrong, the punishment is flogging and fine. If the husband brought baseless charges against her, which in one way leads to her character assassination, the sentence ought to be death, but the law is lenient towards the husband.

אַנְשֵׁי עִירָהּ (*men of her city*) – The punishment is executed by the men of her city, even though she is married to a man of another city. The reason for such an act is because of her fornication, while living in her father's house.

נְבָלָה בְּיִשְׂרָאֵל (*disgraceful act in Israel*) - The Hebrew word נְבָלָה indicates conduct resulting in gross disorder, outrage, disorderly foolish and deplorable act.[409] It is an expression found in different parts of the Old Testament (Gen.34:7; Josh.7:15; Judg.19:23; 20:6-10; II Sam. 13:12; Jer. 29:23). This noun often indicates sexual crime such as rape and adultery.

The Deuteronomic Code considers the family life not merely a matter of sexual morality, rather a fundamental aspect of the Covenant community, where drastic measures must be taken to ensure purity. Unfortunately, unlike other Deuteronomic passages, the women referred to in this text were not treated as persons, having an adequate status and rights. The judgment taken against the man (if found accused) contradicts within the law ('talionic retribution'- Deut 19:16-21). The male domination is heavily marked in this text, where woman passes on from her father to husband and then back to her father. The male members are the decision makers and the female members are at the mercy hand of their male counter parts. Even, for producing the proof of her virginity, the father of the girl is given the time and space to defend, and her mother is mentioned as a secondary person (v.15). However, the law also provides a stringent action against her husband if the charge made is false, though not

---

408 Tigay, 206. Also refer Anthony Philips, "Another Look at Adultery," *JSOT* 20 (1981): 10. Cf. CH §21.

409 Mayes, 311; Philips, *Deuteronomy*, 149.

as severe as the woman (if found accused). Thus, the law provides security to her future by making him marry her; otherwise her condition will be most vulnerable to her name and status. Hence, the ruling appears to be unique comparing to other parallel codes and in all of the Ancient West Asian legislations.

Deuteronomy 22:22 (Law on Adultery)

Translation/Textual Comments

22 If a man is found sleeping with the wife of another man, both of them shall die[410], the man who sleeps with the woman, and the woman; so you shall purge the evil from Israel.

Comments and Explanation

Like the previous section, this law also is casuistic in style (Cf. Deut 5:18). Unchastity with a married woman is punished by death. According to the Deuteronomic legislation, women are equally liable along with men. Originally only the man was liable to execution, and if woman was found in this act, the punishment meted out to her was divorce. The Deuteronomic reform changes the law making both party equally responsible. The Law did not support for a double standard.[411]

In Israel, adultery carries with it death penalty (Cf. Ezek. 16:38-41; 23:45-47). Other law collections from the Ancient West Asia prescribe or pronounce death penalty for adultery (CH §129; MAL §§14-16; HL §§197-198).The Deuteronomic Code considers this act as destroying the very fabric of social order in which family is pivotal and adultery endangers its very existence. The pronouncement of death to both man and woman will purge the evil from Israel.

---

410 The method of execution is not specified, but the formula 'so you shall purge the evil from Israel' possibly indicates death by stoning (Clements, "The Book of Deuteronomy," 455. Cf. v. 24).

411 Philips, *Deuteronomy*, 150. The Deuteronomic legislation is different from Ancient West Asia legislation, for instance in the Code of Hammurabi, both the parties are thrown into the water [AWAT: CH §129 (If the wife of a seignior has been caught while lying with another man, they shall bind them and throw them into the water. If the husband of the woman wishes to spare his wife, then the king in turn may spare his subject) Cf. MAL §§13-14]. The Holiness Code also gives equal judgment (20:10).

Deuteronomy 22:23-29 (Laws on Sexual Intercourse with a Betrothed and Unbetrothed Girl)

Translation/Textual Comments

23 If there is a young woman betrothed to a man, and a man finds her in the city and he sleeps with her, 24 then you shall take both of them to the gate of that city, and you shall stone them to death with the stones, the young woman because she had not cried for help in the city and the man because he violated his neighbor's wife; so you shall purge the evil from the midst of you.

25 But if in the open country a man finds a young woman who is betrothed, and he overpowers her and lies with her, then only the man who lay with her shall die. 26 But to the young woman you shall do[412] nothing[413]; the young woman has not committed an offence punishable by death, for this case is like that of a man attacking and murdering[414] his neighbor; 27 for he found her in the open country, the betrothed young woman cried for help but there was no one to rescue her.

28 If a man meets a virgin[415] who is not betrothed and seizes[416] her and lies with her, and they are found[417], 29 then the man who lay with her shall give to the father of the young woman fifty shekels of silver, and she shall be his wife because he has violated her; he cannot divorce her[418] all of his days.

---

412 The Samaritan Hebrew Pentateuch, Septuagint, Syriac, Targum Pseudo Jonathan read תַעֲשׂוּ 'you(pl.) shall do', whereas MT read תַעֲשֶׂה 'you (sg.) shall do'. Septuagint (Codex Alexandrinus) read ποιήσεται 'it shall be done'. Though the text certifies her as innocent, her future status is not specified, i.e., whether her future husband will take care of her needs.

413 Septuagint MS and Syriac add כִּי 'for' (You shall do nothing for….)

414 It indicates a violent intentional act.

415 A girl of marriageable age.

416 The verb תפש means hold, handle or catch.

417 In MT, the verb is in plural whereas Septuagint reads it as singular 'he is found'.

418 The Verb שַׁלְּחָהּ is in Piel infinitive construct. Few manuscripts and Vulgate adds ל to the beginning of the verb (v. 19). Grammatically, the absence of ל before the infinitive construct is common. Possibly it is a haplography or dittography caused by the preceding word לֹא־יוּכַל.

Form and Structure

This section of law also comes under casuistic form. Unchastity with a betrothed woman is also punishable. However, unlike the previous section (v. 22), here there is a difference. The place where the offence is committed is taken into consideration. If in a city, both are equally responsible and punished by death. But, if it is in an open country, man is responsible and will be awarded death. And if the girl is not betrothed, he has to pay fifty shekels of silver to her father, and must marry her (cf. Exod 22:16f[419]). Unlike other Deuteronomic passages, women are placed under the authority of men, first to her father (paying 50 shekels as a bride price) and then to her husband (allowing him to marry her).

The crime against a betrothed woman and against an unbetrothed woman is also found in Ancient West Asian legal documents. In the Babylonian law code (CH §130), a betrothed woman who has been raped is freed while the rapist is executed. The deuteronomic law is more specific (if it is within the city, both the rapist and the woman will be stoned to death and if it is in open country, the rapist will be executed). The Middle Assyrian law (§55) deals with the rape of an unbetrothed virgin who is staying in her father's house. The rapist must pay a fine to her father for the loss of his daughter's virginity and the father has the right to force the rapist to marry his daughter and is not permitted to divorce her later.

Comments and Explanation

The betrothed girl is considered favourably and equated as wife, and her sexual relation with another man is considered as adultery which prescribes capital punishment.

419 In the Exodus passage, the bride-price is not specified. And the right of the father is given an upper hand, i.e., he has the right to give her daughter in marriage or to refuse the marriage and take the bride-price. In Deuteronomic Code, the accuser has to pay the bride-price and must marry her, which serves as her rights and security.

Verses 23-24 (Seduction of a Betrothed Women in the City)

נער נַעֲרָה בְתוּלָה מְאֹרָשָׂה לְאִישׁ (*young woman betrothed to a man*) -The position of betrothed women comes in between a virgin and a married woman. Her betrothed status is considerably more than merely engagement. Her status is almost of a wife (v. 24). The completion of all legal arrangements preceding the marriage including the bride-price is taken place. [420]

בעִיר (*in the city*) - a woman not willing for sexual intercourse would cry out and people will hear her cry and will rescue her. If she does not cry out, it points to her consent. Hence, the women's consent to the act was assumed.[421]

וְשָׁכַב עִמָּהּ (*and he sleeps with her*) - The betrothed status is equivalent to marriage, and having sexual relationship with a betrothed woman is equivalent to adultery. The words 'and he lies with her' is different from the words 'he seizes and lies with her' (v. 25). In the former case, it need not imply force and points to her consent, whereas in the latter case it points to force and violent act.[422]

Verses 25-27 (Seduction of a Betrothed Woman in the Open Country)

When the betrothed girl is seduced in the open country, it is assumed that the woman had been raped and she screamed, but no one was there for her rescue. Since, she is innocent, only the man shall be put to death.[423]

For Mayes, the original law is probably concluded with verse 25. The following verses (26f) add merely an explanation. Probably, it is a deuteronomistic addition.[424]

---

420 Mayes, 311-312.

421 For different interpretation (Philo, Josephus and others) refer Tigay, 207.

422 Wright, 244.

423 The verb used here is 'seize'. C.f. AWA Laws (CH §130; EL §26; MAL A §12; HL §197).

424 Mayes, 312.

Verses 28-29 (Seduction of a Woman who is not betrothed)

Having intercourse with an unengaged virgin is also considered as offence. However, the quantum of punishment differs from the case of the betrothed woman. It is not clear, why the law prescribes only a fine, as it will tempt people to lead for such an act especially in case where the man has an eye upon her and woman not willing to marry him. Moreover, the fine taken from the accused person is half of the amount demanded from the one who wrongly accused his wife's virginity (v.19).

אֲשֶׁר לֹא־אֹרָשָׂה (*who is not* betrothed) - The verb is in Pual perfect third person singular unlike Pual participle feminine singular absolute. The more accurate translation ought to be *who has never been betrothed.*[425]

When a virgin who is not betrothed, is seduced, the accused shall pay to her father the bride-price which he might normally expect and must also marry the girl. The death penalty is not issued as no legal obligations are involved here.

The Deuteronomic Code is different from the parallel code (Exod 22:16-17), even though the structure and style are similar (*If a man... a virgin who is not betrothed...*). Here, the law gives the father no other option, for instance, receiving a second bride price, which can be a possibility in Exodus. Moreover, the Deuteronomic law protects the girl from further harm and ensuring that she is not left single. It also guards her by not permitting the seducer to divorce her. Hence, the Deuteronomic Code unlike the Covenant Code curtails the power of male (all-male decision) and gives the offender no other option.

425 Ibid. See Exod 22:16-17; MAL §55. Alexander Rofe is not in favor of the translation 'who had never been betrothed'. His argument is that the biblical use of the perfect expresses an action which continues into the present. And in order to negate an action by the word לא, a finite verb, rather than participle is used (c.f. Rofe, 170-171.)

Deuteronomy 24:1-4 (Law on Remarriage with a Former Wife)

Translation/Textual Comments

1 If a man takes a woman[426] and he marries/possesses her and she finds no favor in his eyes because he finds something obnoxious[427], and he writes for her a certificate of divorce[428] and he gives in her hand[429] and sends her from his home, 2 and she goes out from his house and she goes[430] to become another man's wife, 3 and her second man dislikes her and he writes for her certificate of divorce and gives in her hand and he sends her from his house or if the second man[431] dies that he took her for him as wife[432], 4 then her first husband who sent her away, may not take her again to be his wife after she has been defiled[433]; for that is detestable before the Lord[434], and you shall not bring guilt[435] on the land that the Lord your God is giving to you as a inheritance.

---

426 The Samaritan Hebrew Pentateuch adds ובא אליה 'and he comes to her'.

427 Literally it means 'a naked thing'. The word ערוה is from the root ערה 'to be naked'. It is commonly used with the 'nakedness' or 'genitals' particularly of a woman (Christensen, "Deuteronomy 21:10-34:12," 566.). c.f. J Carl Laney, "Deuteronomy 24:1-4 and the Issue of Divorce," *Bibliotheca Sacra* 149, no. 593 (1992): 5-6.

428 Lit., 'a document/writ of cutting off' (cutting off the wife's hem or garment, which is a ceremonial act of divorce).

429 Septuagint reads plural. Targum Pseudo Jonathan and Syriac read לה 'to her'.

430 Septuagint omits מִבֵּיתוֹ וְהָלְכָה 'from his house and she goes' [καὶ ἀπελθοῦσα γένηται ἀνδρὶ ἑτέρῳ]

431 The Samaritan Hebrew Pentateuch read בעלה 'her husband' (as v.4). Some Septuagint adds αὐτῆς 'her'.

432 Vulgate omits הָאַחֲרוֹן אֲשֶׁר־לְקָחָהּ לוֹ לְאִשָּׁה 'the second that he took for him as wife'.

433 It is a Hithpa'el form which generally communicates a passive idea (means 'was defiled').

434 Septuagint adds τοῦ θεοῦ 'your God' to κυρίου 'Lord'.

435 The Samaritan Hebrew Pentateuch and Septuagint (μιανεῖτε) read 2nd person plural.

Form and Structure

The law is in casuistic form with the first three verses in protasis which state the conditions of the contemplated case (cf. Exod.21:1-6) and verse 4 as apodosis which states the law. The style of this law is 'If (v. 1)....then (v. 4)'. The law is set out in different conditions so that the protasis of the conditional sentence takes up three verses.[436] The clause 'then' clearly points out that the law does not deal with divorce or advocates for divorce rather prohibits the woman for remarrying to a man who has been separated before (case of remarriage).

Comments and Explanation

The law that prohibits remarrying her former husband who divorced her is wholly unclear. This law is not found anywhere else and has no parallelism with Ancient West Asian Codes.

Verse 1

כִּי־מָצָא בָהּ עֶרְוַת דָּבָר (*because he finds something obnoxiousin her*) - The literal meaning is 'the shameful thing' or 'the nakedness of a thing'. The Septuagint translation is 'ἄσχημον πρᾶγμα' (unpresentable thing). The possibility of adultery is not the case, as the law for such an act is death, not divorce (cf. 22:22; Lev.20:10). It indicates something which was offensive or unpleasant to her husband (cf. 23:14- violates the purity and holiness, i.e., impure).[437]

סֵפֶר כְּרִיתֻת (*a certificate of divorce*) - The certificate of divorce is a proof that her marriage had been terminated. It is very strange to note that in Israelite legal system, the husband has the right to divorce his wife at any time and for any reason, while a wife could never divorce her husband how genuine the case is.[438] In the words of Bird, 'Divorce was an exclusively male prerogative'.[439] The present text is a clear

436 Thompson, "Deuteronomy," 243. Mayes, 322.

437 Philips, *Deuteronomy*, 159. Mayes feels that the words 'but she finds no favor in his eyes because he finds something indecency' is probably a later addition (Mayes, 322.) c.f. Christensen, "Deuteronomy 21:10-34:12," 566; Nelson, 287; Tigay, 220-221.

438 Philips, *Deuteronomy*, 160.

439 Phyllis A. Bird, *Missing Persons and Mistaken Identities: Women and Gender in Ancient Israel* (Minneapolis: Fortress Press, 1997), 25.

example, where the law maker is not specifying the case that made the husband to write the certificate of divorce. However, the issuing of the certificate of divorce brings protection to her in a sense that no further action will be taken by the man and she has the freedom to marry another man, otherwise she could be accused of adultery leading to death. It is to protect the ill-fated woman.

וְשִׁלְּחָהּ מִבֵּיתוֹ(*and sends her from his house*) - The step to put the divorce into effect is by sending her away from his house.

Verse 4

כִּי־תוֹעֵבָה הִוא לִפְנֵי יְהוָה (*for that is detestable before the Lord*)- Her former husband must not marry her as she had been defiled and to take her back, which shall be an abomination before the Lord, which in turn will bring guilt upon the land (cf. Jer. 3:1-5).[440]

The Deuteronomic legislation sends out a clear message in the interest of woman that there is no easy passage of a man to divorce a woman and then taking her back, which is not possible. She is not a property to be misused, rather she is a person and treating her like a property will lead to the defilement of the woman, which is an abomination before the Lord and thereby it shall increase the guilt upon the land. It protects a woman from further abuse. Here the status of women is elevated. The law makes a significant change in the male dominated power.

Deuteronomy 25:5-10 (The law concerning Levirate Marriage)

Translation/Textual Comments

5 If brothers dwell together[441] and one of them dies and has no son[442], the wife of the dead shall not be married outside the family

---

440 Thompson, "Deuteronomy," 244.

441 The conditional clause probably limited the levirate obligation to the one who stays together. It is applied to those who are close to the property of the deceased.

442 The word son is understood and correctly interpreted in the LXX, Vulgate as child. If child, it presupposes not only a son but also a daughter (cf. Numbers 27:1-11; 36:1-12).

to a strange man (stranger); her husband's brother[443] shall go in to her[444] and take her as his wife, and must do the duty of a husband's brother to her, 6 and the firstborn[445] whom she bears shall carry on the name of his dead brother, so that his name is not blotted out from Israel. 7 But if the man has no desire to take his brother's wife, then his brother's wife shall go to the gate to the elders, and she shall say, "My husband's brother refuses[446] to carry on his brother's name in Israel; he will not perform[447] the duty of a husband's brother to me." 8 Then the elders of his city shall call him and they shall speak to him. If he persists, saying, "I have no desire to marry her," 9 then his brother's wife shall go to him in the presence of the elders and she shall pull his sandal[448] off his foot[449], spit on his

443 The verb יבם means 'to do the duty of a husband's brother (after his brother's death)'.

444 The Samaritan Hebrew Pentateuch reads אֵלֶיהָ 'to her' whereas MT reads עָלֶיהָ 'to her'.

445 The Samaritan Hebrew Pentateuch reads הַבֵּן 'the firstborn son' which is supported by Septuagint Luciani (τὸ πρωτὸτοκον 'the first born son'. Septuagint reads τὸ παιδίον 'the child'.

446 Many Hebrew manuscripts read as מֵאֵן 'he refuses'.

447 Some Hebrew manuscripts Samaritan (Ms), Septuagint (N), Syriac and Vulgate adds waw conjunction וְלֹא 'and not'.

448 The Sandal is a symbol of humiliating oppression, in the sense of treading on someone, and its removal points to humiliating submission to another authority [T. H. Gaster, *Myth, Legend and Custom in the Old Testament* (New York: Harper, 1969), 449-450.] c.f. C. F. Keil, "The Pentateuch," in *Commentary on the Old Testament*, ed. C. F. Keil and F. Delitzsch (Massachusetts: Hendrickson Publishers, 2001), 954-955; Nelson, 299-300.

449 There are different forms of interpretation concerning the removal of shoes: 1) It is regarded as a customary gesture of mourning, as the dead man's brother's refusal points to the end of the family line of her husband and the widow's removal of levir's sandal signifies the mourning, 2) the removal of shoe points to Arabic form of divorce, where the man by removing his sandal states 'she was my slipper and I have cast her off'. In Arabic world, a wife is sometimes figuratively referred to as shoe, 3) It is a symbolic act that the brother had refused his responsibility, 4) The shoe was considered as a symbol of authority and the removal indicates that he has surrendered his authority, 5) The foot was considered as a male symbol and the sandal as a female symbol. The man's refusal points to a breakup of marital relationship and responsibility, 6) the foot was also considered in a euphemistic way to male genitals. So, the removal

face[450] and she shall speak and shall say, "This is what is done to the man who does not build up his brother's house." 10 And his name will be known in Israel, "the house of him whose sandal is pulled off.[451]"

Form and Structure

The form of this law is a precisely expressed and circumspect conditional legal saying by means of which a dispute within a family and local community were to be settled.[452]

This law deals with refusal to carry out the ancient custom[453] of levirate marriage. The custom of marrying a man who dies before having a male child by one of his brother is known throughout Israel and Ancient West Asia such as Hittite and Assyrian.[454] The purposes of such marriage are social and economic matter, i.e., to perpetuate the name of the deceased person (cf. Genesis 38:8-12; Ruth 4:5, 10) and also to keep the family property together. This law goes contrary to the Holiness code where the levirate marriage is forbidden (Lev. 18:16; 20:21).

Comments and Explanation

This law is peculiar in Deuteronomy, though found as early as during the patriarchal period. The law is unique in a sense, as it carries a public disgrace instead of mere penalty.

---

of the sandal is a symbolic exposure of the brother's genital, which is an act of gross contempt (Calum M. Carmichael, "A Ceremonial Crux: Removing a Man's Sandal as a Female Gesture of Contempt," *JBL* 96, no. 3 (1977): 321-336; Clements, "The Book of Deuteronomy," 474-475; Gaster, 449-450; Wright, 269.)

450 It means either to spit on his face or on the ground in front of her brother-in-law.

451 It means barefooted man, i.e., a miserable person.

452 Rad, *Deuteronomy*, 154.

453 The Levirate marriage was known in Hebrew society as far back as the patriarchal age (Gen.38:8ff).

454 In Assyria, this practice was extended even to the one who is betrothed (See Thompson, "Deuteronomy," 251.) See MAL A §30, §31, §33.

Verse 5

כִּֽי־יֵשְׁבוּ אַחִים יַחְדָּו (*When brothers live together*) - Originally the duty of levirate marriage was not restricted to brothers alone, rather it was extended beyond it (Gen.38:1-10; Ruth 4).

Verse 6

יָקוּם עַל־שֵׁם אָחִיו הַמֵּת (*carry on/perpetuate the name of his dead brother*) - It was the belief of the Israelites that after their death their personalities were carried on in the life of their sons who bore their name, while they went to the shadowy half-life of the sheol. And not to have a son means their name is blotted out, which is a misfortune. To have no son, means he has never existed.[455] So, it was the duty of the brother to perpetuate the levirate marriage.

Verse 7

וְאִם־לֹא יַחְפֹּץ הָאִישׁ לָקַחַת אֶת־יְבִמְתּוֹ (*if the man has no desire to take his brother's wife*)-There are few reasons for his refusal: 1) the child would not be his, and 2) the property of the deceased brother if his widow did not marry again, will go back to his family. If the father is dead, naturally the property will be inherited by the surviving brother, so he will have a personal gain even without marrying her.[456]

עָלְתָה יְבִמְתּוֹ הַשַּׁעְרָה אֶל־הַזְּקֵנִים (*his brother's wife shall go the gate to the elders*)-The widow has the right to take his brother to the elders. The elders have jurisdiction in this matter too (cf. 21:19; 22:15).

Verse 9

חָלְצָה נַעֲלוֹ מֵעַל רַגְלוֹ וְיָרְקָה בְּפָנָיו (*she shall pull his sandal off his foot, spit on his face*)-Provision was made for a brother to escape from this obligation by a symbolic act before the elders at the gate. The astonishing act in the law is a public shaming and humiliating ceremony. A sandal was used as a symbolic expression to point to the transfer of rights over property (c.f. Amos 2:6). The action of the widow points out that her brother-in-law has surrendered his right of levirate marriage. Instead of acquiring property by passing

455 Philips, *Deuteronomy*, 169.

456 Craige, 315; Mayes, 329; Tigay, 232-233.

out the sandal, he acquires it through a quite ironical way (cf. Ruth 4:7-8).[457] The shoe which was a symbol of authority is removed off and her brother-in-law surrenders his authority over her. Concerning spiting in his face, there are mixed opinion. It meant spitting on his face or spitting on the ground in front of his face.[458] In either case, both of these acts refer to humiliation (cf. Num 12:14; II Sam 15:30; Isa 20:2; 50:6).

Verse 10

בֵּית חֲלוּץ הַנָּעַל (*the house of him whose sandal is pulled off*) - The unsandaled condition is a sign of dishonor, which will cling to his family for his unbrotherly act.

The law evokes a strong sense of mutual responsibility. It exercises a strong commitment on the patterns of social behavior and is fully sensitive to the moral value of family.

Summary

In the late eighth century BCE, both Judah and Israel were vassals of Assyria. In the year 722 BCE, Israel rebelled against Assyria. The king of Assyria Shalmaneser found out that Hoshea was a traitor, for he had sent envoys to the king of Egypt and he no longer paid tribute. Hoshea was summoned to the king's presence and was thrown into prison. Israel lost political independence and was reduced to the status of Assyrian province (II Kings 17:3-6). Judah too was under the control of Assyria, as king Ahaz instead of heeding the words of prophet Isaiah, sought the help from Assyria (Isaiah 7). During the reign of Josiah (639-609 BCE), the Assyrian power declined. Josiah was able to regain political independence. He began his full scale

457 Philips, *Deuteronomy*, 169. In the book of Ruth, Boaz takes the initiative and the purpose of the ceremony is to redeem the land and to take Ruth as his wife, and the removal of shoe was not for public disgrace. The whole procedure was to acquire Ruth. The redeeming of the land belonging to Elimelech will provide him the base to take Ruth as his wife. In Deuteronomy, the man has no desire to take his brother's wife, which in turn forced the woman to take his sandal off from his foot thereby indicating that he has surrendered from his responsibility. In both of these texts, the land and woman are related [c.f. Carmichael: 324.]

458 Tigay, 233.

reformation by purifying the cult from foreign elements (622 BCE; II Kings 22). The prophecy of the 7th century prophets (Jeremiah and Ezekiel) show traces of the Deuteronomic Code. It is for this reason, modern scholars consider that the Deuteronomic Code was written during the reign of Josiah.

The Deuteronomic Code is not merely a series of legal enactments; rather it gives more importance to ethical and religious issues. It gives emphasis on social issues, more specifically about the poor and the marginalized. It also gives special importance to women, widows, children, and foreigners. The laws on women, marriage and sexuality are given utmost importance in the Deuteronomic Code. The Deuteronomic code as mentioned earlier, probably took its final form in the later period of Manasseh's reign (II Chron 33: 10-16) and during Josiah's rule (II Chron 33, 34). The code appears to be anti-colonial in color and is almost free from the patriarchal structure. Women are given the position of legal independence and are having the right to defend their case. The best example is the levirate text (25:5-10), where a widow has the right to approach the elders, defend her case and even execute the judgment in public.

Chapter 4

The Status of Women in the Holiness Code

The Holiness Code

Title

Since the late 19th century, the Holiness code [Leviticus (17) 18-26] has been considered to be a corpus separate from the rest of the priestly material.[459] The laws in this corpus are distinctively substantiated by Yahweh's self-introduction. The marked feature of this code is that most of the laws are formulated categorically. Scholars like A. Alt, G. Liedke and others label this formulation as apodictic. And when a penalty is stated, it is usually the death penalty or the cut-off penalty, for instance chapter 20. The holiness aspect is given prime importance. Due to these characteristics, Klostermann in 1877 named this corpus *Das Heiligkeitsgesetz*, "the Holiness Code".[460] And

459 Hartley, 247.

460 Ibid., 247-248.

from then on, this name continued to have been referred as Holiness Code.

The Nature of the Holiness Code

According to Gordon J. Wenham, cleanness is the natural state of most creatures. Holiness is a state of grace to which 'men' are called by God, and it is attained through obeying the law and carrying out rituals such as sacrifice. Uncleanness is a substandard condition to which 'men' descend through bodily processes and sin. Every Israelite had a duty to seek release from the uncleanness through washing and sacrifice, because uncleanness was quite incompatible with the holiness of the Covenant people".[461]

But, Mary Douglas, the feminist theologian goes further to Wenham. For her, holiness is not merely an act of separation, rather it means more than separation to divine service. It means wholeness and completeness. She quotes Lev. 21:17-21, listing imperfections that block one from acting as a priest, and puts forward in nutshell as , 'He must be perfect as a 'man', if he is to be a priest'.[462] So, for her, holiness is exemplified by completeness. It requires that individuals should conform to the class to which they belong, and it requires that different classes of things shall not be confused. The idea of wholeness or normality as the notion implicitly assumed to be essential to holiness and cleanness is the key for determining the divisions of the animal kingdom.[463] For Wenham, holiness is something given by God and human being can achieve it, by obeying the law, and it can be done through sacrifice. But, for Douglas, it is not limited only for divine service; rather it has to do with wholeness and completeness.

Form and Structure

The Holiness code is categorized from Chapter 17 to 26. But, among the Scholars, there is a debate regarding Chapter 17, whether

461 Gordon J. Wenham, "The Book of Leviticus," in *The New International Commentary on the Old Testament*, ed. R. K. Harrison (Grand Rapids, Michigan: William B. Eerdmans Publishing Company, 1979), 23.

462 Mary Douglas, *Purity and Danger* (London: Routledge, 1966), 51.

463 Ibid., 53.

it belongs to the section of Holiness code, as the phraseology of Chapter 17 varies from the rest of the chapters, and an introduction to a new corpus is lacking at 17:1. So, it is doubtful, whether Chapter 17 belongs to the following chapters as part of the Holiness Code.

– D. Hoffman pointed out that Chapter 17 seems to be integrally related to what precedes, and not with what follows.[464]

– R. Kilian points out that Chapter 17 is quite distinct from the rest of the Holiness Code. He argues that this chapter was placed at the head of the Holiness Code by a priestly redactor, who used the Covenant code and Deuteronomy as the pattern. And this priestly redactor did not include a separate heading for this block of material, as he was incorporating it into the priestly material. [465]

– For G. J. Wenham chapter 17 lacks most of the phraseology characteristics of chapter 18ff, and has certain features common with the preceding material. He prefers to place chapter 17 as a hinge linking the two halves of the book of Leviticus. Chapter 1-16 contains the ritual regulations for public life and worship, and chapter 18-26 regulates the personal and private affairs of the individual.[466]

Now, scholars such as Beretholet, Eissfeldt, and Bentsch place chapter 17 as part of the Holiness code, as they defend it by implying the practice of ancient codes, which put cultic laws at the beginning of the legal material. For substantiating their argument, they mentioned few examples: Exod. 20:24-26 for the Book of the Covenant; Deut.12 for Deut 12-28; Ezek. 40-42 for Ezek 40-48; and Exod 25-31 for the priestly material. They also note that the language of Chapter 17 ties to the Holiness Code, for instance, the use of the divine first person (vv. 10-12, 14; cf. 26:3, 6, 17), the formula 'any Israelite' (vv. 3, 8, 10, 13), the "cut off" penalty in the divine first person (v. 10; cf. 20:5), and the penalty 'he is held responsible' (v. 16). At the same time, it must be noted however that, this chapter reflects the style of the priestly writer, such as, 'the tent of

464 D. Hoffman, *Das Buch: Leviticus* (Berlin: Poppelaver, 1906), 469.

465 R. Kilian, *Literarkritische Und Formgeschichtiche Untersuchung Des Heiligkeitsgesetzes* (Bonn: Hanstein, 1963), 176ff.

466 Wenham, 241.

the meeting' (vv. 4, 5, 6, 9), eating blood (vv. 10-14), 'a sweet aroma to Yahweh' (v. 6) etc.[467]

In our observation, the very form and structure of chapter 17 comparing to remaining section (18-26) may place chapter 17 not as a part of the Holiness code. The Holiness code can be mentioned as 17(18-26). Above all, it seems that a priestly redactor redacted chapter 17, and so we do see the emergence of both priestly and also ethical and cultic matters. The author agrees with Wenham that, chapter 17 plays the role of hinge in the book of Leviticus between the two halves of the book, chapter 1-16 (ritual regulation for public life and worship), and 18-26 (personal and private matter of the individual).

After analyzing the contribution of these scholars, it can be concluded that the Holiness Code, which is presently seen as single, was not originated from so earlier age but was of widely varying ages. The work of the priestly redactor is visible in the text. These texts such as Chapter 17 might have been composed to supplement and strengthen the other existing text.

The Jubilee[468]

What is the inner core of the term Jubilee? The main purpose is to protect the debtors from the hand of the creditors. In biblical times a man who incurred a debt that he could not repay could be forced to sell of his land or even his personal freedom by becoming a slave. And when this process was left unchecked, that led to a great social division, with a class of rich land owners exploiting a mass of landless groups.[469] So, the Jubilee is being observed to check the unbridled exploitation of the poor. The goal of Jubilee was to maintain the solidarity among the tribes of Israel by keeping alive the equality and unity of all Israelites irrespective of their position under the covenant.

---

467 Hartley, 250-251.

468 Jubilee is one of the main events in the life of the Israel community. It is specified only in Holiness Code. It involves the whole community. Since, it deals with land and people, and freedom for all, the author strongly feels to have a separate section.

469 Wenham, 317.

Observance of the Jubilee

– For Finkelstein and Wiseman, in the Old Babylonia times (19th/17th century BCE) as evident from Mesopotamia, some kings did make administrative decrees, whose effects were similar to the Jubilee laws.[470]

– Westbrook suggested that the Jubilee was the invention of Nehemiah's day. He argues that the only feature of the Jubilee law that is late and impracticable is the idea of a regular 50-year cycle of releases.[471]

– R. North has made a strong case for supposing that the followers of Moses were more likely to have embraced such idealism than the dispirited men who returned from exile.[472]

The original intention of the Jubilee was for the welfare of the weaker section, and the year duration had to do with the administrative decrees of the neighboring states as indicated by Finkelstein and Wiseman. Though it appears that it was originated with a proper intention by the followers of Moses directed by Yahweh, however, the hand of the post-exilic group behind the final shaping of the text can't be negated. The differences between native and foreign slave is one of the reasons for this argument.

The following sections will be an exegetical study on selected texts. Though the Law of Holiness is from chapter 17 through 26, the two texts on cleanness regulations (Lev.12:1-8 and 15:16-31) are added in our study as it deals with woman. The exegetical study of these two texts will help us to know, how it differs from the laws of Holiness.

Leviticus 12:1-8 (Laws on Ritual Purity of a Woman who has given Birth)

The Book of Leviticus contains a series of regulations and laws. The major part of the book deals with laws on ritual purity (11-15) and holy living (17-26).The section (Lev. 11-15) contains a series of laws

470 J. J. Finkelstein, "Ammisaduqa's Edict and the Babylonian 'Law Codes'," *JCS* 15 (1961): 91-104; Wiseman: 161-172.

471 R. Westbrook, "Jubilee Laws," *Israel Law Review* 6 (1971): 209-226.

472 R. North, *Sociology of the Biblical Jubilee* (Rome: Pontifical Biblical Institute, 1954), 204ff.

that emphasize on ritual purity, i.e., clean and unclean, whereas the section 17-26 deals about holy living, i.e., holy and common. In between these two sections, the regulation for the day of atonement is stated (Lev.16).Though the two texts selected for the research, i.e., Leviticus 12:1-8 and 15:16-31 come under the section on ritual purity (Priestly Code) and are outside the holiness code [17(18-26)], they are interconnected[473], and moreover associated with and literally connected with the cause of women. The author strongly feels to have it along with the texts on Holiness code.

Translation/Textual Comments

1The Lord spoke to Moses[474] saying, 2 say to the sons of Israel, saying, when a woman conceives[475] and bears a male child, she shall be ceremonially unclean seven days, as the days of her monthly period, she shall be unclean. 3 On the eighth day, the flesh of his foreskin shall be circumcised[476]. 4 Then she shall wait (remain) thirty three days in the blood of her purifying; she shall not touch any holy thing, or come into the sanctuary until the days of her purifying are completed. 5 But if she bears a female child, then she will be unclean two weeks, as in her period; and she shall wait sixty-six days in the

473 The Priestly Code like Holiness Code was compiled almost at the same time (exilic or early post exilic period). It is assumed that the Priestly writer or a final redactor would have incorporated the Holiness code as both had almost same theological stance (Rao, 39-40.) For Hartley, there is an interconnection from chapter 11 through 26. Chapters 11-15 deal on the state of uncleanness, chapter 16 is a regulation for the day of atonement that removes the state of uncleanness, and chapters 17-26 set forth series of ethical integrity and cultic purity, a forgiven community has to follow.

474 The absence of Aaron's name in the introductory formula is striking (cf. Lev. 11:1, 13:1; 15:1) since it deals with ritual purity.

475 תַזְרִיעַ - Literally, the word means 'produce/sow seed'. The Samaritan Hebrew Pentateuch and Septuagint have a niphal form 'to become pregnant, to conceive' whereas MT uses hiphil form (c.f. Gen 1:11-12 'plants bearing seed'). The hiphil form is used probably to emphasize the procedure 'to conceive a child (Produces offspring)' [c.f. Walter C. Kaiser, "The Book of Leviticus," in *The New Interpreter's Bible*, ed. Leander E. Keck (Nashville: Abingdon Press, 1994), 1085.]

476 The Samaritan Hebrew Pentateuch adds את, the sign of the definite direct object. The MT is in Niphal imperfect form 'he is to be circumcised'.

blood of her purifying. 6 And when the days of her purifying are over, whether for a son or a daughter, she shall bring to the priest at the door of the tent of meeting a lamb a year old[477] for a burnt offering, and a young pigeon or turtledove for a sin offering. 7 And he shall offer it[478] before the Lord, and make atonement for her[479], and then she shall be clean[480] from her flow of blood. This is the law for her who bears a child, male or female. 8 But if she cannot afford a lamb, then she shall bring two turtledoves or two young pigeons[481], one for a burnt offering and the other for a sin offering; and the priest shall make atonement for her, and she shall be clean.

Form and Structure

The law of the purification of birth is only mentioned in Leviticus. It deals with ritual defilement and purity with regard to the birth of a male and female child. It starts with introductory formula (v.1) followed by the regulation to be taken concerning the birth of a male child (vv. 2-4) and female child (v. 5), which includes the time of impurity, separation, restrictions etc. The sacrifices for purification after birth are given utmost importance (vv. 6-7). If the woman is financially weak to meet the requirement, she can offer turtledoves or pigeons (v. 8), which is considered as an appendix.[482] The role of husband is totally missing out, as probably they have nothing to do with this ritual.[483] The main case is introduced by כִּי, whereas the subsidiary case is introduced by אם.

477 Lit., Son of his year (cf. Exodus 12:5; 29:38; Lev. 23:12, 18, 19; Num 6:12, 14; 7:15, 17, 21, 23, 29).

478 The expression 'it' refers to both burnt offering and sin offering.

479 The Hebrew manuscripts, Samaritan Hebrew Pentateuch, Septuagint, Syriac and Targum pseudo-Jonathae add הַכֹּהֵן 'the priest' (cf. v. 8).

480 The Septuagint has και καθαριει'αυτήν 'and it cleanses her'.

481 The Samaritan reverses the order of these sacrifices.

482 Refer Hartley, 166-167.

483 Erhard S. Gerstenberger, "Leviticus," in *The Old Testament Library*, ed. Carol A Newsom and David L Petersen James L Mays (Kentucky: Westminster John Knox Press, 1996), 147.

Comments and Explanation

The law in chapter 12[484] defines the ritual status of an Israelite mother (cultic uncleanness) following the child birth. The reason for such purification is not specified in the text. The text makes a distinction between the birth of a male child (vv. 2-4) and a female child (v. 5). The period of uncleanness for a female child and the time period for a mother to keep herself away from holy activities is double than that of a male child. The text is not stating the reason for such a distinction. After stating the distinction between the male and female child, the law adds an instruction about the offerings to be brought to the priest for cleansing, which is same both for a male and female child (vv. 6-7). Verse 8 deals with a provision if she is poor and cannot afford a lamb.

The sexual activities and childbirth were understood as unclean. The reason for such understanding is because of some mysterious powers and activities.[485] This belief is known throughout Ancient West Asia. Is Israel inclined to such belief? If marriage is ordained by God, why sexual activity and childbirth are phrased as 'unclean'? Why must the woman only enact a purification ritual when she has not sinned? The creator had told the human being to 'Be fruitful and multiply, and fill the earth', then why should a woman be considered unclean when she obeys and follows the command of God.[486] How can the given text contradict with the command of God? We cannot any longer know the reason for such changes in the custom as the text has not specified here or anywhere else.

The issue here is not only to know how this practice of discriminating against women came into Israel, rather why distinction is made between male and female child. Why mother has to appear before the priest for offering and not her husband? Throughout Ancient West Asia, there is a belief that the birth of a female child was more dangerous for the mother than that of a male child, and they also consider that hostile supernatural beings

484 Chapter 12 and 15 deal with the impurities female incur in giving birth and genital discharges both male and female incur respectively.

485 Noth, *Leviticus*, 97.

486 Wenham, 187.

are doubly active during this time.[487] The inferiority of female child is clearly expressed in the text in stating the double 'uncleanness' period.

Verse 2

שִׁבְעַת יָמִים – Why do we have seven days for a male child and fourteen days for a female child ?/why is the time for a mother's purification doubled for a female child? There are two main opinions: Rabbi Simeon ben Yohai, Hoffmann, and Shadal argue that the seven days for a male child is to have circumcision on the eighth day for which holiness is needed. Rabbi Simeon ben Yohai believes that originally like female child, mother of a male child too was impure for fourteen days, but that was reduced to seven to allow circumcision on the eighth day. For Walter C. Kaiser, 'the circumcision of her son cuts her days of purification in half'.[488] However, the other possibility is the practice among the Hittites, where the impurity for the mother giving birth to a male child was shorter than that of a female.[489] If the seven days is resulted due to circumcision, it is considered as a holy ritual. The pertinent argument then is, if circumcision makes way for a male child to purity, then what about the female child, for whom no such rite is performed? Does it have to do with Hittite practice? That could be a possibility as seventh day ritual for a newborn was practised among the Hittites.[490] Some argue that the longer period of impurity in case of a girl child is due to ancient belief that women will be subjected by the strong attacks of the demon. Other argument is that the discharges in case of a girl last longer than male. It has

---

487 A. W. Streane and A. T. Chapman. *The Book of Leviticus* (Cambridge: University Press, 1914), 67. N. H. Snaith, "Leviticus and Numbers," in *The Century Bible*, ed. H. H. Rowley (London: Thomas Nelson and Sons Ltd, 1967), 90-91.

488 Kaiser, "The Book of Leviticus," 1084; Walter C. Kaiser, "The Book of Leviticus," in *The New Interpreter's Bible*, ed. Leander E. Keck (Nashville: Abingdon Press, 1994), 1084.

489 Jacob Milgrom, "Leviticus 1-16," in *The Anchor Bible*, ed. William Foxwell Albright and David Noel Freedman (New York: Doubleday, 1991), 744, 750. C.f. Samuel E. Balentine, "Leviticus," in *Interpretation*, ed. Patrick D. Miller (Louisville: John Knox Press, 2002), 100-102.

490 Milgrom, "Leviticus 1-16," 744.

also been suggested that the birth of a female child was considered less valuable and therefore, required longer period.[491] The text is not clear. The possibility appears to be the social standing of female, where women are placed much lower than that of men.

כִּימֵי נִדַּת דְּוֹתָהּ– Literally 'as the days of her monthly period'. The stress of the particle כִּי is not that it merely equates with the length of the menstruation period, rather to stress the gravity of uncleanness.[492]

Verse 3

This verse is a parenthesis as it switches from mother to a male child. A careful reading points to the continuity of verse 2 as verse 4, since both of these verses deal with the length of impurity. The editorial addition is to emphasize the uniqueness of circumcision. The text on one hand emphasizes the circumcision rite and its uniqueness and on the other hand it highlights the ritual to be performed by a mother for her impurity.

Verse 4

תֵּשֵׁב 'she shall wait/remain'- This refers to isolation or to abstain, probably sexual abstinence. She is not permitted to partake of sacred food and was not given the access to enter the holy sanctuary.

שְׁלֹשִׁים יוֹם וּשְׁלֹשֶׁת יְמֵי (thirty three days)- The days of impurity for a mother bearing a male child is altogether 40 days (v. 2 –seven days and v. 4-thirty three days). The number 40 was one of the chief sacred numbers before the exile (See Exod 24:18).[493] The number 40 is not only prevalent in the scripture, but also in many other cultures such as Greek and Persians. The rules of separation from religious rites are also found in Hittites and in India, though the period of 40 is not practised. However, in Israel a difference can be seen. In Israel, only the mother is considered impure, whereas in Hittite and many other cultures both the child and mother are impure.[494]

---

491 Gorman, 79; Hartley, 167.

492 Milgrom, "Leviticus 1-16," 744.

493 J. R. Porter, "Leviticus," in *The Cambridge Bible Commentary*, ed. A. R. C. Leaney P. R. Ackroyd, J. W. Packer (London: Cambridge University Press, 1976), 94.

494 Milgrom, "Leviticus 1-16," 750.

Verse 5

וְאִם־נְקֵבָה תֵלֵד (But if she bears a female child) - The word וְאִם introduces a second case. The first case is male. The word used for female is נְקֵבָה. It comes from the verb נקב meaning pierce or bore. It refers to the sexual organ of the female, which is the only indication of the gender at the time of the birth.[495]

וְשִׁשִּׁים יוֹם וְשֵׁשֶׁת יָמִים (sixty six days) - The impurity period for a mother bearing a female child is double than that of a male child (sixty six days and fourteen days). The reason for such prolonged uncleanness as mentioned earlier, is probably due to the attack by the demons.[496] The text gives no explicit answer.

Verse 6

וּבִמְלֹאת יְמֵי טָהֳרָהּ (And when the days of her purifying are over)- The word מְלֹאת is in qal infinitive construct form, literally means 'the completion of', i.e., 41st day and 81st day.

לְבֵן אוֹ לְבַת (son or daughter)- Since, the 40th and 80th days are over, the word son and daughter are used.

Though the distinction aspect for impurity is stated in the preceding verses, the offerings to be brought for either son or daughter are same. The issue in this verse is asking a woman and not her husband to bring sacrifice after childbirth. The confinement of a woman and thereafter offering possibly points to her as a sinner. The text is silent in this issue.The silence points to a male dominated tradition where woman are subjected to confinement. The text here is not clear, but in the episode of Hannah, she appeared in the sanctuary at Shiloh only when her son Samuel is weaned (I Sam 1:22).

---

495 Ibid., 755.

496 Wenham, 187. Various reasons are proposed by the scholars. C.f. Keil, 571; Mark F. Rooker, "Leviticus," in *The New American Commentary*, ed. E. Ray Clendenen (Nashville: Broadman& Holman Publishers, 2000), 183; Ross, 267.

Verse 7

When the priest offers both the burnt offering and sin offering and makes atonement on her behalf, then only she will be cleaned from her flow of blood and is eligible to make contact with the sacred objects. The mother bearing male child has to separate herself for 40 days and make an offering to become clean, and in case of bearing female child, she has to dissociate for 80 days and offering, which clearly brings out the picture of confinement and domination.

Verse 8

This verse is considered as a supplement. The reasons for such an argument are based on 7b 'This is the law for her who bears a child, male or female', which is a concluding statement and the reversal in vocabulary 'turtledove and pigeon' (v. 8) instead of 'pigeon and turtledove' (v. 6).

Why should a birth cause such a prolonged uncleanness which even makes her in confinement? The practice of confinement can be seen in many other cultures. As mentioned earlier, in the Hittite culture, both the child and mother are considered impure. The purification period for the female in the Hittite like biblical culture is longer in comparision to the male.[497]

The rituals laid down by the priest show clearly the status of women in ancient Israel. This practice is found in different cultures throughout the world. It is a universal issue that has evoked criticism positively and negatively throughout the globe. Since holiness is a cultural-historical issue, probably the nations around Israel considered holiness as a supreme duty. Probably Israel (Priestly class) too got influenced by the thinking of her neighboring cultures. This disparaging approach can be supported by chapter 27:1-7, where the redemption price of a female is half of that of man.

However, there are opinions favoring for a longer period for female. One of the arguments laid down by them are that both the female, mother and newborn daughter are more vulnerable. The

497 Milgrom, "Leviticus 1-16," 763-765.In Indian culture too especially in Manu, all relatives of a newborn child and the house are considered as impure (Manu 5.58). The Hindu women are barred from temples and are confined inside the house during their menstrual period.

mother's loss of blood and even daughter who will lose in future some of her life leaves them weakened and potentially to death. The male also by losing semen experiences the same risk, however, the circumcision on the eighth day protect them from the risk as they enjoy the covenant with God.[498] If so, the woman is vulnerable as she has not received the privilege of being a covenant partner. The male members are the covenant partners with God, and female members are considered as partners with their male counterpart. The woman's rights and status are governed by the male members of the household. Hence, it could be the rationale of the priest and lawmaker.

The women are playing a crucial role in the procreative activity. They are in a way playing a dominant role in the generative process entrusted by God. Hence, woman must not be intrinsically treated as inferior beings susceptible to danger, rather a key person in continuing the plan and promise of God. The birth of a female child and thereby doubling of the time is not a sign of lesser social standing.All these ritual and practices were a creation of male dominated and male controlled society. The role of priests can't be negated, as they were holding an important role in the Israelite society.

Leviticus 15:16-31 (Law on Uncleanness from Bodily Emissions)

Translation/Textual Comments

16 And if a man has an emission of semen, he shall bathe his whole body in water and he will be unclean[499] until the evening. 17 And every cloth and every skin that has semen on it will be washed with

---

498 Balentine, 102-103. The other argument for the doubling is found in Jubilees 3:8-14 and the Mishnah. The etiological differences explained in these texts are based on the creation day and entrance to Garden of Eden by Adam and Eve. It says Adam was created at the end of the first week of creation and entered Eden on the 41st day, while Eve was created at the end of the second week and was finally admitted to the Garden of Eden on the 81st day (c.f. Kaiser, "The Book of Leviticus," 1085.)

499 The projection of semen as unclean marks the differences between Israel and Ancient West Asian legislation. In Ancient West Asian legislation, sexual activity was performed within the sacred precincts among the worshippers as it was believed that such an act would activate the gods into fertilizing the soil with rain (Rooker, 203.)

water and will be unclean until the evening. 18 And a woman[500] with whom a man lies and has an emission of semen, both of them shall bathe in water, and they will be unclean until the evening.

19 When a woman has a discharge of blood which is her regular discharge from her body, she will be in her impurity for seven days[501], and whoever touches her[502] will be unclean until the evening[503]. 20 And everything upon which she lies during her impurity will be unclean; everything upon which she sits will be unclean. 21 And whoever touches her bed shall wash his clothes and bathe with water[504] and will be unclean until the evening. 22 And whoever touches anything[505] upon which she sits[506] shall wash his clothes and bathe in water, and will be unclean until the evening; 23 whether it[507] is the bed or anything upon which she sits, when he touches it

500 Samaritan Hebrew Pentateuch reads אִישָׁהּ'her husband' instead of אִישׁ . 'man' (MT reading). In MT, woman is placed as the subject even though her case begins in next verse. If we observe carefully, the law starts with abnormal male discharges followed by normal male discharges. With a break of one verse (v. 18), start the normal female discharges instead of abnormal discharges (ab-b1a1). This chiasmus brings out the unity of the text. The centre verse (v. 18) instead of beginning with man followed by woman, goes the other way and instead of word כִּיuses the word אֲשֶׁר (v. 2, 16, 19 and 25). It is purposefully structured by the legislator showing a well balanced law. Hence, the MT reading is valid.

501 Seven days is the normal period of the menstrual flow.

502 It means contact with her body.

503 The instruction to take bathe is missing (cf. 21, 22). Probably it is a scribal error.

504 The MT has 'bathe with water' whereas Septuagint adds τὸ σῶμα αὐτου 'his body' i.e bathe his body with water [verse 21 καὶ πᾶς ὃς ἐὰν ἅψηται τῆς κοίτης αὐτῆς πλυνεῖ τὰ ἱμάτια αὐτοῦ καὶ λούσεται τὸ σῶμα αὐτοῦ ὕδατι καὶ ἀκάθαρτος ἔσται ἕως ἑσπέρας]

505 The Samaritan Hebrew Pentateuch, Targum and Targum Pseudo-Jonathae secundum adds article on כְּלִי.

506 'בְּכָל־כְּלִי אֲשֶׁר־תֵּשֵׁב עָלָיו (anything upon which she sits)' is absent in Targum.

507 The Samaritan Hebrew Pentateuch reads הִיאin place of הוּא (MT reading). For Hartley the word הוּאrefers not to a specific antecedent, but to a situation (Refer Hartley, 204.) Refer also for further detail Milgrom, "Leviticus 1-16," 938-939. It refers to any uncontaminated object.

he will be unclean until the evening. 24 And if any man[508] lies [509]with her and her impurity is on him, and he becomes unclean[510] seven days; and every bed on which he lies will be unclean.

25 If a woman has a discharge of blood for many days, not at the time of her impurity, or if she has a discharge beyond the time of her impurity, all the days of the discharge she shall continue in uncleanness; as in the days of her impurity, she will be unclean. 26 Every[511] bed on which she lies all the days of her discharge will be to her as the bed of her impurity; and everything on which she sits will be unclean, as in the uncleanness of her impurity. 27 And whoever[512] touches them[513] will be unclean and he shall wash his clothes, and bathe in water, and will be unclean until the evening. 28 And when she is cleansed of her discharge, she shall count off seven days, and after that she will be clean. 29 And on the eighth day she[514] shall take two turtledoves or two young pigeons, and bring them to the priest at the entrance of the tent of meeting. 30 And the priest shall offer one for a sin offering and the other for a burnt offering; and the priest will make atonement for her before the Lord for her unclean discharge.

508 Refer v. 18.

509 'If a man *lies* with her…' The word 'שָׁכֹב' is in Qal infinite absolute and is placed before יִשְׁכַּב which is in Qal imperfect form. When the infinite absolute is placed before an imperfect form, it intensifies the verbal idea emphasizing the importance of the circumstance (cf. Gen. 2:17- מוֹת תָּמוּת).

510 The Samaritan Hebrew Pentateuch reads יטמא 'he becomes unclean' instead of וְטָמֵא 'and he becomes unclean'. This variant is based on the frequent confusion of *waw* and *yod* at the various stages of the Hebrew scripture (cf. Verse 8a) [refer Hartley, 204.] This judgement is in contrast with 20:18, where the punishment for both party is cut off. The holiness code is harsh towards both the man and the woman.

511 A few Hebrew manuscripts Septuagint (textus Graecus originalis), Syriac and Targum Pseudo-Jonathae secundum have waw at the beginning of the verse.

512 Two manuscripts and Septuagint omits copula (the vav).

513 Few manuscripts and Septuagint read בה 'her' instead of בם 'them'.

514 The woman is holding a significant stand in Israel's cult like man where she is having access to make an offering.

31 You shall separate[515] the sons of Israel from their uncleanness, so that they do not die in their uncleanness by defiling my tabernacle that is in their midst.

Form and Structure

The text (15:16-33) comes under the instructions on uncleanness from bodily emissions (15:1-33). This regulation is an instruction on uncleanness from normal or abnormal discharges from a person's genitals. This regulation is in a conditional form (case and consequences). The structure of this chapter is equally divided between male and female. The form and content complement each other. It starts with an introductory formula (v. 1) followed by a series of regulations treating uncleanness of both persons and objects that comes in contact directly or indirectly with a person with a discharge (vv. 2-30). The regulation ends with an exhortation (v. 31) and summary statement (vv. 32-33). The main section vv. 2-30 has four subsections, each introduced by the particle כִּי [vv. 2-12 (2), 16-17 (16), 19-24 (19) and 25-30 (25)].[516] Each of these subsections carries the consequences and an appropriate requirement.

Comments and Explanation

Chapter 15 like chapter 12 deal with genital discharges and the general opinion among the scholars is that both can be joined together.

Chapter 15 deals with male and female discharges. Both section (2-17 and 19-30) are dependent to each other and are considered as mirror to each other as the language and content are same. In between these two sections verse 18 is placed which deals with marital intercourse. Verse 18 stands as the rhetoric centre of the two main sections where ruling on sexual intercourse between a man and a woman is stated. In this chapter, women are not alone placed as unclean because of their discharges, but also men. Men or women

515 The verb וְהִזַּרְתֶּם is in Hiphil form which means ' to cause that a person keeps detached from uncleanness. Probably to be read with Samaritan Hebrew manuscripts and Syriac as והוְהַרתם 'You will warn'. Septuagint reads καὶ εὐλαβεῖς ποιήσετε 'and you will show discretion/prudence (c.f. Hartley, 204.)

516 Ibid., 205-209. C.f. Hartley, 205-209; Noth, *Leviticus*, 113; Ross, 304-308; Wenham, 216-217.

with discharges are unclean, contaminating anyone who touches them and anything he or she touches. They require ritual purification for restoration and to lead a normal life. The only difference is the duration. For male, in normal discharge until evening but for female, the time period is 7 days. Though the woman's impurity lasted seven days, no purificatory rite is proposed or demanded.[517] For abnormal case, after healing, both male and female have to wait seven days followed by a purification and burnt offering on the eighth day.

Though the laws are straightforward and are equally placed both for man and woman, it is difficult to understand the logic behind all these rituals, as to have a bodily discharge is a normal condition for human kind. This is what even the creator had intended for human kind. If so, why do the bodily discharges make someone unclean? Is this ritual known only to Israel or prevalent to other cultures? The rituals for discharges are found in almost every culture (Egyptians, Hittite, Babylonian, Arab, Persians, Greeks, and even Hinduism).[518] The entire ancient world is unanimous in this regard.

In this law, once again we can see the priestly dominance where the advantages are for man who imposes harsh social and religious control over women. The form of discrimination was also seen in Gospel writings. It is remarkable to note that Jesus like other Jewish rabbi did not rebuke the woman suffering from bleeding for long 12 years, when she touched Jesus (Mt 9:20-21; Mk 5:25-33; Lk 8:43-48). The approach of Jesus was contrary to the Levitical laws. In the eyes of Jesus, the attitude and approach of woman was weightier than the stipulated and rigid regulation.

Leviticus 19: 20-22, 29 (Laws for Holy Living)

Translation/Textual Comments

20 If a man sleeps[519] with a woman who is a slave, betrothed to another man but not ransomed[520] or given her freedom, an inquiry

517 Porter, 121.

518 Milgrom, "Leviticus 1-16," 932, 957-968.

519 The Hebrew word שִׁכְבַת־זֶרַע means carnal relations.

520 The MT וְהָפְדֵּה is a hophal infinitive absolute (c.f. 2 Kings 3:23). For Hartley, since the verb הָפְדֵּה stands before a verb נִפְדָּתָה which is in Niphal perfect form, it is more meaningful to repoint it as a niphal infinitive absolute. The Infinitive

shall be held.[521] They shall not be put to death,[522] because she was not free; 21 but he shall bring a guilt offering for himself to the Lord, to the door of the tent of meeting, a ram for a guilt offering. 22 And the priest shall make expiation[523] for him with the ram of the guilt offering before the Lord for his sin which he has committed; and the sin which he has committed shall be forgiven him.

29 Do not degrade your daughter by making her a prostitute, so that the land may not turn to prostitution and the land shall be full of depravity.[524]

Form and Structure

The law deals with the sexual relations between a man and a betrothed slave (vv. 20-22),[525] and it is against selling a daughter into prostitution (v. 29). These two laws are placed in between the command 'you shall keep my Sabbaths (v. 3 and v. 30). The Holiness aspect is projected highly in these regulations, where the Israelites are expected to practice holiness in all aspects of their daily life. The

---

absolute is used to emphasize the contract. The hophal form communicates both that her owner is duty-bound to let her be redeemed and that her would be is duty-bound to pay the price for redemption (Hartley, 305.). c.f. Milgrom, "Leviticus 17-22", 1667.

521 The Samaritan Hebrew Pentateuch adds לו 'to him' and Septuagint adds αὐτοῖς 'to them'.

522 The MT has the verb in Hophal plural form, whereas the Samaritan Hebrew Pentateuch reads a singular form. The following verses support the singular form '*he* shall bring a guilt offering for *himself* (v. 21) and 'the priest shall make atonement for *him* ...... for *his* sin which *he* committed; and the sin which *he* has committed shall be forgiven *him*' (v. 22). Since these two verses point seven times to the ravisher, the proposed translation must be 'he shall not be put to death'.

523 Wiped clean of impurities.

524 The Hebrew word זמה 'to plot or conspire' usually refers either to sexual immorality or, as a metaphor to Israel's infidelity in community idolatry [Baruch A. Levine, "Leviticus," in *The Jewish Publication Society Torah Commentary*, ed. Nahum M. Sarna (Jerusalem: The Jewish Publication Society, 1989), 122.]

525 For Milgrom, verses 20-22 are an insertion [Jacob Milgrom, "Leviticus 17-22," in *The Anchor Bible*, ed. David Noel Freedman William Foxwell Albright (New York: Doubleday, 2000), 1595.]. Verses 20-22 unlike all other laws are in Casuistic style. Also refer Noth, *Leviticus*, 142.

recurrence of the word שׁמר 'to keep' (v. 3, 19, and 30) signals the importance of the laws in the life of Israel, i.e., the first and the last deals with Sabbath and the central part points to decrees. Each of these laws ends with a self-introductory formula 'I am Yahweh your God/I am Yahweh' (vv. 2, 3, 4, 10, 12, 14, 16, 18, 25, 28, 30, 31, 32, 34, 36, 37). These repeated expressions project Yahweh as holy and He expects the people of Israel to be holy. The holiness must carry the love towards God and fellow human beings. The word love, fear and holiness are interwoven in these regulations. [526]

Comments and Explanation

Verses 20-22 and 29 are placed under miscellaneous duties (vv. 19-29). These laws are about man's relationships with animal, field, garment (v. 19), slave woman (vv. 20-22), land (vv. 23-25), body (vv. 26-28) and daughter (v. 29). The laws on slave woman and daughter are placed along with other properties.

Verses 20-22 (The Betrothed Slave Woman)

The laws in verses 20-22 is related to the seventh commandment as it has to do with adultery, but since the victimized person is a slave woman and not received freedom, the accused person got escaped from death penalty.

The slave woman in this text is not a freed person. Now, if she had been freed, the law would have been different, i.e., death penalty (*they shall not be put to death* cf. Deut 22:23-27). And if she was not betrothed, there would have been no penalty, as the slave was treated as property/ chattel. Who is the man who had sexual relation with the slave woman? Is he the owner, member of his household or a person not connected to the owner? The man who had sexual relations with her probably is her owner or member of her owner's household. If not, the penalty would have been paid to her owner, as it has caused a loss to her master.[527] Few questions to be answered: The slave woman is betrothed but not freed, if so, who controls her? Owner or the one to whom she was betrothed! Why the law of

526 Hartley, 307-312.

527 Levine, 131.

adultery is not applicable? Is it because of her position in the society? A closer scrutiny is warranted.

אִישׁ כִּי־יִשְׁכַּב (*If a man sleeps*) - Who is the man involved in sexual relation with the betrothed slave woman? There are two opinions among the scholars: One opinion argues that the accused man is none other than her owner and the other argument disagrees by stating that if owner, the text would have read 'if a man has sexual relations with a woman *who is his slave*'. Now, if we disagree that the accused man is the owner, the pertinent question will be, why the text does notpoint compensation to the owner?

אִשָּׁה (*woman*) - The absolute אִשָּׁה always refers to any woman (18:17, 18, 19, 22; 20:13, 14, 16, 18).[528] Does this refer to a married woman or an unmarried woman? Since, she is betrothed; her position is not as an unmarried woman, rather it is equivalent to a married woman.

שִׁפְחָה (a *slave*) – The word שִׁפְחָה is derived from מִשְׁפָּחָה meaning 'family, clan'. The law here uses the word שִׁפְחָה instead of אָמָה. The Hebrew word שִׁפְחָה is found nowhere else in a legal enactment.[529] Both words are equivalent and have almost the same legal status (for, e.g., Hagar is addressed as שִׁפְחָה (slave girl) in Gen 16:1, 3; 25:12 and as אָמָה (slave woman) in Gen 21:10, 13).[530] Who is this slave? There are mixed opinion[531]:

1. She is an Israelite betrothed to a Hebrew slave.
2. A non-Israelite slave woman betrothed to a Hebrew slave.
3. A non-Israelite slave woman betrothed to a non-Israelite slave.

The higher amount of possibility is either the second or third one, a non-Israelite betrothed to a Hebrew slave or non-Israelite slave. The first option is not possible as it will contradict 25:39, where the legislation prohibits making fellow Hebrew brethren as slave.

528 Milgrom, "Leviticus 17-22," 1666.

529 A. T. Chapman, 110.

530 Milgrom, "Leviticus 17-22," 1666. For Allen P. Ross, שִׁפְחָה is a woman servant who could become a concubine (Ross, 363.)

531 Milgrom, "Leviticus 17-22," 1666.

נֶחֱרֶפֶת (*betrothed*) - The verb used here differs from the commonly used verb אֹרָשָׂה (Exod 22:15, Deut 22: 23). The verb אֹרָשָׂה carries higher legal force than the verb נֶחֱרֶפֶת as it carries death penalty.[532]

לְאִישׁ (*to another man*)- Who is this man? The possibility is either a Hebrew slave or a non-Hebrew slave. There is an argument that the slave woman is betrothed to her owner. This opinion must be rejected. There are two valid reasons: If owner, definitely the consequence would have been at least to pay an amount as fine, since the slave was considered as property, secondly, the text would have been 'to her owner' instead of 'to another man'.

וְהָפְדֵּה לֹא נִפְדָּתָה (*but not ransomed*) – The waw indicates contrast, i.e., although she is betrothed, she is not redeemed/ransomed.[533] The understanding behind these words is that though she is betrothed, her owner has power over her. It is the duty of her prospective bridegroom to pay the amount to her owner and ransom and free her from the control of her owner.

בִּקֹּרֶת (*an inquiry*) - Unlike Deuteronomy where it opts for death (Deut 22:22-25), the law here recommends for an inquiry. The prospective husband must have the same rights as the actual marriage, and having sexual relation with a betrothed girl is adultery and is liable to death penalty.[534] But here the punishment is not death, as she is not redeemed or freed. This clearly shows the power of her ravisher both in the social and economic spheres and a woman wholly at the disposal of her owner.

לֹא יוּמְתוּ (*they shall not be put to death*) - The judgement 'they shall not be put to death' because 'she was not free' seems to be illogical. The logical judgement should be 'He shall not be put to death'. The reason

532 Ibid., 1667.

533 Ibid. For Milgrom, 'since it is a combination of Hophal and Niphal, it has two contrasts: 1) The owner's responsibility to enable her to be ransomed (c.f. Exod 21:8), and 2) the prospective bridegroom's obligation is to ransom her'. He prefers 'the word 'ransom' in place of 'redeem' as the latter in the priestly texts refers to the obligation of the owner or his nearest relative to redeem his lost property. Anyone else performing the same act is considered as *ransomer*'. The Rabbinic sources designate her as 'redeemed but not redeemed' and characterize her status as 'partly slave and partly free' (1667-1668).

534 C.f. Wenham, 270.

for such an argument can be answered by addressing the question, If she is free, what the judgement will be? The judgement stated in the text carries the power of the owner over her slave. Since she is not free, the punishment is a lighter one (v. 21). Here the judgement is in favour of the owner, as she is the property of her owner. Though she is betrothed (betrothal and marriage are equally subjected to a capital punishment), being a slave (having not received freedom), the accuser is asked to bring a guilt offering for the atonement of his sin (vv. 21-22). The approach of this law is similar to Exodus 21:7-8, where the law is focussed solely on a person considered as property not as a human being.

Verse 29

In this verse, the daughter is equated with the land. Profaning a daughter by making her a prostitute will yield the land to prostitution and depravity. The pertinent question here is: Is it referring to a cultic prostitution or secular one? Who is this daughter? The daughter is an Israelite. Probably an Israelite due to heavy debt was tempted to sell his daughter into prostitution to clear his debt. This form of practice may even tempt the greedy father to sell off his daughter to accumulate wealth, which in turn defiles the land.

The Old Testament has ample references of cultic prostitution (Gen. 38:20-23; Deut 23:17-18; I Kings 14: 23-24; 15:11-12; 22:47; II Kings 23:7; Hos 4:13-14). What made the woman to prostitution? Is it practiced to have fertility rites? The text is not clear. This form of practice was customary among the Canaanites, where a father devoted his daughter.[535] There is a possibility that the Israelite got influenced by the Canaanite cult.

לְהַזְנוֹתָהּ (*to make her prostitute*) - Why did the text narrate 'Do not *degrade* your daughter by making her as a *prostitute*'. The word 'degrade' and 'prostitute' is a deliberate choice to deprive the right of the woman. This double word is throwing her away from her rights. It brings out the rights and vested interest of her father. Her reputation is completely diminished.

535 Kaiser, "The Book of Leviticus," 1135; Noth, *Leviticus*, 143. For Porter, cultic prostitution was the object of promoting fertility, and hence the reason for prohibition is primarily religious rather than moral (Porter, 158.)

וְלֹא־תִזְנֶה הָאָרֶץ (*so that the land may not turn to prostitution*) -Does this refer to land or people of the land? Does it refer to the economy of the land? The land sometimes is referred to as people of the land (Gen. 41:36; Ezek 14:13). In this text, it is referred to in a collective way, i.e., the people of the land will yield themselves to prostitution, which in turn will lead the land to pollution and depravity.

The law in Leviticus takes it in a lighter way unlike the Deuteronomic code, where it is condemned and considered as abhorrent to the Lord (Deut 23:18-19 c.f. Hos 4:14; Amos 2:7).

Leviticus 20:10-14; 17-21 (Laws for Sexual Offence)

Translation/Textual comments

10 If a man commits adultery[536] with the wife of[537] a man who[538] commits adultery[539] with the wife of his neighbour, both the adulterer and the adulteress shall be put to death[540]. 11 If a man lies with his father's wife, he has uncovered his father's nakedness; both of them shall be put to death[541], their blood is upon them. 12 If a man lies with his daughter-in-law, both of them shall be put to death; they have committed perversion, their blood is upon them. 13 If a man lies with a male as with a woman, both of them[542] have committed an abomination; they shall be put to death, their blood is upon them. 14 If a man takes a wife and her mother also, it is wickedness; both

536 The verb is in singular.

537 MT repeats *if a man who commits adultery with the wife of.* The words אֵשֶׁת־ אִישׁ אֲשֶׁר יִנְאַף אֶת 'a man who commits adultery with the wife of' is absent in Septuagint (codices minusculis scripti). The MT has resulted from an error of dittography.

538 Few manuscripts like Septuagint, Syriac, Targum and Vulgate read a vav on אֲשֶׁר 'who'.

539 The verb like the preceding verb is in singular form.

540 Septuagint, Syriac and Vulgate read a plural instead of singular (MT). The same form occurs also in verses 11-13.

541 Unlike the preceding verse, the word מוֹת־יוּמַת is in plural form but the dependent clause is in singular form.

542 The Samaritan Hebrew Pentateuch, Septuagint and Arabic version transpose the word שְׁנֵיהֶם (Pl.) 'both of them' after יוּמָתוּ.

he and they shall be burned with fire, so that no wickedness will be among you.
17 If a man takes his sister, a daughter of his father or a daughter of his mother, and he sees her nakedness, and she sees his nakedness, it is a disgrace[543], and they shall be cut off before the eyes of their people; he has uncovered his sister's nakedness, he shall bear his punishment[544]. 18 If a man lies with a woman having infirmity, and uncovers her nakedness, he has made naked her fountain[545], and she has uncovered the fountain of her blood; both of them shall be cut off from their people. 19 You shall not uncover the nakedness of your mother's sister or of your father's sister[546], for that is lay bare one's own flesh[547]; they shall bear their punishment. 20 If a man lies with his uncle's wife, he has uncovered his uncle's nakedness; they shall bear their sin[548], they shall die childless[549]. 21 If a man takes his brother's wife[550], it is impurity; he has uncovered his brother's nakedness, they shall be childless[551].

Form and Structure

The laws are in casuistic form. These laws deal with the illegal sexual relationships and its consequences (vv.10-14) and sexual relationships

543 Targum Onkelos reads it as shame. The word here and in Prov 14:34 refers to as 'disgrace or shameful' and in all other places it means 'steadfast love/ goodness/loyalty' (For more interpretation on חֶסֶדrefer Levine, 138; Snaith, 139.)

544 Septuagint reads ἁμαρτίαν κομιοῦνται 'they will receive back their sin'.

545 Many manuscripts of Targum (Tg Mss and Tg J) add a conjunctive waw with the direct object אֵת.

546 The Samaritan Hebrew Pentateuch and Septuagint reads אחות אָבִיךָ וַאֲחותאִמְּךָ 'your father's sister or your mother's sister' instead of MT reading וַאֲחות אָבִיךָ אחות אִמְּךָ 'your mother's sister or your father's sister'.

547 Literally, 'for he has laid bare his own flesh'.

548 Septuagint omits the words חֶטְאָם יִשָּׂאוּ 'they shall bear/receive back their sin'.

549 The Samaritan Hebrew Pentateuch reads יומתו 'they shall die'. The root meaning is 'stripped', i.e., 'stripped of children or posterity (unfruitful)'.

550 Is it referring to Levirate marriage? The Holiness Code opposes Levirate marriage and the punishment for such an act is childless instead of death or cut off. Hence, it discourages for such marriage.

551 The Septuagint reads ἀποθανοῦνται'they shall die' as in v. 20.

that bring disgrace and dishonor (vv.17-21). Each of these laws carries generally four elements: a) the case, b) the penalty, c) the reason for the penalty, and d) declaratory formula. The severity of penalty is in a descending order. Verses 10-14 carry the death penalty. Verses 17-18 carry the penalty of 'cut off from the assembly', Verses 20-21 carry the penalty of 'childlessness'.[552]

Comments and Explanation

Leviticus 20 is similar to Leviticus 18, as both chapters strongly warn Israel to avoid pagan religious practices. Leviticus 18 is apodictic in style, whereas Leviticus 20 is casuistic in style. In Leviticus 18, the warning for the people of Israel is not to conform to the abomination of Egypt and Canaan whereas in 20 the concern is about her influence to pagan fertility cult (Molech) and necromancy.

Verse 10

אֲשֶׁר יִנְאַף אֶת־אֵשֶׁת רֵעֵהוּ (*who commits adultery with his neighbour's wife*)- אִישׁ אֲשֶׁר יִנְאַף סתאפרֵ תמ (a man who commits adultery with the wife of). Is it a dittography? This additional clause has been variously argued[553]:

1. It is original and not an addition.
2. This addition was added to project one's own wife.
3. This clause addresses both the engaged and married woman.
4. It was added to stress the gravity of the crime.
5. It is a stylistic device common in Hebrew poetry.
6. It is to limit the jurisdiction of the law to an Israelite.
7. It is to stress that committing adultery with neighbour's wife is to commit adultery with one's own wife.

מוֹת־יוּמַת הַנֹּאֵף וְהַנֹּאָפֶת (*both the adulterer and the adulteress shall be put to death*)- The verb is in singular instead of plural, which indicates that originally only the man was put to death; the wife was added later. The death penalty for a woman conflicts with Numbers 5:12-31,

552 Hartley, 329-332.

553 Milgrom, "Leviticus 17-22," 1747.

where the punishment for such an act is sterility.[554] A contradiction can be seen here. Is she in a helpless situation, where every decision is governed by a male dominated society? The text is not clear. The woman is in a disadvantaged position, where she is apprehended by the male member of the society.

Verse 11

אֶת־אֵשֶׁת אָבִיו (*his father's wife*) - Targum Pseudo Jonathan secundum understands this words as 'his own mother' (cf. 18:7-8). To have sexual relationship with one's mother is a heinous crime, which leads to death penalty. Having sexual relations with mother, daughter or sister was abhorred throughout Ancient West Asia.[555] The laws are addressed to the man, as he initiates the sexual act.

עֶרְוַת אָבִיו (*his father's nakedness*) – These words emphasize that to have incest with one's mother is also his father's wife. The word עֶרְוַת intends his father's wife (cf. 18:8, 14, 16). To have sex with one's father's wife is to uncover the nakedness of his father, which brings dishonour to his father, as they are considered as one flesh.[556]

גִּלָּה (*uncover*) - Literally it means to see genital, i.e., the nakedness is exposed (Gen. 9:20-21; Lev. 18:6-19; Ezek. 16:36; 23:18). It is punishable by death.

מוֹת־יוּמְתוּ שְׁנֵיהֶם (*both of them shall be put to death*) –The text is not clear whether her consent is there, since he initiates the act (v.11a). The word שְׁנֵיהֶם doesn't presume her consent.

דְּמֵיהֶם בָּם (*their blood is upon them*) – It is an idiomatic language, which assures that the convicted person is responsible for his/her death. The one who executes the judgment will not be held responsible. This idiom also implies that the accused person will face death whether or not the executor puts him/her to death.[557]

554 Ibid., 1747-1748. For Noth, the singular מוֹת־יוּמָת refers to the adulterous man, the interpretation for woman as adulterous was brought later (Noth, *Leviticus*, 150.)

555 Milgrom, "Leviticus 17-22," 1749.

556 Ross, 374.

557 Jacob Milgrom, *Leviticus: A Book of Ritual and Ethics* (Minneapolis: Fortress Press, 2004), 255.

Verse 12

תֶּבֶל (*perversion*) – The term is unclear. It reflects Israel's shame culture.[558]

Verse 13

The law prohibits homosexual acts. It is the violation of divine order of life. This act is considered as abomination to the Lord (cf. 18:22; Gen 19:4-8).

וְאִישׁ אֲשֶׁר יִשְׁכַּב אֶת־זָכָר (*If a man lies with a male*) – The law opposes homosexual acts. Who is this male? Is he a fellow Israelite or a non-Israelite? The text is not clear.

Verse 14

וְאִישׁ אֲשֶׁר יִקַּח (If a man takes) – The verb יִקַּח has multiple meanings such as lay hold of (seize), acquire (buy), marry (take a wife) and snatch (take away). If the verb is read as 'lay hold of, acquire or snatch', it indicates that she is in a vulnerable position and under the authority of the man. The important question is: why the verb יִקַּח and not שָׁכַב is used (cf. v. 17)? Why both women should be put to death as one among them is a legal wife? If it is in their consent, the death penalty is justified, but if the second wife was forced to marry to have a child or for sexual pleasure, the penalty of death is not justified.

בָּאֵשׁ יִשְׂרְפוּ (*they shall be burned with fire*) – Why this form of punishment and not מוֹת־יוּמָת? Execution by burning was taken place to deprive the wrongdoer of a decent burial.[559] For Noth, the substitution of the judgment from death to burning indicates that the verse did not belong to the basic form of the list of offences, i.e., death.[560]

Verses 17

יִקַּח (*takes*) – Refer v.14. If the verbs points to other than marry, the case will be different. If so, the violator is man, and if marriage took

558 Milgrom, "Leviticus 17-22," 1749.

559 Hartley, 339; Milgrom, "Leviticus 17-22," 1751.

560 Noth, *Leviticus*, 150.

place on the basis of contract and consensus, the punishment is justified.

וְרָאָה אֶת־עֶרְוָתָהּ וְהִיא־תִרְאֶה אֶת־עֶרְוָתוֹ (*and he sees her nakedness, and she sees his nakedness*)– The double euphemism indicates that the marriage took place in agreement by both parties and are ardently involved. Both are equally guilty.[561]

וְנִכְרְתוּ לְעֵינֵי בְּנֵי עַמָּם (*they shall be cut off before the eyes of their people*) –They acted in secret, and they will be punished in open (cf. David and Bathsheba in II Sam 12:12). The community will witness their fate, and their line will be cut off.

עֶרְוַת אֲחֹתוֹ גִּלָּה עֲוֹנוֹ יִשָּׂא (*he has uncovered his sister's nakedness, he shall bear his punishment*) – It is puzzling to note that the verb is in singular instead of plural. The Septuagint version reads it as plural. If we accept MT, the question to be answered is, why punishment to his wife, since he is responsible for the act?

Verse 18

אֶת־אִשָּׁה דָּוָה (*woman having infirmity*) - This refers to any genital flow.

Unlike other verses, where male are stated guilty, here both the parties are held guilty. The reason cited here is that he has exposed her discharge and she has uncovered the source of her discharge.

Verses 19

This verse is different from the preceding and following verses in style. It is in apodictic style and in second person (v.19b however is in third person).[562] The content and style of this verse is different from the preceding and following verses, for instance all other verses start with וְאִישׁ אֲשֶׁר whereas this verse begins with וְעֶרְוַת אֲחוֹת (cf. 18:12-13). The word אֶת־שְׁאֵרוֹ (one's own flesh) is not found in chapter 20, but is seen in chapter 18 (vv.12-13, 17). Unlike other verses, the consequence for such an act is not specified.

561 Milgrom, "Leviticus 17-22," 1753.

562 Ibid., 1756; Noth, *Leviticus*, 151.

כִּי אֶת־שְׁאֵרוֹ הֶעֱרָה (*for that is make naked one's own flesh*) – Verse 19a is in second person and 19b is in third person. The change of subject indicates that the focus has shifted from the person to the act.[563] The word שְׁאֵר refers to a blood relation.

Verse 20-21

In both of these verses, the punishment for such an act is childless. The words stated in both of these verses are עֲרִירִים (childless) but with a difference. In Verse 20, 'they shall die childless' and in verse 21 'they shall be childless'. The penalty stated here is of childlessness, which is opposite of the custom of marriage where the continuance of family life is insured.[564]

Then the question to be addressed is who will die or be childless? Has this crime taken place due to childless uncle and brother (in case of brother to accumulate his deceased brother's property)? Has the consent taken place by both parties? The text is not clear. If it is by the consent of the childless uncle and brother, the punishment must be to the one who has initiated, and not to the one who is subjected for such an act. If so, the crime is of adultery and the punishment is death.

Lev 25:39-46 (Laws on Slavery)

Translation/Textual comments

39 If your brother becomes poor beside you, and sells himself/sold[565] to you, you shall not make him serve[566] as slave. 40 As a resident hireling he shall be with you. He shall serve with you until the year of the jubilee; 41 Then he shall go out from you[567], he and his children with him go back to his own family and to the possession of his father he shall return. 42 For they are my servants, whom I brought

563 Milgrom, "Leviticus 17-22," 1756.

564 Hartley, 340.

565 The verb נִמְכַּר is in niphal perfect form. This verb is also read and translated in reflexive (Hithpael) form (cf.v.47-48).

566 The MT reads תַעֲבֹד בּוֹ 'you shall make him serve' whereas the Septuagint reads δουλεύσει σοι 'he will serve you'.

567 Unlike Exodus 21:2 and Deut 15:12, the word חָפְשִׁי 'free' is purposefully omitted as he is treated as hireling and not as a slave.

forth out of the land of Egypt, they shall not be sold as slaves are sold. 43 You shall not rule[568] over him with harshness[569], but shall fear your God[570]. 44 As for your male and your female slaves[571] whom you may have, you may acquire male and female slaves from among the nations that are around you. 45 You may also buy from among the strangers who sojourn with you and their families that are with you, who have been born in your land; and they shall become your property. 46 You may keep them as a possession for your children after you, for them to inherit as property. These you may make them slaves[572] for life, but as for your fellow Israelites, no one shall rule over the other with harshness.

Form and Structure

The content of this chapter can be classified into two major sections: (1) the Sabbatical Year with some laws dealing with the land (vv. 2-7), and (2) the year of Jubilee with several extensive laws (vv. 8-55). The second section includes the law on selling of the land (vv. 23-24), laws about loans to poor Israelites (vv. 35-38), and laws on slavery caused by debt (vv. 39-55).

An analysis of the structure reveals of two major sections: (a) the Sabbatical year and the year of Jubilee with some laws (vv. 2-22), and (b) legislation regulating the גְאֻלָּה "laws of redemption", pertaining to property and slaves in relationship to the year of Jubilee (vv. 23-55).[573]

With the year of Jubilee, three laws dealing with the rights of the sale and redemption of property (vv. 25-34), loans to poor Israelites (vv. 35-38), and slavery resulting from debt (vv. 39-55) are

568 In Septuagint the word used is κατατενεῖς (hold down right). The word here means 'drive hard'.

569 This verb means 'ruthlessly'. The meanings in Aramaic, Arabic and Akkadian is mentioned by Milgrom, "Leviticus 23-27," 2227-2228.

570 MT has מֵאֱלֹהֶיךָ 'your God'. The Septuagint has κύριον τὸν θεόν σου 'the Lord your God' (c.f. Verse 17a).

571 The Samaritan Hebrew Pentateuch reads as plural, whereas MT read singular (c.f.6a-a).

572 The words בָּהֶם תַּעֲבֹדוּ'you may make them slaves' is absent in Septuagint.

573 Hartley, 422.

interrelated, because that year is the terminal date for such contracts. Each of the three series of laws begins with the same case "if your brother or kin becomes poor". This symmetry in style clearly indicates that these three sets of laws have been arranged for this speech. And it serves as an integral part of the liberating power of the year of Jubilee. Two brief parenthesis verses are in the structure in order to motivate Israel to comply with these laws (vv. 42, 55).[574]

Now, the question to be raised is: Why these laws are incorporated in the year of Jubilee? The primary reason is that debt is the greatest internal threat to the very social foundation of the equality of all Israelites, based on the enduring right of every family to its patrimony. These laws will guard both the fortunate and the misfortunate ones, who in course of time became rich and poor. The legislator through cultic legislation sought to prevent the slave class in Israel by having a set time, when all debts were forgiven, and every patrimony was returned to its original owner.[575]

The composition of this chapter is marked by three distinctive styles: impersonal laws (vv. 26-34, [41], 42, 48-54), laws in the second person singular (vv. 3-5, 6-7, 8-9a, 14a, 15-16, 17bα, 25, 35-37, 39-40, [41], 43-44a, 46b, 47, 53b), and parenthetic and legal material cast in the second person plural (vv. 2, 9b-13, 14b, 17a, 17bβ-24, 38, 44b-46, 55b).[576] Literary critics use these variations of style as the evidence of variety of sources. Martin Noth with regard to the styles, judges that this passage was the result of a long, gradual development, but at the same time, for him the various stages are no longer discernible. And for the dating, he concedes that the directions for Jubilee and restoration of land to its owner is of the era, when Israel settled in Canaan, and concludes that this chapter reached its present form in the exile before the finalization of chapter 23, for here the year begins on the tenth of the seventh month (v. 9; contrast 23:24b-25).[577] R. Kilian argues for three strata in Lev 25. In the first two strata, he claims that a priestly author made a few editorial changes to the document, and judges the legislation of redemption

574 Ibid., 424.

575 Ibid., 424-425.

576 Ibid., 425.

577 Noth, *Leviticus*, 184-185.

to be quite distinct from the material on the year of Jubilee. The latter comes from a source unattested elsewhere in the Holiness Code.[578] So also Elliger, and Cholewinski stand and support for a redactor work in the Holiness Code. Basing on these comments, Hartley analyses that, this chapter went through at least two editions. The first edition is discernible by the use of second person singular forms at the structural seams. The laws on the sabbatical year form a block. However, the year of Jubilee has two distinct layers: it begins with second person singular (vv. 8-9a), and then shifts to the second person plural (vv. 9b-13). He suggests that, the material from different sources has been joined. The legislation on redemption is cast in three distinctive styles. Both the laws dealing with land leasing (vv. 25-34) and redemption of an Israelite debtor-slave (vv. 47-54) are impersonal casuistic laws except for the statement of the case (Second person singular). The laws on poor Israelites (vv. 35-37) are in second person singular, while the laws on Israelites holding slaves (vv. 44-46) are formulated in the second person plural. This all clearly reveals that these sets of laws were taken from different portions of the priestly legal material.[579] The whole structure is shifted from second person singular to second person plural. It seems that there is lack of uniformity throughout these laws, which is a clear indication of editorial and redactional work. In this section, it seems that the priestly redactor has included few verses to motivate the Israelite to adhere to the law such as vv. 42, 45 etc.

Comments and Explanation

The Law on slavery in Holiness Code differs from the parallel codes (Exod 21:2-11 and Deut 15:12-18). In the Covenant Code, the freedom is for the male slave after 7 years and in Deuteronomy code, the freedom is entitled both for male and female slaves after the same duration. The Holiness code is totally different in relation to nature and time duration. If a debtor enters the household of the creditor, his status will be not that of slave but of a resident hireling. They shall serve until the year of jubilee. Then he and his children are to be released. The method of release is identical to buying back one's own

578 Kilian, 145-148.

579 Hartley, 426.

land (25:25-28). However, the non-Israelites be treated as property/ slaves.

In the Holiness code, there are major differences between an Israelite slave and a non-Israelite slave. The Israelite must not be treated as slave but as a hireling (vv. 39-40) whereas the non-Israelite can be bought and be treated as slave (vv. 44-45). In the year of Jubilee, the Israelite and his family are released as they are freed from the land of Egypt by Lord God (vv. 41-42) whereas for the non-Israelite there is no freedom as they are owner's property (vv. 45-46). The Israelites shall not be ruled with harshness which is mentioned twice (vv. 43, 46), which emphasizes the preference of Israelite over non-Israelite. The treatment for a non-Israelite is not specified, which possibly implies that the owner has every right upon them.

Verses 39-40

This section has a deal in favor of the brother(Israelite) who has become poor. The poverty/debt forced him to sell himself. This situation makes him as the property of the owner. But the legislation lays down the rule in favor of the slave. He is to be treated not as slave but as 'hired servant' or 'sojourner'.

וְכִי־יָמוּךְ (*And if he becomes poor*) - The word impoverished or poor, may be due to poor harvests, plagues, personal illness, or other difficult circumstances. As a consequence, he has to sell himself in servitude to another person. This would have been true, when during the days of judges; the Israelites began their occupation of Canaan with limited capital and limited experience in farming. Losses inflicted by marauding bands were a recurring problem that caused great hardship and threatened many with the loss of patrimony, which the Book of Judges attests.[580]

They shall be treated as hired laborers. When an Israelite put himself in the service of another Israelite, his master must treat him as hired laborers, and not as a slave. Israelite servant must not be dealt harshly. They were to be treated humanely. Now, here raises the question of discrimination between the Israelite servant and those from outside (Compare v. 39-40 with 44-46).

580 Ibid., 440-441.

וְנִמְכַּר־לָךְ (*sells himself to you/sold to you*) -This word can be translated in two ways: As reflexive (Hithpael) and as passive (Niphal). If Hithpael, the translation will be 'If your brother becomes poor besides you, and *sells himself to you*', which implies that the sale is voluntary, and if Niphal, the translation will be 'If your brother becomes poor besides you, and *sold to you*.'

לֹא־תַעֲבֹד בּוֹ עֲבֹדַת עָבֶד (*lit. do not enslave him with the enslavement of a slave*)- The threefold use of עבד indicates the repulsion of slavery in the mind of the legislator, as the Israelite cannot be a slave of another Israelite because all are God's slave.[581]

שָׂכִיר (*hireling*) - The hired servant receives wages. The wages which he receives would help him to free himself from the debt and status.

כְּשָׂכִיר כְּתוֹשָׁב (*resident hireling*) - The addition of תוֹשָׁב brings a different picture. The debtor will not be like a daily wager, who works for each day and earns his daily wage and returns home (19:13; Deut 24:14-15), rather he will be a person who stays with his owner for a longer period of time.[582]

עַד־שְׁנַת הַיֹּבֵל יַעֲבֹד עִמָּךְ (*he shall serve with you until the year of Jubilee*) - The Holiness Code unlike the Book of Covenant Code and Deuteronomic code promotes for Jubilee instead of 7 year period. For Levine, the law in Leviticus is most severe comparing the parallel codes and allows for almost lifelong indenture.[583] Moreover, the law misses out the redemption or self redemption clauses. The text even misses out to state the possibility of a relative who can redeem him by paying off his debt. Even there is no indication of the redeemer who is reluctant to redeem him.[584] It is surprising to note that the redemption provision is mentioned to only property (vv. 25-33) and to an Israelite who falls into slavery to an alien (vv. 47-52). The redemption for an Israelite who falls into slavery to an Israelite owner is not specified. Is it purposefully missed out? If not, will the Israelite love to fall into slavery to an alien or to an Israelite where there is no redemption clause? The clause in vv. 39-46 is not justified to the

581 Milgrom, "Leviticus 23-27," 2220.

582 Ibid., 2221.

583 Levine, 179.

584 C.f. Milgrom, "Leviticus 23-27," 2216-2217.

cause and welfare of the debtor. It is highly colonial in taste where the powerful plays an upper hand over his fellow brethren. Though the debtor is treated not as slave but as hireling, he/she has no freedom until the Jubilee.

Verses 41-42

הוּא וּבָנָיו (*he and his children*) – The freedom for wife is not specified. Is it missed out like redemption clause (taken for granted), not taken as hired person or is it purposefully missed out? The same approach can be seen in v. 54. Now concerning non-Israelite, twice female slaves are mentioned along with male slaves and that too in one verse (v. 44), but for Israelite hired servant the position of wife is missed out.

מִשְׁפַּחְתּוֹ (*his* clan) -Norman Gottwald identifies מִשְׁפָּחָה as '*protective association of extended families*'.[585]

During the time of Jubilee, the Israelites return to the status of free citizens and return to their own clan/family and to their property. Now, how to relate it with Exod 21:2-6 and Deut 15:12-18, where the release is on the seventh year? Does there will be freedom in the year of Jubilee to those, who renounced his freedom on the seventh year? For Josephus and many others, this declaration of liberty in the Jubilee includes those, who have bound themselves to their master at the seventh year release.[586] In contrast to Exodus, the laws in Holiness Code do not differentiate between the Children born before the servitude or during the time of servitude. The caution is given to the Israelites at v. 42. This law is for the remembrance to Israelites that they are slaves to Yahweh. However, as mentioned before, the status of wife is not specified.

Verse 43

לֹא־תִרְדֶּה בוֹ בְּפָרֶךְ (*You shall not rule over him with harshness*) - The master is not to רדה, "rule over", with פרך, "ruthlessly" (cf. Exod 1:13-14). The root פרך means *grind down* (qal) and *crush, break in pieces, rub off* (piel). When it is related to slave, it means toil, which breaks

585 Norman Gottwald, *The Tribes of Yahweh: A Sociology of the Religion of Liberated Israel 1250-1050 B.C.E* (London: SCM Press 1980), 257-267.

586 Josephus, *Antiquities* 4.8.28.

the body and grinds down the spirit (forced labor).[587] Here the law appeals the master not only to treat an Israelite as hired servant, but also not to treat him harshly.

Verses 44-46

וְהָיוּ לָכֶם לַאֲחֻזָּה (*they shall become your property*) – In ancient laws, the legal status of slaves were equated with land. As the land is passed on from generation to generation, so also the slaves were treated as property.[588]

The Jubilee release is not applicable to foreign slaves (vv. 44-46). A clear discrimination is seen here. A theological reason underlies for it. God redeemed his people from Egyptian slaves, to become his slaves (vv. 42, 55). It is therefore unfitting, that an Israelite should be resold into slavery, especially to a foreigner.[589]

Here comes the indiscrimination between the native and the Israelite slaves. The Israelites servant must not be treated harshly, and in order to treat harshly, the law permits them to take the slaves from neighboring countries. The native slaves are considered as property (chattel slaves). They are to be passed from generation to generation, as other properties. They will be permanent slaves.

The year of Jubilee was a year of restoration. The people who lost the land received back the land. The land which was in the hand of the rich and powerful has been given back to the original owner. This aspect of restoration can be seen in Persian Imperialism. The Persian Empire instead of deporting the captive people brought the captive people back to their own land. They were given freedom to practice their own religion. The aspect of restoration can be seen both in the year of Jubilee and in the strategy of Persian Imperialism.

Summary

The Holiness Code though has elements of pre-monarchic and monarchic times, reached its present state during Persian imperialism. The Persian regime unlike Assyria and Babylon was more open to smaller nations.The Persian Empire adopted strategies different from

---

587 Hartley, 441.

588 Levine, 180.

589 Wenham, 322.

Assyria and Babylon. Unlike Assyrian and Babylonian strategies of deportation and replacing the land with people of other nations (II Kings 17:6, 24-27), the Persian Empire greatly encouraged the people to return to their homeland. They adopted the strategy of rebuilding and resettling instead of deportation. The Persian regime permitted the people of other nations to worship their god/gods. They even helped in restoring or reconstructing the temple. Freedom was given to exercise their faith and ritual practices.[590] The religion and priesthood in Judah got restored under Persian Empire. The strategy of freedom and restoration adopted by the Persian Empire,on one hand,was to make their boundaries strong and on the other hand, to extract tribute and loyalty from the conquered nations.[591] The intention behind freedom and restoration was to dominate Judah both politically and economically.

The Holiness Code had a strong influence of Persian imperialism, as it gave the people of Judah a new sense of identity. The office of priesthood regained their former strength and glory. The high priest had upper hand over the community. With the support of priest, the rich people enjoyed the privileges of the Persian Empire. This created a gap between the powerful and the powerless. It had its effect on the weaker sections of the society specially the women.

In our observation, the Holiness Code falls between the Covenant and Deuteronomic code. Though it falls closely with the Covenant Code, however, in few cases it has resemblances with the Deuteronomic code. While the Holiness code emphasizes on holiness and the penalty laid down is either death or cut off from the community, the yardstick adopted for women specially the female slaves differs from the male. A superficial reading shows that the laws in relation to female slave are almost similar to the Covenant Code where she is considered as the property of the owner (Lev. 20:20-22 cf. Exod 21:7-11). Nevertheless, in some cases, the holiness code stands much better than the Covenant Code, for instance the freedom of

590 Martin Noth, *The History of Israel* (London: Adam and Charles Black, 1960), 302.

591 Jon L Berquist, *Judaism in Persian's Shadow: A Social and Historical Approach* (Eugene, Origen: Wipf and Stock Publishers, 1995), 25-26.

female slave. In the Covenant Code, the freedom for female slave is not specified. In the Deuteronomic Code, the freedom is both for the male and female slave. In Holiness Code, the freedom is both for Hebrew male and female slave with few differences. Nonetheless, the time period in Holiness Code differs from the other two codes and the treatment between Hebrew and non-Hebrew slaves are clearly specified in the Holiness Code, which is missing in the other two Codes. A closer reading shows that the Holiness code appears to be ambivalent in nature.

Chapter 5

The Status of Women in the Book of the Covenant Code

Introduction

The Book of Exodus projects the life of Israel from 'Egypt, the Land of slavery' to 'Tabernacle, the place of worship'. In between these two stages of Israelite life, a series of events took place. The giving of the law at Mount Sinai plays a pivotal role in the life of Israel.

The Book of Exodus played and still plays a major role in the life of the Church and Society and serves as a paradigm for the people of the Church and Society. The different forms of theology are based on the liberation experiences of Israel. The passages such as the story of baby Moses and his miraculous saving from the hand of Pharaoh and the river Nile episode, Israelite walking through the Red Sea on dry land, the provision of water and Manna brought inspiration throughout the centuries and are the constitutive events for the Christians. However, the legal texts (20-23) are not taken seriously by the Church and are left aside and neglected as if they have no bearing to the life and activity of the Church. This chapter will help the readers to know the importance of legal text as it will bring the community to a well balanced knitted family where social stratification has no importance. The author will read the legal text in a Postcolonial womanist perspective.

The Book of the Covenant Code

The Book of the Exodus pictures Yahweh as a Liberator. Yahweh comes into the history to liberate the oppressed. The history projecting God as liberator starts from the book of Exodus. Political, social, economic and spiritual freedoms are projected in this book. The expression 'bringing forth out of Egypt' (Exod 1-15) is not merely the point of departure but a mighty deed of God as a liberator. Hence, the liberation aspect is social, economic, political and spiritual. This aspect runs throughout the scripture and in the present time. Prophets in the Old Testament highlighted the events of Exodus to motivate, challenge and encourage the Israelites to remain faithful and loyal to Yahweh (Isa 43:14-17; Jer 2:2-3; 6:16; Hos 2:14-15; 11:1-4; 12:9; Amos 2:10; 3:1-2; Mic 6:4-5). The New Testament cites the Exodus event to the community of faith to strengthen herself in the midst of struggles and temptation (I Cor.10:1ff; Gal 5:1; Heb.11:27-29). Moving further to the 20th and 21st century, Liberation theologies like Latin American Theology, Dalit theology and feminist theology used the Exodus event as a paradigm to fight for their rights in a power dominated culture and society. Historical critics too considered the Exodus event as the historical and theological starting point of ancient Israel.[592] Hence, the Exodus event is an ongoing experience.

Though the Exodus event in the Book of Exodus has highly influenced both the Jewish and the Christian world and is considered as a paradigm for different movements, for instance, the liberation movements, the laws in the same book seem to be highly androcentric in nature. The laws related to women are male constructs and are heavily sexist, racist and classist. Hence, a postcolonial womanist reading is a possible alternative for understanding the content of the Law system.

---

592 Susanne Scholz, "The Complexities of 'His' Liberation Talk: A Literary Feminist Reading of the Book of Exodus," in *Exodus to Deuteronomy*, ed. Athalya Brenner (Sheffield: Sheffield Academic Press, 2000), 21.

The passage Exod 20:22-23:19 is a collection of judgments (*Mishpatim*). Unlike the theophany narrative (19:1-20:21), it differs both in form and content. Based on 24:7, this section is known as the Book of the Covenant. The Book of the Covenant has some affinity with the Codes of Mesopotamian civilization such as the code of Hammurabi. The text deals with civil laws such as property, protection rights and theft (Exod 21:1-22:17) and religious, cultic, and moral instruction (Exod 22:18-23:19). A closer reading leads us into a discussion that the code of laws (the civil laws) is heavily andocentric and imperialistic in perspective. This section will explore the position of women.

Title

Why and how the term Book of the Covenant (*sefer ha-berit)* came into being? The passage 20:22-23:33 has traditionally been entitled by the term *Book of the Covenant* in the light of the reference in 24:3. The earlier literary critics observed in 24:3 the double reference, *all the words of Yahweh*, and *all the ordinances*, which clearly marks a distinction between the Decalogue and the Book of the Covenant.[593] So, these passages gain its name from the supposition that they represent the actual terms upon which the covenant was ratified, as mentioned in 24:7. However, in the modern times, the distinction has been retained.

Scholars' Approach on the title 'Book of the Covenant': Origin of the placement of the Book of the Covenant Code

For John Durham, the title occurs outside the collection (24:7), and though that title, along with *all Yahweh's words and all guiding decisions* (24:3), is commonly applied to Exodus 20:22-23:33, there is no way to determine exactly how much of this collection was suggested by the title at any given point in Israel's history.[594] Werner H. Schmidt states that the collection of laws in Ex. 20:22-23:33 has been introduced at a later date into the Sinai pericope by means of preceding and following narrative devices, and it is from

593 Childs, 451.

594 John I. Durham, "Exodus," in *Word Biblical Commentary*, ed. John D. W. Watts and James W. Watts (USA: Nelson Reference & Electronic, 1987), 315.

this new setting that the collection gets its name as the Book of the Covenant.[595] Ronald E. Clements feels that the Book of the Covenant Code formed a separate and self-contained collection of laws which has been inserted into the Sinai narrative.[596] Martin Noth views that probably the Book of the Covenant Code was an independent book of law which has been inserted in a later period into the Pentateuchal narrative.[597] However, for Alan Cole and Albright, the Book of the Covenant deals with the problems of bronze-age society. And due to this, extreme critics favor for an early date for this section, the period of the judges at latest.[598]

In our observation, the text Exodus 20:22-23:33 was a separate collection, which has been inserted in the Sinai narrative. The title 'Book of the Covenant' was given at a later period to connect the independent book of the law (20:22-23:33) with the Sinai narrative. However, its structure and especially its origin make it a subject of ongoing debate, which will be focused in the following paragraph.

Sources[599]

In which literary sources 'the Book of the Covenant' has to be assigned?

- Julius Wellhausen assigned it to the J source, but retracted his opinion in 1889 in the light of the Kuenen's criticism.
- Julicher assigned it to the E source.
- B. Bantsch's monograph of 1892 turned the whole claim upside down, where a growing consensus had emerged that the Book of the Covenant was an older collection of laws, which was independent of the usual critical sources.
- For Brevard Childs, the secondary framework into which it was placed was that of E.

595 Schmidt, 134.

596 Clements, *Exodus*, 127. Clements writes that the collection of laws in Exodus resembles with the law codes of Ancient West Asia such as Code of Hammurabi, Laws of Eshnunna, Assyrian and Hittite laws (c.f. 128).

597 Noth, *Exodus*, 173.

598 Alan Cole, *Exodus:An Introduction and Commentary* (England: Inter-Varsity Press, 1973), 162.

599 Childs, 452.

Form Criticism

In the initial stages, the centre of attraction was based on the question of literary sources, but later the interest has been shifted on the question of analyzing the different forms in which the laws of the Book of the Covenant appear. Though the different literary forms within the Book of the Covenant had been taken into consideration long before, it was only after the rise of the form-critical method the full implication of the stylistic observations and approach were drawn. The Book of the Covenant consists of a diversity of forms such as case law, apodictic, divine exhortation and promises. The major part is case laws, which is in impersonal style with legal sanctions (21:1-22:20).

Scholars' Observation

Literary critics, such as B. Bantsch, distinguished between the ordinances in 21:1-22:16, and the words in 20:22-26; 22:27-29; 23:10-16. The former had the casuistic form of case law, and it regulated the secular affairs of an economic and social order, whereas the latter were given in a direct, apodictic style, and deal with cultic and moral life and nature. He felt that the Deuteronomic redactor had combined the apodictic and casuistic forms of law.[600]

Jirku had undertaken a detailed study on the legal forms within the Book of the Covenant. He distinguished ten different formulations of legal material within the Pentateuch, out of which five occurs in the Book of the Covenant. Jirku refined Bantsch's two larger categories into significant subheadings. He distinguished the singular and plural forms of the apodictic laws (22:17; 22:20; 22:27 and 22:21; cf. 20:18), isolated the characteristic conditional formulation of ordinances (21:7-11; 21:14), recognized the important participial formulation (Ex. 21:12,15,16,17), and designated a 'when you…' formulation, which appeared to combine elements of the casuistic with those of the apodictic (21:2; 22:24).[601] The

600 Ibid. [Childs cited from B. Bantsch, *Das Bundesbuch Exod XX.22-XXIII.33*, (Halle, 1892).]

601 Ibid. [Childs cited from A. Jirku, *Das weltliche Recht in Alten Testament*, (Gutersloh: Bertelsmann, 1927).]

disappointment concerning his study is that it never went beyond the detailed analysis.

A. Jepsen[602] though went far deeper into the analysis of the forms, failed to rid itself of a predominantly literary approach. Above all, it did not prove to be qualitatively different from B. Bantsch.

A. Alt overcame the deficiency of his predecessors by establishing an organic connection between literary form and historical function. He first simplified Jirku's classification by arguing that the Book of the Covenant Code is marked by two types of biblical law and thus retained only two major categories of laws: casuistic (protasis) and apodictic (apodosis). The casuistic law is dominant in the first half of the Code (21:1-22:17) and this form dominates also in most Ancient West Asian Codes. The second half of the Code (22:18-23:19) is stated in apodictic form, which are the direct commands stated in second person. Unlike the Casuistic law, the apodictic law is uniquely Israelite in origin, though this view is not widely accepted. He also suggested that the casuistic law had its setting in the secular case law of the Ancient West Asia, whereas the apodictic arose out of the unique covenantal setting of early Israel. For Alt, the subsequent fusion of legal material far from being a late literary activity reflected the institutional life of Israel during the early period of the Tribal League in which Israel appropriated common Ancient West Asian law from the Canaanites and brought it under the control of her unique covenantal law. [603]

Werner H. Schmidt has explored an interesting approach with regard to the structure of the Book of the Covenant 20:22-23:19(33). The body of the laws is set within a probably late framework, which is either theological or based on cultic law and also seeks in various ways to effect a clear differentiation from Canaanite religion (20:22-26; 23:10-19). The Prologue, with its more recent form of the prohibition against images (20:22f) and its law regarding the altar, precedes the superscription or title (21:1). The calendar of feasts (23:10ff) reveals close contact with the cultic Decalogue (34:10ff).

602 Ibid., 453. [Childs cited from A. Jepsen, *Untersuchungen Zum Bundesbuch*, (Stuttgart, 1927).]

603 A. Alt, 'The Origins of Israelite Law', *Essays on Old Testament History and Religion* (Oxford: Blackwell, 1966), 81-132.

Besides this, a differently structured concluding section, a speech of dismissal by Yahweh (23:20-33), has been added.[604] So, he proposes the Book of the Covenant as indicated above as 20:22-23:19(33). This complicated structure might hardly have been due to the will of a legislature seeking to give shape to his thought, but is rather to be explained by the gradual growth of the Book of the Covenant.

Though we do find more complex analysis of the forms by Gese, E. Gerstenberger, Kilian, Schulz, and others, the basic insight introduced by Alt in combining form and function in discovering a *Sitz im Leben* for a law, has provided a sound methodology for critical study and research.

Book of the Covenant and Sinai Narrative

The relationship of the Book of the Covenant to the Sinai narrative is one of the most difficult questions in the critical scholarship. It is primarily based on the area of form, unity, and historical setting of the Book of the Covenant. However, it must be noted that, most modern critical Scholars have reached a consensus that the Book of the Covenant was not initially or originally a part of the Sinai tradition, but only secondarily spliced or interweaved into the Sinai narrative. Brevard S. Childs[605] has cited mainly four reasons for the Book of the Covenant being not original in the Sinai narrative:

1. The Book of the Covenant interrupts the narrative sequence of 20:18-21; 20:1-17; 24:3, this is thought to be and considered by many as the original outline of events.
2. The reference in 24:3 to the Book of the Covenant is redactional, as the phrase *all the words,* which formed the basis for the Covenant ceremony originally referred only to the Decalogue.
3. The inner structure of the Book of the Covenant shows an independent history of development and redactional history distinct from the Sinai tradition.

604 Schmidt, 135.

605 Childs, 453-454.

4. Above all, the very content of the Book of the Covenant shows no original relation to the Covenant, rather points to a settled life in Palestine, long after Sinai.

Problems of the Present Position of the Book of the Covenant

Mainly on two distinct levels, namely on the literary and oral level, we do find problem.

Oral Level

In the whole book of the Covenant, two different blocks of material, casuistic (21:1-22:16) and apodictic (22:17ff) can be seen. A careful study on the historical setting of the apodictic style reveals the period before the rise of the monarchy. For instance, compare 23:10 ff with 34:18ff. Now, in the casuistic part, the introduction in 21:1 would also point to its being a unified collection.

For Childs, the fusion of the two halves of the Book occurred at the literary stage. The *mispatim* were joined to the cultic laws, which already had received a place within the Sinai narrative.[606] So, it seems that the redactor rearranged the material and gave the law its present leading position.

Literary Level

The present position of the Book of the Covenant clearly shows many signs of redactional activity. The transition from the Sinai narrative in 20:22 indicates every sign of being a secondary connection, which was strongly influenced by Deuteronomy. The present order of the laws is due to a redactional ordering and so not original. It is clearly sustained from the two different sorts of material, which have been interwoven together. The ordinances begin in 21:1 with an obvious superscription, and this collection continues through 22:16 in a strictly uniform style. The other material in a different style partly precedes and partly follows the ordinances. Within the body of the ordinances only once has there been a serious interpolation, in 21:12-17. The conclusion of the Book of the Covenant, 23:20-33, is also secondary, and it did not belong to the original layer of the laws. Above all, there is a series of Deuteronomic glosses, which have

606 Ibid., 458.

entered into the text secondarily, such as 22:20b, 23, 23:9b.[607] So, the redactional activity on the literal level is an asset in understanding the later stage in the development of the text.

Exodus20 (The Decalogue)

Title

The title Decalogue carries no designation as such in this chapter. The commonly known title 'The ten commandments' is traditionally derived from the Hebrew phrase עֲשֶׂרֶת הַדְּבָרִים (cf. Exodus 34:28, Deuteronomy 4:13, 10:4). The Hebrew term מִצְוָה 'commandment' is not employed in the present context. The Jews of ancient Alexandria in Egypt translated as 'The ten words' literally into Greek as *δεκα λογοι*, which gave rise to the title 'Decalogue'. [608]

Source

There are two different opinions concerning the Decalogue: 1) the Decalogue is a product of later development in the culture of Israel and is based on the teaching of the prophets. 2) It should be attributed to Moses in its original form. This opinion is based on the study of the ethical teaching of the Ancient West Asia (the negative confession of the Egyptian 'Book of the Dead' dated around 15th century BCE and the Mesopotamian Penitential texts in the *Surpu* series dated of the same period or slightly later). However, there is a general opinion that the short lapidary sentences like 'I am the Lord your God', 'Remember the Sabbath day' so on are original and others were added in the course of time, under the inspiration of the Book of Deuteronomy.[609] In our observation, the argument for a later date is a possibility because the Book of Deuteronomy supports

---

607 Ibid., 454.

608 Nahum M. Sarna, "Exodus," in *The Jerusalem Publication Society Torah Commentary*, ed. Nahum M. Sarna (Jerusalem: The Jewish Publication Society, 1991), 107. Hebrew הַדְּבָרִים appears in the introductory verse as well as in the epilogue.

609 Cassuto, 235-236. For Clements, *Exodus*, 124. and Noth, *Exodus*, 164., the explanation of the commands in verses 9-11 are added later. It has been argued that the Decalogue covers the period from Moses (Gressman, Driver, Schmidt) to the exilic (Beer) or even to post-exilic (HÖlschr) [Durham, 282.]

for equality and justice for all (cf. 20:8-10), which is missing out in the Book of the Covenant Code.

The content, style and language points to the Decalogue into two distinct groups- The first group (vv. 2-12) deals with the relation between Yahweh and Israelite; the second group (vv. 13-17) governs human relationships. Interestingly, the first group is characterized by the phrase 'the Lord your God' (vv. 2, 5, 7, 10, 12) which is missing in the second group. The first part is unique to the religion of Israel, while the second which carries a series of prohibitory statement is not unique for Israel, rather is of universal and has several parallels in literatures of Ancient West Asia.[610] This is possible as the book of Deuteronomy supports equality and justice for all.

Exodus 20:8-10, 17

Exodus 20: 8-10

The day of rest in Exodus (Exod. 20:8-11) differs from Deuteronomy (Deut. 5:12-15) with respect to the motivation of the commandment. In Deuteronomy unlike Exodus, the rest is commanded, and the reason for rest is to remember their days of slavery in the land of Egypt (v. 15). In Exodus, the day of rest is related to creation (v. 11). In Exodus, the seventh day of rest is expected for all members of the community including the aliens (v. 10). However, in Deuteronomy like Exodus, the rest includes to all members, but the additional clause 'in order that your male slave and your female slave may rest as well as you' is missing in Exodus (Deut. 5:14; Exod. 20:10). In both texts, the day of rest points not only to a religious observance, but also has a social and humanitarian flavour.

---

610 Sarna, 108.

Translation/Textual Comments

8 Remember[611] the Sabbath day to keep it holy[612] 9 Six days you shall labor and do all your work[613] 10 but the seventh day[614] is a Sabbath to the Lord your God; you shall not do[615] any work, you, your son or your daughter, your male[616] or your female slave[617], or your animals[618], or the alien in your gates[619].

Form and Structure

The verses 8-11 are the longest command in the Decalogue. Verse 8 introduces the positive command and the verb is in infinitive absolute form which functions as a strong command. Verses 9-10 are dependent on verse 8 describing the way to observe the Sabbath. Verse 11 provides a motivational clause (*ki*) for the command and also the implication of Yahweh's action.

Comments and Explanation

The text 20:8-10, though part of the law is outside the Covenant Code text. In the Covenant Code text, the position of women,

---

611 The Samaritan Hebrew Pentateuch reads שׁמור 'keep' cf. Deut. 5:12 (Along with the word 'observe/keep' it also adds a clause 'as YHWH your God commands to you'). The LXX reads 'remember'. In MT, the verb used is זכוֹר 'remember' which is in Qal infinitive absolute (c.f. Exodus 13:3). It is read as an 'emphatic imperative' (legislative command).

612 *Soph pasuq* is absent in L, but found in number of Manuscripts (see Durham, 277.) לְקַדְּשׁוֹ has preposition ְל, the infinitive form of the verb.

613 *Soph Pasuq* is again missing.

614 The Nash Papyrus and a few manuscripts Septuagint and Vulgate read 'in the seventh day'.

615 The Nash Papyrus, Septuagint, Syriac and Vulgate add בה for more lucidity as the restriction is applied only on the seventh day.

616 The Targum and many manuscripts codices minusculis scripti Syriac read 'nor your male slave'. The Parallel version in Deuteronomy also adds w. (Deut.5:14).

617 The Nash Papyrus and Septuagint follow Deut 5:14.

618 The Samaritan Pentateuch reads 'your animal' and is absent in Targum Pseudo-Jonathan. The Septuagint includes 'your ox and your ass'.

619 The Septuagint has 'ο παροικων ἐν σοι 'the one residing with you/who dwells with you'. This verse is also without *soph pasuq* in L.

slave (male and female) are in a lower status and in a disadvantaged position, whereas in the Decalogue the freedom is given to all.

זכר - The law of Sabbath commences with the 7th letter of the Hebrew alphabet ז and the beneficiaries are not the elite group, rather the whole society (you, your son, your daughter, your male slave, your female slave, your animal and your guest/sojourner who is in your gate), which are 7 categories.

שבת - There are different opinions among the scholars concerning the origin of Sabbath. For Cassuto, the name of the Sabbath was already known in the Orient before the people of Israel came into being. However, for the Israelite the Sabbath held a new character, identity and significance and emerged as a new and original institution.[620] Sarna argues that the Sabbath is altogether an Israelite innovation and there is nothing analogous to it in the entire Ancient West Asian world. However, he makes a point that the seven day units of time are well known throughout the region but the Israelite understanding of Sabbath unlike the Ancient West Asia completely dissociates itself from the notion of the movement of celestial bodies.[621] In our observation, there is a possibility that Israel being a newly formed nation borrowed it from the neighbouring nation and gave a new colour. The word Sabbath is given more importance in priestly ritual and regulation (cf. Genesis 2:1-3).

קדשׁ - Holiness means separateness. The form is in Piel infinitive construct with the suffix in third person singular, which means 'to make holy'.

In these verses, the narrator enlists 7 categories of living beings probably having the number seven (Sabbath) in his mind- you, or

620 Cassuto, 237.

621 Sarna, 111. The Hebrew word שבת has some similarity with her neighbouring nation. The Akkadian has a word *shabattum* which is designated as the 15th day of the lunar month (full moon). This is described as the day of the quieting of the heart (of the god). In Mesopotamia the lunar calendar of the 7th, 14th, 21st and 28th days of certain months corresponding to the four phases of the moon, were regarded as days controlled by the evil spirits. During these days, special magical rites were performed and all sorts of activities were refrained. The King in particular refrained from his duties. In Israel, the 7th day was not considered as evil day, rather a holy day to desist from labour (112).

your son or your daughter, your male slave or your female slave, your animal or your alien who is in your gate. If we go deeper, the order of creation is of 7 days (cf. Genesis 2:1-3) and the categories of living beings are 7 and the word starts with the 7th letter of the Hebrew alphabet, which clearly defines the social pattern and are woven into the fabric of the society. The Decalogue unlike the Book of the Covenant Code delimits human self-rule and restores human beings irrespective of his/her social standing to a position of freedom. The law promotes human liberty and human equality. The cause of social justice is highly pointed out by issuing the decree and advocating the unchallengeable right of every human being irrespective of his/her societal standing.

Hence, in this law, the whole society irrespective of the standing of each member is given equal opportunity and rights to keep the Sabbath and to partake in it.

Exodus 20:17 (Law of Covetousness)

Translation/Textual Comments

You shall not covet the house of your neighbor[622]. You shall not covet the wife of your neighbor[623], or his male servant or female servant, or his ox or donkey[624], or anything that belong to your neighbor.

Form and Structure

This law is in command form (apodictic) and comes under the Decalogue. This law is unique as it forbids coveting neighbor and his/her belongings, which are listed as seven like the command of Sabbath.

---

622 Septuagint and the parallel passage in Deuteronomy (5:21) has wife first and house second. The Deuteronomic passage puts wife before house showing the importance of woman in the eyes of law.

623 Nash Papyrus and few manuscripts Samaritan Pentateuch and Septuagint add 'his field' before 'male servant'. The Deuteronomic passage also has field before male servant (5:21).

624 Septuagint adds 'or any of his livestock'. It is very interesting to note that the things not to be coveted like 20:8-10 are seven in numbers. The Decalogue starts with 'I am the Lord your God' ends with 'neighbor and his belonging', which clearly points to the importance of neighbor and his belonging in law instituted by God.

Comments and Explanation

חָמַד – The exact meaning of לֹא תַחְמֹד (you shall not covet) is a subject of dispute. The word covet means 'wrongful attitude, desire, yearn for, lust after someone or something specifically for one's use or gratification'.[625] According to Wallis, 'the word *chāmadh* refers not to the 'desire' that is inherently human, but the specific act of desire that is generated by emotion.[626] Many scholars consider that it connotes practical action, i.e., you shall not do anything in order to acquire what belongs to your neighbour (cf. Exod 34:24; Josh 7:21, Prov 6:25 and Mic 2:2).[627] This word could also be employed as a position of power and unfair rivalry to acquire other's property.[628]

The question here arises is, whether the verb חָמַד points to action like the previous nine commandments, or suggests for desire, or points to action as well as desire. If desire, is it possible to put it as a command or legislation? The preceding commandments are full of actions such as 'Do not murder, do not commit adultery, do not steal and do not bear false witness against your neighbour'. Does the tenth commandment (verse 17) go further than the previous commandments pointing that the desire before action is forbidden? This is a possibility as desire for neighbour's property and wife may lead to stealing and adultery. Here, the law clearly forbids the power

625 Durham, 297. For Scholars opinion (such as Hyatt and A. Philips) see Durham, 297-298. C.f. Cornelis Houtman, "Exodus," in *Historical Commentary on the Old Testament*, ed. Gert T. M. Prinsloo Cornelis Houtman, Wilfred G. E. Watson and Al Wolters (Leuven: Peeters, 2000), 68-69.

626 Hale G. Wallis, "Chāmadh," in *Theological Dictionary of the Old Testament*, ed. G. Johannes Botterweck and Helmer Ringgren (Grand Rapids, Michigan: William B. Eerdmans Publishing Company, 1980), 454. For Wallis, 'the semasiological range of *chāmadh* covers the entire human sequence from viewing through perception of pleasure or even delight and inward longing to the desire to possess…'(454). The word *chāmadh* in the scripture have positive (Psalms 19: 10; Prov 21:10), negative (Exod 20:17; Deut 5:21; Josh 7:21), and neutral (Gen 27:15; Psalm 39:11) component (456-457).

627 Cassuto, 248. J. Hermann, E. Sellin, Leipzig argues that the verb *hmd* includes the action which stems from the emotion [cf. Childs, 425.] Martin Noth describes this verb as an attempt to attach something to oneself illegally (cf. Noth, *Exodus*, 166.)

628 Wallis, 459.

over others (the possession of neighbour). This perspective is totally missing out in the Covenant Code (cf. Deut. 10:17-19, 23:7-8; Lev. 19:13, 17-19).

If we go further by comparing it with the parallel code (Deut. 5:21), differences can be seen especially concerning 'wife'. In Deuteronomy, the word תַחְמֹד is used only for wife. The desire for other things is expressed by means of תִתְאַוֶּה. Do these changes refer to sexual desire, stealing or to gain possession of something that belongs to another? It is difficult to bring out a conclusion. In our observation, in Deuteronomy 'the wife' is highlighted as the main object, and all other, i.e., house, male or female servant, ox and donkey are supplemented, which shows that woman is a full and equal partner of her husband and has rights in society. Unlike Deuteronomy 5:21, in Exodus the place of wife is counted along with male or female servant, ox and donkey. The wife is considered as the property of the husband and is categorized under house 'בֵית'. The Septuagint version of the Exodus text too supports for Deuteronomistic readings where 'the wife' is mentioned as the main and given a place of her own (οὐκ ἐπιθυμήσεις τὴν γυναῖκα τοῦ πλησίον σου οὐκ ἐπιθυμήσεις τὴν οἰκίαν τοῦ πλησίον σου οὔτε τὸν ἀγρὸν αὐτοῦ οὔτε τὸν παῖδα αὐτοῦ οὔτε τὴν παιδίσκην αὐτοῦ οὔτε τοῦ βοὸς αὐτοῦ οὔτε τοῦ ὑποζυγίου αὐτοῦ οὔτε παντὸς κτήνους αὐτοῦ οὔτε ὅσα τῷ πλησίον σού ἐστιν). It points out a clear picture of woman's subordination and her status as a property in the Covenant Code.

Exodus 21:2-11 (Laws on Slavery)

> ***If I have rejected the cause of my male or female slaves,***
> ***When they brought a complaint against me;***
> ***What then shall I do when God rises up?***
> ***When he makes inquiry, what shall I answer him?***
> ***Did not He who made me in the womb make them also?***
> ***And did not one fashion us in the womb? Job 31:13-15***

Background Studies

In this section, the author will be stressing mainly three areas: The meaning and general idea of Hebrew word עבר (Slave), Slavery in the Ancient West Asia, and Slavery in the Old Testament.

The Meaning and General Idea of עבד

The Brown Driver Briggs Hebrew and English Lexicon gives various meaning for עבד such as slave, servant, subject, worshipper, etc. It is derived from the verb עבד, which means to labor, to work, to serve, as well as to serve as subjects, to be slaves of another, to worship, to serve God, and so on.[629]. The Hiphil or the causative form of the verb has the connotation of compelling someone to labor as slaves, for, e.g., Israel under Egyptian bondage (Exod 1:13; 6:5 cf. 6:6; Ezra 9:8-9).[630] In the LXX it is referred to as δουλοs, which is the most general attributive of a slave, and sometimes οικετηs, a household slave. The Hebrew אנאשׁר (fem. נערט), literally means boy, lad, youth, and for noun feminine damsel, girl. The word סאמה (amah) takes the meaning as a slave woman among the ancient women.[631]

Slavery in the Ancient West Asia

Slavery in ancient Israel must be studied against the background of the Ancient West Asia, and should not be compared or interpreted in the light of slavery in ancient Greece, Rome, or of Latin America or any other concept.

Ancient West Asian Laws and Israelite Law concerning Slavery

All the law collections of the Ancient West Asia deal with the law concerning slavery. Slave though had a close daily contact with his/her owner, in reality was treated and considered as a chattel and property, weighed in terms of monetary value. They were bought with a price, used for a price and sold for a price. They could be leased, exchanged or inherited. They were treated and used more harshly than animals. It is quite surprising to note that the laws of Ancient West Asia including Israelite law system nowhere prohibited or discouraged slave market/ slavery. However, in all of these laws distinction was made between the native and foreign slaves.

---

629 Francis Brown, *The Brown-Driver-Briggs Hebrew and English Lexicon* (Massachusetts: Hendrickson Publishers, 2000), 713-714.

630 Rui de Menezes, "Was There Slavery in Ancient Israel?," *Vidya Jyothi Journal of Theological Reflection* 63 (1999): 799-800.

631 Muhammad A. Dandamayev, "Slavery (Old Testament)," in *Anchor Bible Dictionary*, ed. David Noel Freedman (New York: Double day, 1992), 62.

Concerning the native and foreign slaves, the Ancient West Asian law codes as well as the laws of Israel made a clear distinction between the two groups. They looked at the foreign slaves as real slaves, and when applied to native, the term had totally different connotation. In the Old Babylonian period, a distinction was drawn between them. According to the Code of Hammurabi (§280), citizens who had been carried off to foreign countries were subject to redemption. [632]
As far as the source of slavery is concerned, similarity can be seen in both Ancient West Asia and Israel. Debt Slavery was one of the basic sources of replenishing the slave population. The Babylonian King Ammisaduqa in the 17th Century BCE issued an edict, according to which all inhabitants of his kingdom, who had been compelled by debt to become slave, should be released together with their families.[633] In early Mesopotamian periods, debt-slavery was usually limited by law to a specific period, usually to 3 or 6 years. The Code of Hammurabi (§ 117) stipulated that debt slavery should be limited to 3 years, but no such limit existed in Assyria.[634]

The slave, particularly the women slave in Ancient West Asia, had no freedom whatsoever. The women slaves were treated and considered as mere property or things, and they were not at all treated as human beings. If injustice and atrocities were done against them, they were not compensated; rather their owner gained the benefit. Though they were physically and mentally tortured, no compassion was rendered towards them. The settlement was usually brought between the slave owner and the one who had done the harm. In short, the slaves had no right whatsoever. They were strictly under the jurisdiction of their owner. Now, the question to be raised is: How were the slaves treated in the Old Testament? Did the slave system in Old Testament have something to do with Ancient West Asia? The following section will deal with this issue.

---

632 Muhammad A. Dandamayev, "Slavery (Ancient near East)," in *Anchor Bible Dictionary*, ed. David Noel Freedman (New York: Double day, 1992), 59.

633 Ibid.

634 Meek, "The Code of Hammurabi," 170-171.

Slavery in the Old Testament

In this section, we will be focusing mainly on two areas: 1) Biblical law (Its social norms and debt slavery, its stand concerning native/ Hebrew and foreign slave, in which way it is related to AWA, female slave etc), 2) Was the slave law in the Old Testament purely religious and social, or had something political in taste? and above all was it originally Israelite or influenced by AWA legal tradition? What do the Scholars have to contribute towards the Biblical or Israelite law?

Israelite Slavery

Slavery as it was in Ancient West Asia was an accepted institution in ancient Israel. This institution was not abolished in ancient Israel. An Israelite might fall into slavery due to different reasons: 1) He might be sold by his parents; 2) He might be sold for theft or bankruptcy; 3) He might be indebted by poverty to sell himself; and 4) as war captives.[635] There are ample references in the scripture promoting/ advocating slavery directly or indirectly (Exod 21:5-6; Exod 21:37-22:3; Lev 25:39-43; Num 31:7-12; Deut 15:15-17; Deut 21:10-14; II Kings 4:1; II Chr 28:8; Neh 5:5). The prophets though spoke against the brutalities of slaves, did not advocate for the eradication of this form of practice [Isa 50:1; Jer 34:8-22; Joel 3:2 (Eng 2:29); Amos 2:6, 8:6].

Social Norms and Debt Slavery

We can find certain social norms that have striking parallels between Biblical and AWA Laws, for e.g., Kidnapping and sale of the abducted person (Exod. 21:6; Deut 24:7; CH §14, and HL §19-§20).

With regard to Debt-Slavery, both in Israel and in the AWA, social problems and dislocations were caused by economic disparities and hardships. The problem of debt was so severe that it forced them to give up their property, home, fields, and eventually their freedom. In Bible, there is a concern about persons who are enslaved because of their debts, and such a person must be released or given freedom after six years (Exod 21:2-11; Deut 15:12-18). In Babylonia, the

635 S. R. Driver, *The Book of Exodus* (Cambridge: Cambridge University Press, 1929), 209; Roy Brasfield Herron, "The Land, the Law, and the Poor," *Word and World* 6, no. 1 (1986): 80.

freedom is after three years (CH §117). In the Assyrian laws (AL A §39, §48) and in the Bible (Exod 21:7-11), we do find attempts to mitigate the consequences of debt slavery for unmarried women. [636]

Slavery: Hebrew/Native and Foreign Slave

Biblical laws make a clear distinction between the slaves of Hebrew and foreign descent. Debtors who were Hebrews and who sold themselves due to utmost need could be held in slavery, but only for 6 years, after which they should be set free without any pay (Exod 21:2; Deut 15:12; Jer 34:14). Exodus 21:2-11 indicates clearly and explicitly about Hebrew Slave (c.f. Deut 15:16-17; Lev 25:39-41, 47-54; Neh 5:8).

Having foreign slaves was an integral part of life throughout Ancient West Asia. Slaves were imported and exported. The supply of war captives and native-born slaves was common. In later periods of Israelite society, the influx of prisoners of war was very limited, and for this reason, the basic source of slave was natural production. The next source was obtaining slaves through purchase from neighboring nations, and such slaves were legally considered the absolute property of their owners, and above all their status was permanent. Non-Israelite or foreign slaves were legally considered movable property of their master, who could dispose of them as they wished (c.f. Mal 1:6), and they were categorized as part of valuable property along with cattle, gold, silver etc (Gen. 12:16; 20:14; 24:35; 30:43; Exod 20:17).[637]

Female Slave

The status of a slave woman differs from that of the free woman's status. The legal status of a slave both male and female was that of a chattel. The female slave unlike male slave was not merely considered as a commodity that could be sold, leased, exchanged and even inherited but was also subjected in many other cases primarily the exploitation by the male members of her master's household and were subjected to the abuse of their male masters[638]. Young female slaves were sold for

636 Greengus, "Law," 250-251.

637 Dandamayev, "Slavery (Old Testament)," 64.

638 Herron: 81.

two purposes-as maids to their mistresses and as concubines to their masters. The highest position of a female slave is to be a concubine to her master and the lowest to be used as a professional prostitute. They were also used as a means to increase the number of slaves by mating them with the male slaves. This practice was not uncommon throughout Ancient West Asia. However, in Israel and in Nuzian, the parents sold their young girls into conditional slavery (Exod. 21:7-11). While Babylonian and Assyrian parents sold of their children without condition, the Nuzians and Israel sold of their children with a condition that their purchaser would give them into marriage.[639]

Hebrew Female Slave

Hebrew has two terms for the female slaves, i.e., אמה and שׁפחה. The former is used by Elohistic literary strand of the Pentateuch, while the latter was found in the Yahwistic author. Now, the question is, whether they are same or different. Scholars indicate a real distinction between the two terms. For H. W. Wolff, אמה is a female slave who has been treated like a concubine by her master or his son, and the שׁפחה is the virgin maid whom the bride brought with her at the time of marriage (Gen 29:24-29).[640] Israelite law forbade the selling into slavery of a female slave who had been treated as a concubine. The Code of Hammurabi too forbids the sale of such slave-girls (CH §146), but if she did not bear children, her mistress may sell her (CH §147).[641]

Exodus 21:2-11 (Slave Law)

Translation/Textual Comments

3. When you buy a Hebrew slave, six years he shall serve[642] and in the seventh (year) he shall go out free for nothing. 3. If he will enter

639 Isaac Mendelsohn, *Slavery in the Ancient near East* (New York: Oxford University Press, 1949), 3-10, 50-52.

640 H. W. Wolff, *Anthropology of the Old Testament* (London: SCM Press, 1974), 199.

641 Menezes: 802.

642 The Samaritan Hebrew Pentateuch, Septuagint, Syriac, and Vulgate adds a pronominal suffix 'you'.

in body (single)[643] he shall go out in his body; if husband and wife (married), his wife shall go out with him. 4. If his owner[644] gives to him a wife she bears to him sons or daughters, the wife and her children shall be her[645] master's and he shall go self (alone)[646]. 5. But, if the slave plainly says[647], I love my master, my wife, and my children[648] ; I will not go out free, 6. then his master shall draw near him to God[649] ; and he shall draw (bring) him to door or the door post; and his master shall pierce his ear through an awl; and he shall serve him forever. 7. When a man sells his daughter as a maidservant, she shall not go out as the male slaves go forth. 8. If she does not please her master, who has appointed her for himself[650], then he shall let her be redeemed; he shall have no right to sell her to a foreigner, since he has dealt deceitfully (unfaithfully) with her. 9. If he betrothed her for his son, he shall do justice to her as his daughter. 10. If he takes another wife to himself, he shall not diminish (restrain) her food, her clothing or her marital rights. 11. And if he does not do these three (things) for her, she shall go out freely (for nothing), without money.

Form and Structure

The passage 21:2-11 can be grouped into two subunits- vv. 2-6, and 7-11.

The structure of both is more or less same. In the first paragraph, after the principal case that is introduced by the word כִּי (*when, if*- v. 2), four secondary cases are cited, prefaced by אִם (*if*) or וְאִם (*and*

643 Samaritan Pentateuch reads *in his back or self.* The word בְּגַפּוֹ literally means 'with his body', i.e., alone. The Septuagint translates it as 'If he comes in single' (ἐὰν αὐτὸς μόνος εἰσέλθῃ).

644 Septuagint, Syriac, and Vulgate read *his master.*

645 Samaritan, Textus Graecus Originalis (Septuagint), Syriac, and Vulgate reads *his.*

646 Or in his back or self.

647 The Hebrew word וְאִם־אָמֹר יֹאמַר is emphatic.

648 In verse 4, for Children ילדים is used, whereas in verse 5, בתי is indicated. There is no specific and clear reason for a change.

649 Septuagint reads *to the God's judgment.*

650 Samaritan adds *to him.*

if or *but if*). It is the case of vv. 7-11. It begins by stating a principal case, commencing with the word וְכִי (*and when*), followed by four secondary cases, introduced by the word אִם (*if*) or וְאִם (*and if*). So, in these ten verses of two paragraphs, there are ten subsections on the laws of slavery, like the number of ten words (Decalogue).[651] So, the structural form of these two paragraphs is similar, which shows the sign of unity, and of same source.

Comments and Explanation

Verse 2

Here the law deals regarding the treatment of the slaves within Israel, most probably native slaves. The principle is introduced by *when,* but the lesser clauses are introduced by *if.* In this passage, the problem to be addressed and tackled first is what is meant by the phrase עֶבֶדעִבְרִי (Hebrew Slave)? This phrase is debatable and grammatically can be understood in different ways.

1. It can mean either a Hebrew (man) servant or (man) servant of a Hebrew.[652] In the latter case the servant can be either a Hebrew or a foreigner. If we compare the parallel law in Deuteronomy 15:12, the slave is a Hebrew. The question arises now is: who is an עִבְרִי (Hebrew)?
2. עִבְרִי has a very distinctive significance. It has been taken both as a designation of a native slave, an Israelite slave, and also an underprivileged social group, disadvantaged persons who fall easily into the oppression of slavery.[653] For centuries, the term עִבְרִי has been associated with a

651 Cassuto, 267, 269. In the Hebrew, the primary cases are introduced by כִּי and the subordinate ones by אִם. c.f. Noth, *Exodus*, 177.

652 William H. C. Propp, *Exodus 19-40*, ed. William Foxwell Albright and David Noel Freedman, The Anchor Bible (New York: Doubleday, 2006), 186-187.

653 Durham, 320. The general consensus among the scholars (M. Greenberg, B. S. Childs and others) is that the term Hebrew is not an ethnic term but a disadvantaged social group within the Ancient West Asian society of the second millennium BCE. They were the landless people who were dependent on wealthy people for survival. For von Rad, from a sociological point of view they were the fluctuating element of the population and from legal and economic point of view a lower class [Rad, *Deuteronomy*, 107.] c.f. Anthony Philips, "The Laws of Slavery: Exodus 21:2-11," *JSOT* 30 (1984): 51-66.; Lemche:

> Jew. The table of the nations in Gen 10:24-25 include an individual named Eber which is also pronounced as עֵבֶר. Does this name עֵבֶר refers to all the עִבְרִים? If so, it refers not only to the people of Israel but also to all Eber's sons which include the Arameans, Moabites, Ammonites, and Edomites etc. Interestingly, Abram is addressed as Hebrew (Gen 14:13). If so, it refers to the descendants of Abram.[654] Recent study has made it clear that the term does not designate an ethnic/racial group, but rather a pejorative designation of a legal or social status within the Ancient West Asian society of the second millennium BCE (who became slaves). The Hebrews were the disadvantaged peoples, considered inferior, having more or less no rights in the society, and were employed in the menial laboring jobs.[655] So, Hebrew is not necessarily ethnic but probably a depressed social class.

The term עִבְרִי is mentioned in the scripture in two contexts: a) in the mouth of foreigners; b) describing slaves. Whatever their nationality is, they were slaves with a certain hope of freedom after a set term of servitude. So, they can't be categorized as full citizens, or as full slaves. At the end of six years, whatever the cause of servitude is, עִבְרִי was free[656] to go. For Alan Cole, the slave mentioned in the text is an indentured laborer bound for six years, and when his seventh year comes to an end, he must be released.[657]

129-144.; Noth, *Exodus*, 177. and G. Henton Davies, *Exodus* (London: SCM Press Ltd, 1967), 175.

654 Propp, 186. The term עִבְרִי can also mean 'the one from across'. From a Palestinian perspective, עִבְרִי denotes 'Easterner'. Canaan was included in the region 'across the river'. It also connotes a 'westerner' which refers to the Amorite (c.f. 186).

655 Childs, 468.

656 The term *free* is another disputed term. It designates apparently a social status free of bondage, but somewhat below the category of free citizen. It also seems to denote a definite class in society lying between nobles and slaves. Hence, it is a social term indicating a status higher than slavery, but below a full free Israelite.

657 Cole, *Exodus: An Introduction and Commentary*, 165.

The time bond of the slaves is varied. The slaves of Nuzi were apparently slaves for life, though there is a different view. The Torah, on the other hand, enacts that the Hebrew slave shall serve only a limited time, and thereafter he shall be free. In the Hammurabi Code (§117), a fixed period of three years is laid down only in the case where a Babylonian freeman sells himself, his wife, or his son, or his daughter on account of debts.[658]

Men servant or servant (male and female)? - Septuagint text reads, Ἐὰν κτήσῃ παῖδα Εβραῖον (If you buy a Hebrew servant). παῖ δα Εβραῖον though claimed by Masoretic text as masculine, the author strongly believes after comparing it with Deuteronomy and Septuagint that it can be used in a generic sense[659]. If so, it can't be claimed as exclusively male slave or female slave. It can be either or both. If both, why the text says, six years *he* shall serve you? What about *she*? Whether she has no freedom after six years? Masoretic text says, כִּי תִקְנֶה עֶבֶד עִבְרִי (When or if you buy a Hebrew slave). עֶבֶד is noun, masculine singular. The textual variance can be clearly seen in these texts. In second part of this verse, Septuagint says 'six years he will serve *you*' (δουλεύσει- Future active indicative, 3 person singular); whereas Masoretic reads 'he will serve'. Though here the meaning does not make much difference, the question lies, why Masoretic avoided 'you'? It seems that Masoretic text intentionally avoided the expression 'you', which resulted into an error. If Masoretic text has error in verse 2, why not in Deuteronomy as it also comes under Masoretic? The author argues that the original laws in Exodus 21:2-11 were having concern both to male and female slave. In the later period due to the influence of AWA laws particularly Nuzi

658 Cassuto, 266. U. and J. P. Hyatt, *Exodus* (London: Oliphants, 1971), 228. The Law in Exodus 21:2-6 has its parallel in § 117 of the Hammurabi Code. Lemche and a good number of scholars consider that the laws of slavery has strong connection to Canaanite and Mesopotamian Laws (c.f. N P Lemche, "Manumission of Slaves-the Fallow Year-the Sabbatical Year-the Jubilee Year," *Vetus Testamentum* 26, no. 1 (1976).)

659 Refer F. Wilbur Gingrich, William F. Arndy *A Greek- English Lexicon of the New Testament and Other Early Christian Literature* (Chicago: The University of Chicago Press, 1957), 609. παῖδα can be used with reference to a relation between one human being and another, and ον ending in Εβραῖον can be used sometimes for feminine.

text, the entire notion has changed, and now the existing text is not the original, but an amalgamated one. The author opts for the Septuagint reading and the translation recommended is, *If you buy a Hebrew slave (male and female), six years he/she shall serve you, and in the seventh year he/she shall go forth free for nothing.* The Exodus passage differs from other slave law passages in Bible with regard to female slave (e.g. Deut. 15:12).

Free- The Hebrew word חָפְשִׁי is probably understood as a freedman, a status between nobles and slaves.[660]

He shall go out free, without debt[661] - The provision aspect is missing in this passage, which differs from the parallel Deuteronomic passage. Deuteronomy 15:12 requires that the owner shall not send the slave empty-handed. He has to provide him liberally (economically) so that the slave may not again turn to slavery.

Verses 3-4

אִם־בְּגַפּוֹ יָבֹא בְּגַפּוֹ- The word בְּגַפּוֹ is disputed. The general understanding of this word is 'single', i.e., if he comes alone. However, there are other derivations too. Rashi considers the word as garment, i.e., if a slave came with only the garment on his back. Jacob refers it as 'staff' (Gen 32:11). Bekhor Shor refers it as 'body'. For him, the word *begappo* means 'with his body'. Ibn Ezra cites Proverbs 9:3, where the word is understood as an architectural feature, presumably the 'back'. Paul considers it as 'self'.[662] Cole considers the word as 'with his back', i.e., bare back and nothing more.[663] The word means 'if a slave enters as an individual or as a person'. Hence, the slave, if single can go as single, and if he is married during the entry as slave, he can

660 Cole, *Exodus: An Introduction and Commentary*, 165. This is a term used for those group or individual who are freed from slavery but not have attained the full rights of the free citizen. On the basis of its Akkadian *hupshu* and Ugaritic *hpt*, the word *hofsi* seems to be a technical term for one who belongs to the low social class composed of emancipated slaves (c.f. Sarna, 119.)

661 The Code of Hammurabi (§117) says, 'if a man gives his wife, son, or daughter as a slave to work off a debt, they may do this for three years, but shall be free in the fourth'.

662 Propp, 190.

663 Cole, *Exodus: An Introduction and Commentary*, 165.

leave as married.[664] The author strongly agree with the view that the word בְּגַפּוֹ refers to 'single', i.e., he enters his owner's house alone.

If he enters his owner's house with his wife, his wife can go out along with him. The woman is mentioned as the wife of the enslaved man.

But, if the master provides a wife for him and if she bears children, he can go free, but his wife and children belongs to his master. They are obviously the owner's property.[665] It brings out a clear picture that the slaves are treated by the owner not as human being, but rather as a property. This also clearly indicates the freedom from bondage, but not as a full citizen. It is an act of inducement to renounce his right of freedom after six years of faithful service. It also contradicts with Gen. 2:24, 'therefore shall a man leave his father and mother, and shall cleave unto his wife, and they shall be one flesh'. The temporary slave who does not want to be separated from his wife and children will opt for servitude forever, and will swear an oath of loyalty to his owner. How can the law (Exod. 21:3-4) contradict with the commandment of God?

The slave woman also is not given the freedom of choice. The wife mentioned here is presumably a perpetual slave, and therefore the master's own property. Some consider it as a Neolithic matriarchal society here, with the relationship to mother closer than that to the

664 In Nuzi, slaves sometimes enter into servitude along with their families and in other cases their owner gives them wife. The Exodus law follows the same pattern. The dispute between Pharaoh and Moses falls in same line, where Pharaoh was hesitant to permit sons and daughters (Exod 10:8-10, 24-26) [c.f. Propp, 191.]

665 In the Ancient West Asia, it was a common practice for an owner to force or allow a slave to have children from a foreign female slave. It was solely for the purpose of adding house born slaves. The woman and her offspring remained his property. Ur-Namma 4 says 'If a male slave marries a female slave, and that male slave is later given freedom, she/he will not leave the home'. It reflects the very attitude of treating slaves as property rather than persons. In the text, the wife given to a slave is probably a freeborn Hebrew slave who was sold by her father. The Late-Bronze Age site of Emar 16 in Syria treats the issue of what to do when a man, in servitude receives a wife from his master and then leaves the household (c.f. Wells, "What Is Biblical Law? A Look at Pentateuchal Rules and near Eastern Practice," 233-234.)

father.[666] Here, at least the husband has the provision to stay with his wife and children, or to go alone. The wife can be either the property of her slave husband or master husband. This law shows cruelty towards female slave.

לַאדֹנֶיהָ- Comparing both texts, an error can be seen. As a Postcolonial womanist thinker, the author categorizes it as a major error. The author thinks that Septuagint here gives some rights and identity to a male slave by using *his*, whereas Masoretic goes for *her*, which clearly reveals the exclusivist concept, i.e., though *wife* of male slave, but her identity is with master. Here, Masoretic text once again opposes the commandment of God (Gen 2:24).

Verses 5-6

But if the slave plainly says- Is this statement made by the slave induced by slave's free will decision or part of the legal formula? Is the declaration made by the slave meant that his love to his master is out of sheer faithfulness or fear? Does his love towards his master coincide with his love towards his wife and children? The text is not spelling out clearly. Most probably the slave fears for an impoverished state, which may perhaps lead to servitude as he would seldom have enough resources to establish himself as a free citizen and to take care of his family. So, out of fear and circumstantial compulsion he may have made such a statement.

וְהִגִּישׁוֹ אֶל־הָאֱלֹהִים - It is also mentioned to the judges or rulers representing divine authority.[667] Originally the word אֱלֹהִים in the ancient legal tradition of the West Asia denotes the idols standing in the court of justice; among the Israelites the expression remained a

666 Cole, *Exodus: An Introduction and Commentary*, 165-166. The traditional Jewish view traces ethnic identity through mother, whereas all biblical evidence suggests that in Israelite time ethnic identity passed through father.

667 It is referred to in the footnotes (NRSV Bible). In the LXX, it is referred to as προσ το κριτηριον του θεου (before the court of God). There are different opinions among the scholars regarding the word אֱלֹהִים. It always connotes to Yahweh. LXX, Targums, and Syriac refer it to ordinary magistrates. It perhaps refers to judicial setting, as their judgments are believed to be inspired by God (Deut. 1:17; 19:17; II Chr 19:6). In Mesopotamia, symbols of gods were placed by the doorways of private homes and also at temples. Refer Propp, 192-193.

stereotyped term signifying the place of the court.[668] The approach to the sanctuary in the presence of God is presumably to make a solemn declaration, in the presence of witnesses, as to the status of the slave. The words are the actual legal formula, which had to be pronounced before witnesses at a sanctuary so as to prevent enforced or false declarations.[669] Now, the question is whether the door or doorpost is that of the sanctuary, or of the home, which is disputed, as it can be either way. To pierce the ear with an awl is probably a mark that indicates the private property of the owner.[670] It may also mean a public indication of a permanent slavery. Now, if the marking differs from owner to owner, it may be an indication for the property of a particular owner. But, if the marking is same, it may connote the sign or organ of obedience (the obedience of the slave towards the master), and to show the acceptance of life-long voluntary service. So, it may mean obedience (Ps.40: 6), or has religious significance (Exod. 29: 20).

Door or door post- The text mentions door or doorpost, but the location is not stated. There are three possibilities: the master's house, the city gate or the temple. The parallel passage in Deuteronomy 15:17 indicate the place at home. [671] Ibn Ezra argues that the location though not mentioned clearly in the text refers to the city gate, where the elders who were appointed to execute judgment would gather up themselves to exercise legal business (Deut 21:19; 22:24; Ruth 4:1).[672] The door may also refer to the temple, where Yahweh is found (I Sam 1:9, Ezek 41:21, 43:8). Cole rightly considers it as home in view of the nature of the ceremony, which made the slave

---

668 Cassuto, 267; Houtman, 116-117.

669 Davies, 175-176.

670 The Hammurabi Code rules that the ear of a slave who rebelled against his master was to be cut off.

671 Scholars like Trumbell, Van der Toorn, Ehrlich agrees with the opinion that the door points to home. For Scholars Trumbell and Van der Toorn, it is on the rear side of the house, where the ancestral gods were kept. Ehrlich too supports for home as no one can avoid it and everyone leaving or entering has to use it. Moreover, the slave will see the hole in the wood and remember his loyalty towards his owner (c.f. Propp, 193-194.)

672 Ibid., 194.

a permanent member of the household.[673] In the Eshnunna Laws (§37), it is mentioned that in case of a dispute over loss of deposited property, 'the owner of the house shall swear an oath for him in the door of the temple of Tishpak'.[674] Though the text is not clear about its location, the possible location is the city gate or the temple as it reminds the Israelite of their obligation towards God. If home, it becomes a private affair, where the owner will play the upper hand.

Pierce- Why should the ear of the slave be pierced? Does it indicate servitude? In other parts of the Old Testament, piercing was a common act as many Israelites like wearing earrings (Gen. 32:2-3). It was a practice in Ancient West Asia. However, in this passage, it reminds the slave that he is entering into a lifelong bondage. For Mendelsohn, the hole was pierced in the ear of the slave in order to receive a ring to which was fastened a tag made of clay or metal, indicating somebody of the slave, i.e., the slave belongs to someone.[675] The very act of piercing indicates the subjugation of the slave, 'he *must* serve him forever' (Exod 21:6). For William H. C. Propp,

> In Israel, the lifelong slave may have worn in his ear not a label but a cattle- ring, representing the invisible rope binding him to his owner and his household. He must always 'incline his ear' to his master's commands.[676]

Ear- Why ear and not any other part of the body? The possible explanations are:

1. The pain in piercing an ear pains less than any other parts of the body.
2. The slave is expected to hear the call of his owner and to be vigilant.
3. The ear as the organ of hearing implies obedience.

673 Cole, *Exodus: An Introduction and Commentary*, 166.

674 Hyatt, 129.

675 I. Mendelsohn, "Slavery in the Old Testament," in *Interpreter's Dictionary of the Bible*, ed. George Arthur Buttrick (New York: Abingdon Press, 1962), 385.

676 Propp, 195.

4. The priest is set apart as Yahweh's slave by the application of blood to his ear. Similarly the slave after piercing belongs to the owner.

לְעֹלָם– A correct translation of the Hebrew means 'forever', i.e., as long as the slave lives. According to Cole, the Israelite was 'practical, not philosophical, in his approach to life.'[677]

The law identifies a woman as slave either as a slave of her husband or her owner, while men are identified as slave and slave owners. Either the women followed their husbands into slavery or the male slave owner married them to his male slaves. In either case, the women were under the control of man. [678]

Verses 7-11

Verse 7- The structure of verse 7 is different from verse 2. In verse 2 the buyer is the subject whereas in verse 7, the slave is the subject, i.e., the girl's father is the subject. The parallel passage in Deut.15:12 emphasize a generous and liberal approach towards both the Hebrew male and female. In Exodus, the female is placed under male, and is treated as a property that can change hands from one owner to another, whereas in Deuteronomy both male and female are considered as equal partners having same rights.

A man sell his daughter- The text is not clear whether the daughter is minor or of age. According to Rabbinic law only a minor may be sold into slavery.[679] Why a man has to sell his daughter and not son? The son has right to be freed after six years, which is missing in the case of daughter. Daughters are sold due to extreme need.[680] Here, instead of receiving bride price for his daughter, the father is selling his daughter for a price to clear his debts.

אָמָה (*maid servant*) - A maid servant is generally a non-free, working female. They may sometimes be considered as second wife, for instance Hagar. The general practice adopted and expected by the

677 Cole, *Exodus: An Introduction and Commentary*, 166.

678 Scholz, 35-36.

679 Propp, 196.

680 Ibid.

owner is to have her as a wife or to give her in marriage to his son. This practice can be seen in Exodus 21 and in Nuzi. In Nuzi, a daughter is sold into servitude but with a stipulation that she will be married either to the owner or to his son.[681] There are two opinions based on this stipulation:

1. It is designed to protect her and elevate her to a status of wife or concubine.
2. To insure that the female slave would not become merely a prostitute.

For the male slave, freedom is granted after six years but this provision is not applied for female slave. It contradicts with the parallel law found in Deuteronomy 15:12-18. If she faces physical abuse by the owner, what the law will do and how long she has to face? In such case, the law will be brutal.

She shall not go out as the male slaves do- It clearly indicates that unlike male slave, female slave is enslaved for life. The male slaves are having the right to leave after six years and if they are willing can be as slaves for life. In the case of female, there is no provision of release after six years. It appears that the daughters are solely the property of fathers or husbands. It also ensures that the daughter may never leave male control, which shows male supremacy.[682]

---

681 Ibid., 196-197. This practice was in practice in the middle of the second millennium BCE in the city of Nuzi (Hurrian Colony) in Mesopotamia. There is a typical Nuzi contract, where the conditions are made between the girl's father and her father-in-law. The condition is that if the girl is given in marriage to one of her father-in-law's slaves and if her husband dies, she is to be given to another slave of the same household. No matter what the situation will be, she is to remain as a slave-bearing mother and a maid. The sold girl will be prevented from exploitation as a prostitute (Mendelsohn, *Slavery in the Ancient Near East,* 10-11*)*. For further reference read I. Mendelsohn, "The Conditional Sale into Slavery of Free-Born Daughters in Nuzi and the Law of Exodus 21:7-11," *JAOS* 55 (1935): 190-195.) The Nuzian practice is similar to what is written in Exodus 21:7-11.

682 Drorah O' Donnel Setel, 'Exodus', in *Women's Bible Commentary*, eds. Carol A. Newsom and Sharon H. Ringe (Kentucky: John Knox Press, 1998), 38.

Verse 8- *If she does not please her master*...The word רָעָה needs to be explored. If marriage has taken place, it may refer to sexual dissatisfaction, but in the text the marriage has not taken place rather engagement took place, hence it probably refers to unattractiveness or incapability. In either case unlike male slave, the choice and rights lies with the owner.

Verse 9- *If he betrothed her for his son*- It seems the law is supporting the owners' son to have a girl as a concubine in order to protect him from illegal sexual activity. Verse 9 is independent. If dependent, it may give us an impression that the maidservant was not pleasing to the owner and so he handed her over to his son, and that would be offensive.

As his daughter- Does this refer to Hebrew daughter? There are different opinions[683]:

1. It may refer to a free Hebrew woman (Paul, Ehrlich, Childs).
2. It may refer to the rights and responsibilities of fatherhood (William, Cazelles, and Sarna).

The idea behind the phrase 'as his daughter' means she must be treated by the owner like a father to a daughter, i.e., father owner.

Verse 10- *If he takes another wife to himself*– Does the law advocate for polygamy? In Biblical narratives there are references advocating for monogamy however, there are references of polygamy (Gen 3-4, Isa 50:1; 54:6-7; 62:4-5; Jer 2:2; Hos 1-2-monogamy; Jer 3:6-11; Ezek 23- Polygamy).[684]

So, in this section (vv. 7-11), female slave is categorized in a different way as compared to that of the male slave. The rules for the male slave and female slave are opposed to each other. She can't go free after six years (cf. Deut. 15:12-15) because her master-husband still has duties towards her. So, the expectation of seventh-year release was denied to women. Unlike men, women do not enjoy full social equality, as they are regarded as male's property. The code here puts

683 Propp, 200.

684 Ibid.

men as the one who rules over the enslaved women. In other words, they are slaves for life. In Deut. 15:12, both man and the woman is accorded the right of freedom in the seventh year. The verse 7 of Exodus 21 says, when a man sells his daughter as a slave, she shall not go out as the male slaves do. Now, we must keep in mind, the reason behind for selling a girl. It might be poverty, debt, etc. It is the same case with male slaves also. Then, why such discrimination is there between the two? There are scholars such as Cassuto and others who express the girl as of Israelite, but the passage (21:7) is not clear. There seems to be having a selfish motto [a secret male conspiracy] to avoid the release of a female slave. The reason for such stand is due to the fact that, the parallel passages dealing with the slaves express similar notion for both female and the male slaves.

Moreover, three cases are mentioned in these passages, which might threaten her status: verse 8- If she pleases not her master, verse 9- if betrothed her unto his son and in verse 10- if the master takes another wife. In the first case, her own people must redeem her. In the second case, she must be treated after the manner of a daughter. In the third case, she must not be diminished, and must be maintained with her full marital status. Mendelsohn has cited Nuzian sale contracts, which almost parallel the Exodus provisions.[685]

Hence, the Book of the Covenant does not criticize the slavery system; rather it advocates and legitimizes the practice. There is gross injustice in the societal structure, where in to some extent a male slave can decide either to be free or continue as slave, and women are on the mercies of either her husband or owner. The one who has power has every right to act and those who are marginalized are in the hand of the powerful.

685 Mendelsohn, "The Conditional Sale into Slavery of Free-Born Daughters in Nuzi and the Law of Exodus 21:7-11," 190-195. Also see CH §147, §159; HL §30-§33.

Exodus 21:22-27 (The Law Concerning Violence)

Translation/Textual Comments

20 If a man strikes his male slave or female slave with a rod[686] and the slave dies on the spot[687], he shall be punished[688]. 21 But if the slave survives a day or two, he shall not be punished[689], for he is his property[690].

22 If men fight[691] and they hit a pregnant woman and she has a premature birth of her children[692] but there is no further injury[693], the one who is responsible shall be fined[694] whatever the woman's husband demands and the Judge determines. 23 But if there is further injury then you are to take life for life[695], 24 eye for eye, tooth for tooth, hand for hand, foot for foot, 25 burn for burn[696], wound for wound, stripe for stripe.

686 Samaritan Pentateuch omits 'with a rod'.

687 Slave dies immediately.

688 Samaritan Pentateuch has 'he shall be put to death'.

689 Samaritan Pentateuch reads 'to be put to death', i.e., he shall not be put to death.

690 Or for the slave is his property or his money.

691 Or if men who are fighting injure a pregnant woman. The verb *ngp* implies malicious, hostile and deliberate act (Stanley Isser, "Two Traditions: The Law of Exodus 21:22-23 Revisited," *The Catholic Biblical Quarterly* 52 (1990): 39.)

692 Samaritan Pentateuch and Septuagint read 'and her child go/come out'. Birth as a result of accidental hit is mentioned in this text. It is not clear why the phrase expressing the premature birth speaks of children in plural.

693 The Palestinian reading in Jewish tradition interprets אסון as damage or harm, even death (cf. Gen. 42:4, 38; 44:29). BDB gives 'mischief, evil, harm'. In this text, it refers to a fatal injury in addition to the miscarriage. Targum Onqelos and Vulgate translate אסון as death.The LXX version relates the injury not to the mother but to the foetus. However, among the scholars there are mixed opinions. Some argue for foetus and others argues for mother (c.f. Isser: 30-33.)

694 The LXX version reads singular instead of Plural 'If two men fight and strike…., he shall be fined…..'

695 Does life for life refer to the life of the wife of the offender? (CH § 210). If this opinion is considered favourably, the sufferer/loser is woman.

696 Samaritan Pentateuch has 'burn-spot, scar of a burn' instead of 'burning'

26 And if man hits the eyes of his male slave or eyes of his female slave, and destroys it, he shall let the slave go free because of the eyes. 27 If he knocks out the tooth of a male slave or female slave, he shall let the slave go free because of the tooth.

Form and Structure

The text 21:22-27 comes under the section 21:18-32. It begins in typical casuistic style and deals mainly in connection with bodily injury. In some cases the injury results in death for which the punishment differs. Many of the laws opt for compensation rather than retaliation. The nature of compensation depends upon the gravity of injury and the person concerned, the social ranking in which he/she belongs to. The form and nature are in parallel with the Code of Hammurabi and other ancient codes. The Hebrew society recognized only two classes, freemen and slaves, whereas the Babylonian society recognized three: nobleman, commoner and the slave.[697] The difference of judgment between the case of a free citizen and of a slave both in Israel and her neighboring states are striking.

Comments and Explanation

Verses 20-21

If a man strikes his male or female slave with a rod and the slave dies on the spot, he shall be punished- The ill-treatment done towards the slave is not prohibited in the laws. The striking of the slave is projected as a normal practice. The action will be taken, if the slave dies. The nature and quantum of punishment is not clearly stated and is vague. The Samaritan text justifies by the judgment 'he shall be put to death'. The slave, male or female is too human being created in His image and whoever attacks shall be answerable. However, in this text the victim's case is not justified. [698]

---

697 Hyatt, 232.

698 The Jewish interpreters Rashi, B. Jacob and U. Cassuto defend the view by stating that a death penalty is intended in the phrase 'he shall surely be punished'. The Talmud (San. 52b) orders for execution and that too by beheading for such a crime. [c.f. Childs, 471.] The text however, doesn't stand in line with the opinion of the Jewish interpreters and Talmud. The view negating death can be supported with the following verse '...because he is his property.

The treatment towards a slave is a discouraging one. In Verse 12, a man who kills a man is put to death. But if a man kills a slave, he is only punished. The slave is of less value and is considered as a property.

But if the slave survives a day or two, he shall not be punished- The law is lenient towards the owner and harsh towards the slave. The text is not clear in making the judgment 'but if the slave survives a day or two'. The possibility of death is placed in favor of the owner assuming that the death occurred not by the beating of the owner but rather due to some other reason. The law is safeguarding the owner by giving him the benefit of doubt. For R. E. Clements, the benefit of doubt is given to the owner as it is assumed that he would not purposefully destroy his own property. [699] In this text, the law is safeguarding the powerful and justice is not given to the weak. The accuser has been let off with an understanding that he has already received punishment through the loss of his property.

A day or two- This expression means 'a day or more'. The addition of expression 'or two' is necessary, for if the text had specified 'a day', one may have a misunderstanding that if he/she survives more than a day he shall be surely to be punished.[700]

The slave is his property/money

The owner suffers a loss in the death of a slave as he bought him with a price. The death of his slave, which is his property, is sufficient as a punishment.

Does this expression mean that the owner has the rights to beat the slave? Was it due to the imperial values practiced by the Israelite society? The Book of the Covenant legitimizes the slavery and its societal structure. It promotes slavery by supporting the rights of the master by discriminating the slaves. [701] The position of slave as his master's property is not a practice found only in Israel, rather a common practice throughout Ancient West Asia. This imperialistic

699 Clements, *Exodus*, 138.

700 Cassuto, 273.

701 Cole, *Exodus:An Introduction and Commentary*, 169.

tendency practiced by the powerful nations got influenced in the social life of Israel.

Verses 22-25[702]

The law stated in Exodus 21:22-25 consists of protasis and apodosis. The protasis describes the striking of a pregnant woman resulting into miscarriage and the apodosis prescribes the consequences, i.e., the duty of the accused to pay for the damages. An androcentric view can be seen in this passage, where the husband and the judge determine the compensation. There are mixed opinion among the scholars concerning the injury of a pregnant woman who was inflicted in a fight. Usually it is understood as an accident, but scholars like D. Daube[703] argued for an act of malevolent intent.

Fight - The Heb. Word יִנָּצוּ implies the use of physical force (cf. Exod 2:13; Deut 25:11; II Sam 14:6).[704]

The one who is responsible shall be fined whatever the woman's husband and the judge determine- D. Daube argues that the words 'he shall pay as the judges determine' are a later addition, and it was added to limit the power of the victim's husband.[705] The precise amount is not specified. The amount is fixed by the woman's husband and is subjected to the final verdict of the judges. The practice of fine is common to the Ancient West Asian law. The pain and suffering meted out by the woman is not considered, as it is assumed that she got injured due to her intervention in the fighting between men. The amount is decided by the male members of the community.

Whatever the woman's husband - This inexact edict is surprising, as it is difficult to ascertain whether the injury caused to woman was an accidental or a deliberate act. In either case, the compensation is decided by her husband and the judge. It appears that the judge is purposefully placed to make certain that the money demanded by

---

702 Alexander Rofe argues that this law did not originally belong to the Covenant Code but was added to the collection at a later stage (Rofe, 172.)

703 D. Daube, *Studies in Biblical Law* (Cambridge: Cambridge University Press, 1947), 100.

704 Sarna, 126.

705 Daube, 108.

the victim's husband be justifiable. It also brings out a clear picture that the victim being a woman has no voice and the decision makers are her husband and the judge, rulers of the household and society. It points out that 'the women's bodies were not merely controlled but actually owned.'[706]

The Judge determine- The Hebrew word is נָתַן בִּפְלִלִים. S. M. Paul understands this word as the payment to be based on reckoning, i.e., according to the estimated age of the embryo.[707]

The judgment stated here resembles with the law codes of Ancient West Asia with few differences. Some of the laws of Ancient West Asia are:

Sumerian Laws

§ 1-§2 -Two clauses are specified in this law: Penalty for the one who hurts accidently and penalty for the one who strikes intentionally a pregnant woman resulting in miscarriage. In the former case the penalties is ten shekels and in the latter case a third of a mina.[708]

Code of Hammurabi

§ 209- If a man has struck another man's daughter and has caused her to have a miscarriage,[709] he shall pay ten shekels of silver for her foetus.

§210- If that woman has died, they shall put his daughter to death.

§ 211- If by a blow he has caused a commoner's daughter to have a miscarriage, he shall pay five shekels of silver.

§ 212- If that woman has died, he shall pay one-half mina of silver.

§ 213- If he has struck a man's female slave and has caused her to have a miscarriage, he shall pay two shekels of silver.

§ 214- If that female slave has died, he shall pay one-third mina of silver.

---

706 Setel, 38.

707 S. M. Paul, *The Book of the Covenant: Its Literary Setting and Extra-Biblical Background* (Michigan: Ann Arbor, 1966), 100.

708 Cassuto, 273.

709 Lit. "caused her to drop that of her womb (her fetus)."

Middle Assyrian Laws

§ 21 - If a man has struck another man's daughter and has caused her to have a miscarriage, when they have prosecuted him (and) convicted him, he shall pay two talents thirty minas of lead; they shall flog him fifty (times) with staves (and) he shall do the work of the king for one full month. (The clause speaks only of miscarriage, but makes no reference to the case where woman dies).

§§ 50-51 - [If a man] has struck another man's [wife] and caused her to have [a miscarriage], they shall treat [the wife of the man], who caused the (other) man's wife to [have a miscarriage], as he treated her; he shall compensate for her foetus with a life. However, if that woman died, they shall put the man to death; he shall compensate for her foetus with a life. But, when that woman's husband has no son, if someone had struck her so that she had a miscarriage, they shall put the striker to death; even if her foetus is a girl, he shall compensate with a life. If a man has struck another man's wife who does not rear her children and caused her to have a miscarriage, this punishment (shall hold): he shall pay two talents of lead.

Hittite Laws

§§ 17-18 - If anyone causes a free woman to miscarriage-if (it is) the 10th month, he shall give 10 shekels of silver, if (it is) the 5th month, he shall give 5 shekels of silver (Later version- If anyone causes a free woman to miscarriage, he shall give 20 shekels of silver). If anyone causes a slave-woman to miscarry- if (it) is the 10th month, he shall give 5 shekels of silver (Later version- If anyone causes a slave-girl to miscarriage, he shall give 10 shekels of silver). [The law makes no reference to the case where woman dies.]

All of these laws call for monetary compensation for the loss of foetus. However, the Sumerian law distinguishes between accidental and intentional assault. Hammurabi code is more severe if the victim belongs to upper class. In such case, the punishment will be to the assailant's daughter.

But if there is further injury... The text is not specifying the gravity of injury. Verses 23-25 are a dramatic description of retribution, i.e., the law of retaliation [Lev. 24:18ff- in the case of any injury done to the neighbor and Deut. 19:21- to be awarded to a malicious witness). It is an afterthought of verse 22. [710]

Life for life, eye for eye, tooth for tooth, hand for hand, foot for foot, burn for burn, wound for wound, stripe for stripe- The law of retaliation (*lex talionis)* has close parallelism with the Ancient West Asian law (CH § 195ff). This form of law is considered as a 'primitive' element in the Biblical law. However, the works of Finkelstein and S. Paul have changed this understanding. For Finkelstein, Hammurabi introduced these talionic rules to widen the range of criminal law, which will protect the members of inferior social standing and provide justice and equality to all irrespective of their social standing.[711] This will eradicate violence and bring wealthy groups under control as they could no longer escape punishment for their crime by simply paying a fine.

Unlike Ancient West Asian law, there are few differences. Free woman or slave, the action taken against the offender is same. The punishment is to be taken to the one who is responsible not his wife or daughter. However, verses 24-25 don't fit in vv. 22-23. It is strange that in the law concerning miscarriage, the punishment indicated is eye, tooth, foot, burn, wound and stripe which are out of the context. The law for eye and tooth is stated in the following verses, which indicates that some modifications have taken place.

Verses 26-27

The verses 26-27 deal with injuries to one's own slave. The laws in Exodus unlike Ancient West Asia state freedom to the slaves for the loss of eye and tooth, as they consider the cost of eye and tooth with the purchase price of the slave.

---

710 Clements, *Exodus*, 138. Verses 23-25 is a secondary interpolation as it does not fit in verse 22. This form of retaliation can be seen in Code of Hammurabi 196-214. C.f. Noth, *Exodus*, 181-182.

711 Childs, 472; L.Finkelstein, "An Eye for an Eye," *The Menorah Journal* 24 (1936); Paul, "Studies in the Book of the Covenant in the Light of Cuneiform and Biblical Law," 70-77. For Sarna, the Talien list is a citation from some extra biblical compendium of the laws and has been incorporated into the Torah (Sarna, 126). C.f. Bernard S. Jackson, "Problem of Exodus 21:22-5, Ius Talionis," *Vetus Testamentum* 23, no. 4 (1973).

If a man hits the eyes or knocks the tooth of a male or female slave- Why only eyes or tooth are mentioned and no other part of the body? Probably these parts will be lost forever, and all other parts will be healed in course of time.[712] The compensation for such a crime is equated with the purchase price, and not with *talio*, as *talio* is applied only to a free citizen and not to the slaves. It clearly highlights the status of male or female slave in a power controlled society. This form of compensation can be seen in the Ancient West Asian Laws, especially in the Code of Hammurabi (§ 199).

Code of Hammurabi[713]

§ 196- If a man has destroyed the eye of a member of the aristocracy,[714] they shall destroy his eye. [715]

§ 198- If he has destroyed the eye of a commoner or broken the bone of a commoner, he shall pay one mina of silver.

§199- If he has destroyed the eye of a man's slave or broken the bone of a man's slave, he shall pay one-half his value.(There is no law with regard to one who blinds the eye of his own slave).

§ 200- If a man has knocked out a tooth of a man of his own rank, they shall knock out his tooth.

§ 201- If a man knocks out the tooth of a commoner, he has to pay a third of a mina of silver.

Laws of Eshnunna

§ 42- If a man bites the nose of another man and severs it, he shall pay 1 mina of silver. (For) an eye (he shall pay) 1 mina of silver; (for) a tooth ½ mina; (for) an ear ½ mina; (for) a slap in the face 10 shekels of silver.

The law mentions only of monetary payments- a mina of silver for destroying an eye, and half a mina for knocking out a tooth.

712 For more interpretation read Houtman, 171.

713 Cassuto, 275-276, 278. In both Hammurabi and Hittite laws, no penalty was paid by a man who harmed his own slave (c.f. Dobson, 123.)

714 Lit., "the son of a man," with "son" used in the technical sense.

715 Cf. Lev 24:19 ff; Deut. 19:21

Hittite Laws

§ 7- If anyone blinds a free man or knocks out his teeth; he shall give 20 shekels of silver and pledge his estate as security.

§ 8- If anyone blinds a male or female slave or knocks out his/her teeth, he shall give 10 shekels of silver and pledge his estate as security.

Exodus 22:16-17 (Eng.) [15-16 Heb.][716] (Social Laws)

Translation/Textual Comments

16 If a man seduces[717] a virgin who is not betrothed[718] and lies with her, he shall pay the bride price for her and make her his wife.17 If[719] her father absolutely/utterly refuses to give her to him, he shall pay money[720] equivalent to the bride price for virgins.

Form and Structure

This law is casuistic in style and it comes under the social laws.

Comments and Explanation

The Book of the Covenant unlike Deuteronomy does not contain a section dealing with marriage laws (Deut. 22:13-26). The law stated here is about the seduction of a girl who is not betrothed and is placed under property laws. The intention behind the law is not the

716 Alexander Rofe argues that this law like 21:22-25 did not originally belong to the Covenant Code but was added to the collection at a later stage. (Rofe, 172.)

717 By persuasion or by deception but not by coercion.

718 Betrothal was very important in Israelite life and was the first stage of the marriage. Important decisions regarding finance take place during this occasion. The betrothal girl comes almost under the category of married woman and the laws are same for both. Here the text means that she had never been betrothed for if the *mohar* was paid, the girl was considered *me'orasah* (betrothed).

719 Few manuscripts such as Samaritan, Septuagint and Syriac version prefer a conjunction 'And/But'.

720 Septuagint translates it as 'to pay restitution to the father' (ἀποτείσειτῷ πατρὶ)

rights of the girl or the purity of the marriage rather the amount of compensation.[721]

Verse 16

This section comes under the heading "social and religious law". The text is about the law of the seducer. A man has seduced a virgin who is not betrothed. A virgin was considered her father's property and he would receive for her the bride price (*mohar*)[722] customarily paid by the husband-to-be. This amount is against the loss of the daughter's services and potential value to the family (cf. Deut 22:13-19; Lev.21:13-15).[723] By the loss of her virginity, she lost her social status and her value. Her father, as a result has the right to claim for compensation. It underscores that 'the virginity was not ethical rather economic.'[724] For Anderson, 'the rape of an unmarried female injured her father rather than the female herself, which clearly points out that the law do not take into account the female's perspective'.[725]

The seduction by a man is treated as adultery and the punishment for such a crime is death (Deut. 22:23-27).Unlike Deuteronomic passage, the punishment for the man in this text is to pay the bride-price and to accept her as his wife, provided her father agrees to it. The choice to give her daughter is the prerogative of the father. If not, still he has to pay the bride- price. In either way, the woman has no rights to express her opinion and she does not participate in the legal course of action. The text is not clear in stating, if the father accepts the seducer and the woman dislikes him. The seduction of a virgin by a man concerns only her father and the seducer. The upper

721 Davies, 183. Ibn Ezra points out that the sequence of legal topics is from the case of a 'stolen property' to a 'stolen heart'. Both are crimes that result into economic losses and entail compensation (See Sarna, 134.)

722 The origin of the term *mohar* is uncertain. Since it is common to Hebrew, Ugaritic, Aramaic and Arabic, the practice must have been widespread (Cf. Genesis 34). The *mohar* in other part of the Old Testament was paid in services or heroic deeds (Gen 29:15-20, 27-28; Josh 15:16-17; Judg 1:12-13; I Sam 17:25; 18:20-27; II Sam 3:14). C.f. Sarna, 135.

723 Ibid., 134.

724 Setel, 39.

725 Cheryl B. Anderson, *Ancient Laws and Contemporary Controversies* (Oxford: Oxford University Press, 2009), 4, 32-33.

hand on the whole issue lies in the male member of the society and the receiving end is the woman. A clear androcentric approach can be seen here.

He must make her his wife- The Hebrew word מָהֹר יִמְהָרֶנָּה are verbs formed from the noun *mohar.*[726]

The law resembles with Middle Assyrian Laws, where the victims are either the virgin who was ravished by the seducer or the wife of the seducer. MAL §§ 55-56- If a man takes the virgin by force and seduces her........the father of the virgin shall take the wife of the virgin's seducer and give her to be seduced...the father could then give his daughter in marriage to the seducer. But if he is not having wife, the father can ask the seducer to pay third in silver to her father asthe value of a virgin (and) her seducer shall marry her and not cast her off. If the father does not wish, he shall receive the third for the virgin in silver and give his daughter to whom he wishes. If the virgin has given herself to the man, the man shall swear and they shall not touch his wife; the seducer shall give the third in silver as the value of the virgin and the father shall treat his daughter as he wishes. The third in silver is interpreted by some as threefold of the usual amount and others consider it as one-third of the amount. [727]

Verse 17

He shall pay money- The literal understanding is 'weigh out silver', which was the practice until coined money was introduced by the Persians.[728]

The law provides two options and both to victim's father. Either he can demand the bride price and ask him to marry or he may refuse to give his daughter and demand the bride-price for a virgin. The acceptance and refusal are under the control of victim's father. The law restricts the voice of the victim.

---

726 Ibid., 135.

727 Cassuto, 289; Houtman, 208; Hyatt, 241.

728 Cole, *Exodus: An Introduction and Commentary*, 173.

Exodus 23:12, 17 (Laws on Sabbath and Annual Festivals)

Translation/Textual Comments

12 Six days you shall do your works but on the seventh day you are to rest in order that your ox and your donkey may rest and the son of your female servant[729] and the alien may be refreshed/take breathe[730].

17 Three times in the year all of your males shall appear before the face of the Lord God[731].

Form and Structure

The law is in command form (apodictic in style) and is placed under the Sabbath (vv. 10-13) and the Annual festivals (vv. 14-19).

Comments and Explanation

Verse 12

It seems verse 12 is incomplete. The phrase 'the son of your female servant' is problematic as it indicates the son of female servant and misses out the daughter/s of female servant. The Samaritan Pentateuch reads it as 'male and female slave' instead of 'the son of female slave'. The author considers Samaritan Pentateuch version as genuine and reasonable comparing it with 20:8-10 and other passages. Is the Exodus text an error or purposefully placed? If we read the text comparing it with outside the Covenant Code passage, it is possible to consider the text as a misplaced text and a deconstruction is needed.

Verse 17

In this verse, the male has been given the rights and privilege to appear before the presence of the Lord, which is a clear androcentric approach. The rights and privilege of the female is missing. The story of Hannah in I Samuel 1-2 presents a clear picture that women were

729 Samaritan Pentateuch reads it differently: 'your male slave and your female slave like yourself and all your animals'.

730 The verb is in Niphal imperfect- 'to take a break or be refreshed'.

731 Septuagint, Syriac and Vulgate reads it as 'the Lord your God'. Samaritan Pentateuch reads 'ark' instead of 'Lord' (c.f. Exodus 34:24).

permitted to enter the temple and had access to make the pilgrimage. Deuteronomy 16:11, 14 include daughter, female slave and strangers among those who are to appear before the Lord.[732]

Summary

The book of the covenant code reached to its present form in 8th century BCE. The Assyrian Empire which was strong during the reign of Assurbanipal and Shalmaneser III (9th century BCE) became weak between 783 and 745 BCE. Both Israel and Judah became strong during the reigns of Jeroboam II in Israel and Uzziah of Judah. During this period both Israel and Judah underwent great socio-political changes. Probably they were influenced by the presence of Assyria and other neighboring nations. In order to maintain the economic and political position, lot of changes were made. The gap between the rich and the poor increased. These changes can be seen in the covenant code.

If we observe carefully, the covenant code is patriarchal and colonial. The Israelite laws are mainly apodictic and casuistic in style. The apodictic laws are generally addressed through the male members and are patriarchal in approach whereas the casuistic laws are both patriarchal and colonial. The casuistic laws can be seen throughout the Ancient West Asian laws. They portray a man's world where women are merely a class of property. The full membership is limited to the male members of the society (Exod 20:17; 21:7-11). The sexuality of woman was regarded as the exclusive property of the male members of the society. For e.g., having illicit affairs with a married woman was treated as serious crime, not because of the demoralizing and dehumanizing effect on the victim, but as violation against her husband (Exod 20:14, 17; Lev 20). Having forceful extramarital sex with an unmarried girl by a male member can be legally compensated by marrying that girl in marriage and payment of mohar (gift) to the parents. This laws stand in conflict with the liberative experience of Israel where all members experienced God's saving action and freedom in their life. In short, the casuistic laws are more oppressive and repressive in nature, where the powerful dominate the powerless. The voice and rights of women are denied

732 Sarna, 146.

due to androcentric politics.The apodictic laws unlike the casuistic laws though patrirachal are rather egalitarian in nature and the liberating aspect can be seen, which is in line with the Israel's unique history of liberation.

The primary intention of the Covenant law was to treat and take care of those who were in need irrespective of their class and color but over a period of time, most probably the influence of Ancient West Asia (Code of Hammurabi and the Middle Assyrian laws in particular) changed the entire nature of the Covenant Code. The Law which we are having now appears to be not an original one. The Covenant Code especially the casuistic laws related to women are colonial in color as it resembles with the laws of the neighboring nations. The laws on dowry, marriage, covetousness, adultery and slavery are unfavourable to women. Discrimination against women is seen both in socio-political and religious sphere which results in disability and impingement on women's lives. Hence, the laws, which appear to be pro-colonial in color, needs to be deconstructed and more inclusive and life affirming laws are needed which can make the foundations of our society strong. It is important for women to break out from the norms and traditional shackles and actively engage themselves in every activity by experimenting with life. The weaker sections especially the women must claim back the position that they have lost by looking at the Biblical laws with a new eyes.

Chapter 6

Evaluation: A Postcolonial Womanist Reading of Biblical Law Codes

Empire and Law

Empire/s and their Strategies

The motif of the emperors/kings in Ancient West Asia was to reinforce their empire and their personal power. They exploited and manipulated the system and law to serve and meet their end. The empires in order to be strong opted for a strong administrative policy. It served as a strong point in creating and running an empire. Moreover, the necessary day-by-day running of affairs was backed by irresistible might of the empire by setting up the captured land as their garrison. The people if adhered to their policies (laws) were allowed to stay in the land. If not, they were forced to leave their place and move to a strange land.

The prime target of the empire was to accumulate land and to have an economic boost. In order to attain this, strategic war was waged against the weaker nations. The people of other land was enforced to support in the building programs in the large cities or to open up new farmland to provide more produce for the growing urban population. In order to execute it, laws and policies were introduced. The laws and policies were introduced primarily to delimit the opponents and their rights. This deliberate act was not only to keep a check of their activities but also to degenerate them in such a way that they would lose their identity and culture.

Israel and Law

The people and the state of Israel were encompassed within a world/ empire which had already taken its shape. Biblical law emerged in the context of a great legal corpus covering the various empires of the AWA.

Good similarities can be drawn between Israel and her neighboring nations. The Israelite king received from God the virtue of right (mishpat) and justice (tsedaqa). Israelite king, for instance, King Solomon was asking God for an understanding mind to govern the people and to discern between good and evil (I Kings 3:9; c.f. Psalm 72:1). Pharaoh received *Maat* (justice or truth) from Re, the supreme God, the Babylonian king received *kittu* and *mesharu* from Marduk. Like other kings of the Ancient West Asia, the Israelite king expressed his role to protect the weak and the poor, the widows and the orphans. In Mesopotamia and in Egypt, the king was the supreme legislator and the intermediary between the gods and the people. In Israel, the power was vested not only to the kings but also to the prophet and the priest. We could see a tension between the office of prophet, priest and king.[733] It appears that the law in Israel too emerged with an intention to protect the weak and the oppressed, but they became a property in the hand of the male members of the community. The whole of Israelite law specially the Covenant Code favors the male members of the society. The female members on the other hand, are in the mercies of the decision makers and the male members of the household and society.

733 Epsztein, 105.

Observations and Findings

Law: Is it an Independent Entity?

The laws in general were not an independent entity of one particular nation, rather the king/s of each nation for their own benefit and well being either borrowed the laws from her neighboring nations and added, collated and redacted them to suit with their situations, i.e., one's own culture, belief and practices.

The earliest legal law is the Sumerian code of Ur-Nammu. Nammu was the founder of the third dynasty of Ur who reigned around 2112-2095 BCE. Nammu with the help of the god Nanna reestablished equity and justice in the country. The law gave special consideration to the orphans, poor and the widows. The code of Ur-Nammu was followed by the second Sumerian legal text, the code of Lipit-Ishtar. Lipit-Ishtar was the fifth king of the dynasty of Isin. The code of Lipit-Ishtar came about two centuries later than the code of Ur-Nammu. Both of these codes point to the role of the royal power, and the divine will of God in relation to the kings to establish and execute equity and justice.[734] The laws thereafter was borrowed and edited by the respective kings.

a. Laws of Eshnunna- The laws of Eshnunna have certain elements, which is found in the Code of Ur-Numma and Lipit-Ishtar, the Sumerian law.[735]
b. The Code of Hammurabi- Though Code of Hammurabi is known as the available complete law comparing with other law codes; it was also borrowed from the earlier collections of Sumerian laws. For instance, the famous *lex talionis* was already known[736] and was in practice in

734 Ibid., 6-7. It is generally accepted that both Assyrian and Babylonian civilizations were stemmed out from the Sumerian civilization. However, both Assyrian and Babylonians spoke very closely related forms of Semitic language, whereas Sumerians were non -Semitics [c.f. Hooke, x.]

735 Epsztein, 8.

736 This practice was found in Amorite. In Sumerian, it was compensated with fines.

the Sumerian period[737]; the social stratification of *awilu, mushkenu* and *wardu* found in the code of Hammurabi is also found in the laws of Eshnunna.

c. Middle Assyrian laws- In the 11th century BCE, the Middle Assyrian king Tukultiapil-Esharra I with the help of Jurists gathered the existing laws and redacted it. The Middle Assyrian laws are the collection of Old Babylonian law, Amorite Customary law, and decrees of the Assyrian kings.[738]

d. Israelite Law- The laws of Israel too were greatly influenced by the codes of Ancient West Asia. They emerged in the context of the great laws existed in the various regions of the Ancient West Asia. The style and nature of Israelite laws especially the laws of the Book of the Covenant Code are similar. The Casuistic law is secular in nature and the style is similar (Conditional 'If'). The famous *lex talionis* seen in the Sumerian law and code of Hammurabi is also found in the Book of the Covenant Code (Exod 21:22-27). The law for the freedom of the slave is almost similar. The Code of Hammurabi (§117) provides liberty at the end of three years, whereas the Book of the Covenant Code after six years of service (Exod 21:2-11). The Israelite law like code of Hammurabi and Middle Assyrian laws also gives preference to the privileged group. The treatment to the Hebrews differs from the non-Hebrews. The Book of the Covenant code like the Middle Assyrian laws restricts the rights and voices of women (marriage, dowry and

---

737 For instance, the Laws of Ur-Nammu lines §§324-345 states 'If a man cuts the foot of another man, he shall pay ten shekels of silver; if a man in the course of scuffle, smashed the limb of another man with a club, he shall pay one mina of silver; if someone severed the nose of another man with a copper knife, he must pay two-thirds of a mina of silver; and if a man cut off…another man with a … he shall pay x shekels of silver' which is similar to the CH §198, §199, §204. In Code of Hammurabi, the law is in favour of the privileged group, whereas in the laws of Ur-Nammu the law is for all irrespective of his or her social standings.

738 Tetlow, 126. It is said that the Assyrians borrowed law and religion largely from Babylonians (c.f. Hooke, xi.]

other practices).In short, the Israelite law particularly the Covenant Code was modified to address its own ethos.

Reflection and Conclusion

This brings out a clear picture that though each code has differences they are building upon their predecessors. If we observe carefully, the kings were the promulgator of the law. In case of Israel, the role of the king with regard to the law though not clearly expressed, it can't be negated. There is a possibility of the hand of Israelite king towards the execution of the laws. An Imperial display appears to be seen in the legal system. Though the Israelite laws speak about the welfare of the weaker section of the society, particularly in the Covenant Code like AWA laws, the slave and women were treated as property.

Cultures of Ancient West Asia: A Fusion

The Ancient West Asia culture especially of Assyria, Babylon and Israel was a blend of two distinct cultures: The Sumerian culture and Semitic culture. The Sumerian culture was basically matriarchal in nature, where the position of women to some extent was favorable. The dignity of woman was well recognized. They enjoyed the privileges of men, though not of same scale. The Semitic culture was patriarchal in nature, where the status of women was of disadvantage. The father, brother, husband (the male members) of the household played a key role.

The Semitic culture engrafted some of the elements of the Sumerian culture. The Sumerians were subjected to a stronger Semitic influence, ethnically and linguistically.[739] These opposing matriarchal and patriarchal cultures got hybridized resulting into a new culture where discrimination against women became stronger.

In Israelite law, there are references where women were treated well particularly in the Deuteronomic Code; however, the major portions of the laws are unfavorable to women. These differences took place probably due to the fusion of these two cultures.

---

739 Dietz Otto Edzard, "The Third Dynasty of Ur- Its Empire and Its Successor States," in *Delacorte World History-the near East: The Early Civilizations*, ed. Elena Cassin Jean Bottero, and Jean Vercoutter (New York: Delacorte Press, 1967), 173.

Land, Law and Gender: An Agriculture Setting

Almost in every religion, the women are identified and associated with the earth. The earth is depicted in the female imagery. Though in some places of scripture/s women are glorified, there are places where they are portrayed in a negative way. As lands are ploughed to increase productivity so also the women are misused and exploited to attain selfish ambitions.[740] The women and land are considered primarily as property and has strong economic connotation. Both are exploited in an aggressive manner to meet the selfish ambitions of a few. The untold plight of women and their ongoing struggles religiously, culturally, socially and politically have provoked for the emergence of different movements.

Land and Women in Ancient West Asia and Israel

Since time immemorial, the identification of woman with the land/earth has been basic to the popular cultural discourse. In many cultures, the land/earth is addressed as female. Agriculture was a common occupation throughout Ancient West Asia. In order to increase productivity and enhance wealth, the accumulation of land was needed. To take care of agriculture, more people were needed. And to achieve this, women became the target. Women became the means to increase its population and, after the adoption of agriculture, its labor force. Hence, like agriculture, the subordination of women occurred independently in numerous societies and civilizations. Agriculture proved to be an invaluable piece of technology, allowing humans to manipulate their environment, whereas female subordination proved to be an invaluable organizational tool for the complex societies which resulted from an agricultural way of life. Accordingly, agriculture and female subordination are intimately linked, providing humanity with a dangerous mixture of advantage

740 Eco-feminists like Mary Mellor, Maria Miles, Chris J. Cuomo, Vandana Shiva strongly argue that both land and women are exploited by the patriarchy/powerful nations. C.f. Mary Mellor, *Feminism and Ecology* (New York: New York University Press, 1997); Maria Miles and Vandana Shiva *Ecofeminism* (New Delhi: Kali for Women, 1993); Chris J. Cuomo, *Feminism and Ecological Communities: An Ethic of Flourishing* (London and New York: Routledge, 1998).

and detriment. Women and land became the most essential means of production in an agricultural society.

Israel's ancestors lived in tents and moved from place to place (Gen. 13:3; 18:1ff; 31:25, 33f). They were stockbreeders and lived as semi-nomads. Then we could see a transition from semi-nomadic life to a sedentary life. With the settlement, they turned into farmers and villagers. Colonies came into existence, and relations with neighboring nation/s gradually became stronger. Hence, Israel when reached to a settled life got influenced by the way of thinking of Ancient West Asia. This cultural change brought about by agriculture greatly contributed to male dominance and female subordination. As the agricultural way of life permeated her way of life, the social fabric of Israelite culture was drastically and permanently altered. The sedentary and settled lifestyle that was accompanied with agriculture resulted in the dominance of new and different means of social organization. Probably this may be the reason for the subordinate position of women in the Israelite Law system, especially in the Book of the Covenant Code.

This negative approach towards land and woman can be seen throughout the OT, especially in the prophetical books. For instance, when Israel commited sin, the 8th century prophets in order to communicate the word of God employed land and woman (Isaiah 1:8; 3:16; Hos 1-2) as symbolic images representing the people of Israel.

Women and Law in AWA and Israel

The development is a blessing, but if that blessing comes at the cost of domination for a few and subjugation for 'other', can we say it as a development?

In Ancient Mesopotamia labor came to be divided not only on lines of gender, but according to a strict hierarchy based upon military might and religiously based authority. Ruby Rohrlich describes state formation in Mesopotamia as "a complex interaction among the processes of class stratification, militarism, patriarchy, and political consolidation."[741] The predominant pattern of social organization

741 Ruby Rohrlick, "State Formation in Sumer and the Subjugation of Women," *Journal of Feminist Studies* 6 (1980): 98.

that emerged in the sedentary, agricultural communities of Ancient Mesopotamia was based on patriarchy, where female sexual and reproductive liberty was subdued. The basis of the patriarchal socio-political power structure was the legitimization of the patriarchal family.[742]

In Ancient Mesopotamia the elite classes, namely the priests and warriors, manipulated religious ideologies to legitimize their claims to power. The religious ideology was similarly manipulated to legitimize the domination of male deities over female deities, and therefore of human males over human females.[743]

As the early civilizations of Mesopotamia became increasingly urbanized, they established institutions which served to put women in an inferior social class. Women as a whole were doubly disadvantaged by the ideologies propagated by the ruling elite since women were subjected to the constraints imposed by both class and gender. While women of the higher classes were subordinate to all men, women of the lowest class (slaves) were subordinate not only to all men, but also to all free women.[744]

The cultures of the Ancient Mesopotamian societies of Babylon, and Assyria formalized the subordination of women. The religions and laws developed by these civilizations prevented females from asserting control over their reproductive function in society. The social institutions developed in these cultures reduced the social power available to women.[745]

According to Jacqueline K. Hammack, the codified laws of these societies effectively compartmentalized female sexuality and commodified female reproductive capacity, which were crucial steps in the subjugation of the female sex. The social institutions of marriage and religion served to reinforce these cultures' definitions of normal, acceptable sexual activity and, in the process, relegated women's sexuality solely to the realm of reproduction. By formalizing

---

742 Gerda Lerner, *The Creation of Patriarchy* (New York: Oxford University Press, 1986), 54; Rohrlick: 83-84.

743 Rohrlick: 85-87.

744 Lerner, 95-96.

745 Jacqueline K. Hammack, "Women in Ancient Mesopotamia: The Mothers of Female Subordination," (USA: Jackson State University, 2007), 1.

patriarchal inheritance rights and reducing women's control over their own procreative power, women were confined to the private sphere of life; their influence and prestige were made ineffective.[746]

When Israel as a nation was transformed into a settled stage (i.e. from nomadic and sedentary life), new and different social institutions necessarily were developed in response to the changing cultural climate. These cultural changes greatly contributed to male dominance and female subordination. As the settled way of life permeated into their prior way of life which was semi-nomadic, the social structure of Israelite culture was significantly and permanently changed. Probably, Israel too like the Mesopotamian law codes opted for women subordination, which can be seen in Israelite Law System especially the Covenant Code (Casuistic Law).

The King and Administration of the Law

Throughout Ancient West Asia, the king is projected as the one responsible for providing justice and preserving the human rights of all the people. The power structure is rested upon the king, who can easily control or misuse the legal matters. A closer resemblance can be seen both in Babylonia and Israel. In Babylonia, the law was given to King Hammurabi by the sun-god Shamash and he was granted wisdom to execute it. Similarly in Israel though traditionally it is believed that Moses received the law from Yahweh, the request of King Solomon for wisdom and his execution to administer justice cannot be ignored. The reason for advocating the hand of kings is due to the fact that a kingdom cannot be administered based on the law founded during the wilderness period. Moreover, unlike other nations, the Israelite law hasdifferent forms and characters, which questions its authenticity.

Hence, the execution of the law solely rests upon the authoritative person (cf. I Sam 8:14-18). The ability of these authoritative individual depends on his administrative skill and power. If his subjects fail to obey, the king has the power to harm.

Despite the primary intention of the law was to protect the weak, it created boundaries between sex and class within a nation resulting into a reversal, i.e., the privilege class benefited more than

746 Ibid., 5.

the weaker ones. Hence, the law became a tool to serve the interest of the privileged groups.

Discrepancies in the Pentateuchal Law Codes

Each of the Biblical law codes (BC, HC, and DC) is a multifaceted text. The differences in laws especially with regard to weaker groups ask for careful investigation. The acceptance and support of slavery system and the view of women as property ought to be seriously relooked and investigated.

Laws on Slavery

All the three biblical codes like AWA codes support the institution of slavery. The harsh among them is the Covenant Code. The Holiness code is much closer and is parallel to the Deuteronomic Code.

1. In the Covenant Code, the slave law starts with 'when you buy a Hebrew slave…'It projects from the view point of a buyer/owner. The Deuteronomic and Holiness code unlike the Covenant Code emphasize the distressed side of the enslaved person ['If your fellow Hebrew, man or woman is sold to you/sell himself to you…(Deut 15:12)', 'If your fellow brother is reduced to poverty and sells himself to you, you must not use him to work for you as a slave… (Lev 25:39-40)'].
2. In Deuteronomic Code, the freedom for both male and female slave is on humanitarian ground and has strong moral and ethical aspect. The owner is expected to provide them liberally to ensure that they may not enter into slavery. Moreover, the law clearly reminds the Israelite community about their past and cites the reason for the freedom of the slaves (Deut 15:15). The Covenant Code gives no room for liberty. Though the male slave can go free in the seventh year, there is no guarantee that he could live an independent life, as he is sent empty handed. The Holiness Code, on the other hand, ensures freedom in a different way (year of Jubilee) which is closer to the Deuteronomic code. The understanding of "Your

brother/fellow countryman" is not just for kinsman but also any fellow Israelite/Hebrew appears to be taken from Deuteronomy. The Holiness Code like Deuteronomic Code instructs the owner to treat the impoverished individual with an open heart (Lev 25:43). They are to be treated not as slave, rather as a hired man. However, it clearly differentiates the Hebrew slaves and non-Hebrew slaves.

Women and Law: Patriarchal and Colonial Ideology

The majority of the laws 'address the community through its male members.'[747] The Pentateuchal law codes in general treat women as property and she is always subjected to the authority of male members of the society. The Covenant Code is much harsher towards women, where they have no right of freedom and are controlled by their male counterparts. The Deuteronomic Code and the Holiness Code to a great extent provide freedom to women. The Covenant Code appears to be in line with the Ancient West Asian Codes.

The whole of Ancient West Asian laws are patriarchal[748] and colonial[749] in color. Women were constantly addressed and treated as property similar to slaves. The rights and dignity of women were in a low level both in social and religious order. They were directly controlled by the male members of the society. Their sexuality belonged exclusively to her husband. If she failed to bear child, he could marry another wife. The wife in order to safeguard her life and to prevent her husband for another marriage was forced to handover a maid to her husband. The law is silent, if the problem of not bearing

747 Bird, 21. C.f. Anderson, 4-7. Some of the references in apodictic laws are Exod 20:19, 22:22-24, 31. The Casuistic laws generally begin with 'If a man….' For Phyllis, in almost all the laws the full membership is limited to males, in which only a male is considered as a responsible person and all others as dependents/household property.

748 In Patriarchal system, though both men and women participate in day to day affairs, it is 'controlled by men and promotes male privilege by being male dominated, male identified and male centered. The core values of the society is the core values of male members focusing on what men do' (Anderson, 11).

749 Colonialism has resemblance with patriarchal approach but goes beyond it by passing rules over the powerless thereby imposing laws over them.

child lies with the husband. The women were treated as chattel to be bought and sold. The identity of the women was limited to that of a daughter to a father, a wife to a husband, a maid to a mistress. In short, the women were ignored, despised and subverted.

The Ancient West Asian laws including the Book of the Covenant Code are in control of the rich and the powerful people. In order to amass wealth and maintain superiority over other nations, the women were targeted. Land was more important and an integral part in the life of agricultural society. In order to increase labor force, women became a tool. In case of war, the women taken as captives were carried by enemies mainly for sexual reasons and to procreate descendants for the triumphant nations. The unprecedented political and economic importance of the colonial power affected the very fabric of the Israelite society, which can be seen in the legal code. The legal code which is supposed to bring justice and welfare to all became a tool for injustice serving the interest of the powerful and elite at the expense of the powerless and marginalized. Israel perhaps in order to compete with other nations mimicked the social departmentalization of her neighboring nation/s.

Hence, the Book of the Covenant Code in particular must be deconstructed and dismantled, which was adapted from the political, cultural and religious practice of neighboring nations in order to build and construct a new voice to uplift the women and the marginalized from the clutches of powerful ideologies of patriarchy and colonialism. The denigration of women in the Book of the Covenant Code due to political, historical and religious levels that impinge on women's lives should be addressed for justice and peace in the world.

Is the Biblical Law Immutable?

Though traditionally it is believed that the biblical law was handed over to Moses by God and is divine and eternal, but reading the whole of laws tends to question its authenticity. The argument can be supported by the fact expressed both by the successful prophet, priest and Judge Samuel and Yahweh himself. When the people of Israel asked for a king like other nations, the word of Samuel was highly human in nature. He mentions the way in which king will mistreat his subjects (I Sam 8:14-18). The language expressed by Samuel is colonial in nature. Similarly Yahweh made a treaty/covenant with Israel, but Israel failed to obey it, resulting into a change in Covenant (Jer 31:29-30). These two examples clearly indicate that the Israelite law was not static. Hence, a redefining and reinterpretation is needed to ease the tensions and erase the boundaries created between sex and class.

Powerful and Powerless: The Power Play behind the Law

It is generally accepted that the laws of Ancient West Asia had not reached in its present shape initially, rather there was a growth and development based on the changing situation and demands. As mentioned earlier each law codes got influenced by the earlier laws. In all other Ancient West Asian laws except Israelite law, the king played the key role behind the promulgation of the laws. In order to make the laws valid, at the very outset they address god/gods with an understanding that the law is binding and applicable to all. However, in Israel it was not only the king who played the key role, rather the office of the prophet and the priest too played the crucial roles. There were frictions between these offices. Throughout Old Testament prophetical books, we could notice how the prophets attacked the office of kings (for instance, Samuel's rebuke to King Saul), and how theyeven attacked the priest (Malachi 1:6-2:9; Zephaniah 3:4; Micah 6:6-8). The role of the offices of prophet, priest and kings behind the daily life of Israel which includes the legal tradition cannot be negated, as it brought the common people under their control. In a tussle between the powerful groups, the real victims were the weaker sections of society, especially women, who had no voice to raise and fight for their rights. The woman and their rights were totally ignored.

Position of Women in India

"Having a daughter is like watering a flower in the neighbor's garden"- A Proverb

The position of women in India is similar to Israel and Ancient West Asia. They are treated as property and are under the control of the male members of the society. The treatment of women differs within caste and class. The high class white skinned women (Aryans) are in a better place than the bottom class black skinned women (dalits).

Prejudice against women can be seen very clearly right from her birth till death. They are victims of foeticide, infanticide, malnutrition, abuse, violence, traifficking etc. India is considered one among the worst countries in the world for the safety and wellbeing of women. The question to be addressed is, could we reclaim the value and dignity of women in our Indian nation? Could we reinstate the equal and inherent value of a girl child? Could we do a proactive role to ensure freedom, equality and dignity to our women?

Women and Society

The Indian society in general is divided in forms of caste, color and gender. In Hinduism, there are two divisions: Aryans and Dravidians. Rig-Veda[750], one of the most important and earliest written literary sources of ancient history has a hymn, which reveals two hostile groups: the *deva* worshipping Aryans and the *deva*-less and the rite-less *dasas* (*Dravidians*). The former has three classes: Brahmin, Kshatriyas and Vaishyas, and the latter are of two groups sudras (the serving caste) and the slaves (dalits).[751]

---

750 The Rigveda indicates the superiority of the white skinned Aryans over the dark skinned dasas and praises the gods 'who made the *Manus* superior to the *dasas*' and extols Indra for having in hundred ways 'preserved the Aryan worshippers ...and subjected the dusty skinned to the Manus' (Rigveda I 130,8; I 179, 6; II 12, 4; III 34, 9; IV 16, 13; IX 71, 2). C.f. John B. Chettimatam, *Dialogue in Indian Tradition* (Bangalore: Dharmaram College, 1969), 20-22.

751 Ramaprasad Chanda, *The Indo-Aryan Races: A Study of the Origin of Indo-Aryan People and Institutions* (Calcutta: 1969), 3; Suniti Kumar Chatterji, *Indo-Aryan and Hindi* (Calcutta: 1969), 18, 36. For John Chethimattam, the religious interpretation of the caste might have come much later than its historical evolution. *Purushasuta* of Rig Veda (X, 90) points out that the Brahmin originates from the mouth of the purusha, the Rajanya from his arms, Vaisya from his thighs and Sudra from his feet (c.f. Veda VII, 104, 3' Atharva Veda, VIII, 4, 13; Sathapatha Brahmana V, 4, 6, 9). Since the Sudra originates from the feet, they are commissioned for the menial works of the society [John B. Chetimattam, *Dialogue in Indian Tradition*, (Bangalore: Dharmaram College, 1969), 31].

For Devasahayam, Manu is a mischief-maker. Manusmriti marks off the latter group (*dasas*/dalits) as 'untouchable and unseeable, whose shadow, and even sight pollute the people of the other castes. They should shout or ring the bell if a caste Hindu approaches and a Brahmin girl should wash her eyes, if she happened to see a dalit'.[752] Even within *dasya*/dalit, the dalit women are in bad shape as they are the victims of casteism, patriarchy, and capitalism.[753] They are sexually exploited both by the higher caste (men and women) and their men.

According to Khare 'Dalit women are culturally misrepresented, historically misplaced, politically mute, unrepresented, isolated, socially faceless and moreover, their experiences and opinions go unrecorded'[754].

Women and Religion

In earlier time, women enjoyed equality. By the Aryan influx, the equality concept got changed. The Pallavas brought Aryan to this land. They donated the land to the Brahmins by following the Manu Dharma tradition. From this period onwards,the women were treated and subjected as slaves. In order to emphasize subordination, three concepts were introduced: *Path thini* (chaste women), *sumankali* (these concepts see the widow as the cursed ones), and *kudumpa pen* (limits the role of a woman within the kitchen).[755]

Religion and Slavery

Slavery is the very ancient institution of Hindus recognized both by Manu and other Smriti writers who followed Manu's principle. Manu

---

752 V. Devasahayam, "Pollution, Poverty and Powerlessness," in *A Reader in Dalit Theology*, ed. Arvind P. Nirmal (Madras: Gurukul Lutheran Theological College and Research Institute, n.d.), 4.

753 Franklyn J. Balasundaram, "Dalit Struggle and Its Implications for Theological Education," *Bangalore Theological Forum* 29, no. 3 & 4 (1997): 87.

754 R. S. Khare, "Elusive Social Justice, Distant Human Rights: Untouchable Women's Struggles and Dilemmas in Changing India," in *Changing Concepts of Rights and Justice in South Asia*, ed. Michael R. Anderson and Sumit Guha (Delhi: Oxford University Press, 1998), 200.

755 Ivy Singh, "Feminism: Various Approaches and Its Values," *Indian Journal of Theology* 37, no. 1 (1995): 59.

recognized seven types of slaves and Narad recognized thirteen types of slaves.[756] The religious books in general control the minds of the people as they strongly believe that all that is mentioned is divinely inspired one and true. In short, the book of laws is responsible for dividing humanity in name of caste, color and gender.

Women and Church

The women are discriminated against in the Church. Both the Old Testament and Pauline writings[757] in general are unfavorable to women and are also misinterpreted by the leaders and male members. Women have no voting rights, not allowed to preach or even permitted to read scripture in some churches. Though provisions are there for women to be theologically trained, their role is limited to be a minister's wife with few exceptions. They are deprived of their efforts and potentials.

The discrimination against women irrespective of their caste and color is done in a subtle way. Right from their childhood they are trained and taught to be submissive both in private and public places. They have to sacrifice their rights and identities. They are exploited economically, politically, socially and religiously. They have no access to legal provisions. The law though seems to give women provisions to fight for their rights and defense, in reality they are treated as property/commodity to be bought, possessed, used and finally to be disposed.

Women and Land

We are proud of our technology and market economy. Globalization is at the peak level. The competition to become and to be known as super power nation/s is the mark of the day. In spite of all these positive developments, the injustice done both to the land

756 Sukhaedeo Thorat, "Dalit Reality: From an Economic Perspective," in *Dalits and Women*, ed. V. Devasahayam (Chennai: Gurukul - Department of Research and Publications, 1992), 31-32.

757 Paul was heavily influenced by the Old Testament practice, which can be seen in his writings (Eph 5:22-24; Col.3:18; I Tim 2:11-15). His writing in the first letter to Timothy is too rigid, where he says 'A woman should learn in quietness and full submission. I do not permit a woman to teach or to have authority over a man… women will be saved through child bearing…'

and women are proportionally high, which creates disorder and imbalance to the universe. For Vandana Shiva, "the colonial mind is disturbing the peace and tranquility of the cosmos. The necessity of the time is to deracinate the patriarchal and colonial world system built and developed through colonizing women, land and nature. The women and her expertise on nature ought to be recognized by the so called super powers."[758] As prophet Micah (Micah 6:6-8) raises the question: What does the Lord require? The same question must be addressed to us especially in our theological community as we are the custodians of the Scripture and cosmos. Truth, love and justice both to the land and women are the need of the hour. If not, there will be disorder and chaos, which will ultimately end up in anarchy.

Women and Related Issues

It is not justified to bring all women and their issues under one scale. The women can be classified based on caste, class and sex. The high caste women suffer from the hand of their own men. The poor women face exploitation as they are poor and being a woman. The poor dalit women as mentioned by Ambedkar are triple oppressed group, as they are in the lowest and bottom rung of the society.[759] Unfortunately, women of all groups keep silent due to honor or shame and even if they come out are not allowed to express themselves.

Views of Indian Feminists[760]: Marriage, Dowry and Violence

1. Gauri Choudhary of Action India, New Delhi: 'Economic and sociological aspects of dowry are affecting everyone, and despite

---

758 Vandana Shiva, *Staying Alive: Women Ecology and Development* (New Delhi: Kali for Women), 24.

759 T. K. Sundari Ravindran, *Subverting Patriarchy: Workshops for Rural Women* (Chennai: Rural Women's Social Education Centre, 1999), 16.

760 This views were expressed by the feminists in a gathering held on Christ college, Bangalore on the topic "Daughters of fire: India courts of women on dowry and related forms of violence" organized by Vimochana and the Asian women's human rights council on 27-29 July, 2009. The same was published in the News paper 'The Hindu', Bangalore edition dated 28 and 29 July, 2009, 4.

the strength of the movement, the practice of dowry has been increased by thousand-fold in the last three decades'.[761]

2. Aati Mundkur, Alternative Law forum, "The more aggressive the law, the more difficult it is to get justice. We have specific laws that are helping woman yet we are caught in the double bind of law."[762]
3. Veena Talwar Oldenburg, Historian and feminist writer: "I dug into colonial archives. The 1853 census showed an appalling sex ratio, and it pointed out that communities which did not take dowry were doing so." [763]
4. Shiv Vishwanathan, Social scientist, 'There has been much talk of India and China's combined capacity to become economic superpowers, but the one thing that the two countries have been able to do efficiently is eliminate fetuses. This amplifies the sign of globalization."[764]
5. Donna Fernandes of Vimochana, 'The criminal justice system only looks at public violence and has certain parameters by which it judges a case. Violence against woman takes place privately'.[765]
6. Prathiba Kumari, All India Mahila Samskruthika Sanghatane President, 'Obscenity and violence in the electronic media were on the rise. Women were being portrayed as a commodity. With the policies of globalization-liberalization and privatization, the profit motive had taken ugly turns."[766]
7. Shah Alam Khan, "The fight for survival for the Indian female starts in the womb. If she is lucky to be born, she becomes ready meat for men of substance in power- prominent politicians or their siblings or even senior police officers.... It is easy to molest a girl in India than to get a mobile phone connection... Male

761 'Dowry case have gone up', *The Hindu* (Bangalore), 28 July 2009, 4.

762 Ibid.

763 Ibid.

764 Ibid.

765 Ibid.

766 "Curb crimes against women", *The Hindu* (Bangalore), 30 July 2009, 4.

dominance in India is a natural occurrence of birth. Indian society should share this collective blame."[767]

8. Soma Basu, "…'unwanted daughters' is still a stark reality in Modern India. The gender muddle continues to make a mockery of all expectations. Sex ratio is not just a demographic index but reflects society's attitude towards women. Education has hardly impacted traditional mindsets. Technology has aggravated the problem of sex ration in spite of the pre-conception and prenatal Diagnostic Techniques Act and the Medical Termination of Pregnancy Act."[768]

The growth of a severely consumerist culture and the issue of caste and class were among the reason for all forms of injustice.

Is our Society Changing? Few Cases

Due to limitation of space, few recent cases are stated.

1. Sakku Bai, a courageous young high school student from Bellary district says 'If not for my mother and sister who have stood by me and are working hard so that I can continue my studies, I would have been married before I turned 18'. She has resisted pressure from her alcoholic father and the larger community to marry her uncle 'to lessen the burden of dowry. She with the help of her teacher, women community workers and the police had thwarted her father's attempt to marry her off just as she finished standard 7. She is continuing her studies with the help of her mother and sister.[769]
2. Feudal system: An untold tale of a village- The Feudal system, an age old practice is still followed and that too in a Karnataka state known worldwide as an IT hub. Budihalli village of Karnataka's Chitaguda district is a clear

767 "We deify women, yet we treat them as doormat!" *The Hindu* (Bangalore), 11 April 2010, 11.

768 "Daughters: Why this discrimination?" *The Hindu* (Bangalore), 24 August 2010, 14.

769 "Stories of torture, horror and courage", *The Hindu* (Bangalore), 29 July 2009, 4.

example of caste discrimination and bondage. The men of madiga, dalit (scheduled caste) community has to work as bonded laborers in the fields of the landlord to repay the loan taken over by their grandparents (accumulated over generations). Their wife though considered as stigma and untouchables are raped by the landlords. In order to have self respect and a life of dignity, a group of them has to leave their homeland. Unfortunately, Government ruled by higher caste failed to address the cause of these people.[770] The sexual harassment is a cruel form of caste discrimination.

3. Accuser of rape let off with five shoe lashes- A teenage girl in Uttar Pradesh was allegedly raped by a youth of the same village. The matter was placed before the village panchayat. The panchayat decided to blacken the face of the accused and take him round the village. But changed the decision fearing that the police would come to know about it. Finally, he was let off with five shoe lashes.[771] The panchayat controlled by the male members are concerned more about the future of the boy and the prestige of the village, and are least concerned about the dignity of the woman.
4. 'Mandap to Mandi' (place of solemnization to Market) – Daughters from North Karnataka are married off to men from Gujarat, Maharashtra, Uttar Pradesh and Rajasthan for cash, only to be pushed into the flesh trade. Women are treated as a commodity, and they are measured depending on age and beauty. Girls below 18 years are sold for Rs. 1 Lakh to Rs.2 Lakh. For widows or deserted women, the price is below Rs. 50, 000. In some cases, they are even sold for Rs.10, 000. The victims are from lower caste women. These poor innocent women are sold under the guise of marriage and end up to a brothel in

770 "Rape and torture force Karnataka villagers to flee', *The Times of India* (Chennai), 27 August 2010, 11.

771 "Punishment for rape: Only five shoe lashes", *Deccan Herald* (Bangalore), 9 March 2009, 9.

Mumbai or North India. This practice is known as 'Gujjar marriage'. This marriage is a 'one night ceremony', where men from North India pay a certain amount of money to the girl's parents, and get married overnight. They bear all the expenses including jewels for the bride. The next day they take the girl away. After few days, the husbands desert them and end up in flesh trade. In this marriage, only the bride's parents are invited. In all these activities, the agents play a key role.[772]

5. Youths Chop off Dalit Girl's Nose and Ear- A 16 year old dalit girl paid the price for resisting the demonic act. Three youths chopped off her nose, ear and a part of her hand after she resisted a rape attempt. This incident took place at Bindaki in Uttar Pradesh, the state headed by a dalit woman chief minister.[773]
6. Cabbie held for Daughter's rape- A Cab driver raped his 13 year old daughter several time since December 2010. She is the daughter of his second wife. The Child is 14 weeks pregnant. A promising girl doing well at school scoring an average 97 percent is in traumatic condition.[774] This incident took place in Bangalore known for advanced technology and development.

The above mentioned incidences are few cases happening in our shinning nation. It shows clearly that the law though looks promising outwardly is not strong enough to handle violence and crime against women. Dowry, rape, abortion and harassment of various formsare wrecking the lives of women, cutting across class and caste barriers. Globalization and changing developmental priorities is resurrecting dowry in new forms. Technologies are supposed to be for betterment; unfortunately it is misused and ushered for 'unwanted daughters'

---

772 "Curse of the Gujjar Marriage", *The Times of India* (Bangalore), 21 October 2010, 6.

773 "Youths Chop off Dalit Girl's Nose and Ear", *The Hindu* (Bangalore), 7 February 2011, 12.

774 "Cabbie held for Daughter's Rape", *The Hindu* (Bangalore), 11 February 2011, 3.

resulting into sex ratio imbalance. The powerful people and men of higher caste harass women with audacity. If women are looked as a commodity, they will be victims for ageless period, but if they are considered and treated as a part of society, crime against them can be curbed. Situations can be changed through female upliftment, understanding the dynamics of equality and giving due respect to all regardless of class, caste and gender.

Our nation India though claims for strong legislative and judicial system, the number of dowry death and rape is mountingup day by day. The metropolitan and urban cities are not safe. Though there is Protection of Domestic Violence Act 2005[775] (brought into force from 2006), Constitution of Indian Acts 14, 15, and 16 for equality, Dowry Prohibition Act 1961 (304b), section 354 of IPC (outraging the modesty of women) and Hindu Progress Acts 1956, 2005 giving rights to women, the atrocities committed against women both within and outside the house is alarming. For physical and sexual violence, there are laws where the culprit can be drilled, but for emotional and mental violence, there is hardly ways to drill them. Irrespective of all these acts, the judgment is either delayed or quashed. Hence, the whole judicial and legislative system ought to be reviewed periodically and alternative ways must be explored to provide justice to all particularly women. The court must have fair representatives of female advocates for impartial judgment. Unfortunately, the women representatives in parliament and Judiciary are discouraging[776]. In doing so, all forms of discrimination

775 It must be noted that the domestic violence act is used against men and not against women. Recently, a woman named Leelavathi sought to persecute her in-laws (father in-law, mother in-law and sister-in-law). The Karnataka High court held that the provision of the Domestic violence act is only meant for the welfare of the women and could not be used against any women (in this case mother in-law and sister in-law) ["Domestic Violence Act not to be used against women", *The Hindu* (Bangalore), 10 September 2010, 10. Here too the verdict is against the safety of women. The judiciaries are controlled by the male members and unfortunately women in some cases joined hand with the system to isolate women and her causes.

776 According to United Nations 'Women hold just over 18 percent of the seats in parliaments around the world... Prejudices and cultural perceptions about the role of society are among the greatest obstacles to women's entry. Asia has

and exploitations can be eliminated. This will erase the fears among women; thereby we could restore a peaceful home, society, nation and world.

To make it fruitful and effective, few steps should be initiated:

1. A general awareness program is to be introduced periodically in all villages and cities.
2. Subject on family law should be added in school syllabus.
3. Media to a great extent can help by airing programmes related to legislation on dowry, rape, culpable homicide and domestic violence. Since our society is a society of honor and shame, media can also help the victims come out from rigid systems.
4. There need to be a change in societal attitude and the society should adopt an inclusive approach.
5. The government should ensure the effective implementation of legislation to protect and preserve human rights.

Summary

The purpose of God, the creator, who created humankind (male and female) in His image, was to treat both sex as equal partners but in the course of time, Israel got influenced by her neighboring nations, and competed with them by borrowing their culture and practices. The wealth and productivity of the land became a target against women. The same situation can be seen worldwide. The psychological, social, cultural and religious differences between men and women, which are a construct and preponderance of patriarchy and colonial power/s, must be relooked. Hence, the law needs to be revisited, taking all walks of people into consideration. A balanced law can produce a healthy community.

the slowest rate of progress in terms of women's access to Parliament over the past 15 years' ("Gender-less democracies", *The Hindu* (Bangalore), 7 March 2009, 9.

Conclusion

Is the Old Testament Law System Irredeemably Colonial in Color?

Is the Israelite law omnicompetent? The plain answer is absolutely 'no'. For Robert D. Taylor and Ronald J. Ricci, 'Law is not God and therefore cannot be omnicompetent'.[777]

The imperialistic exploitation by the powerful nations like Babylonia, Assyria and Egypt and Israel's own inability and vulnerability to prevent from these political and cultural dominations, encroached the religious and social stand of Israel, which in turn affected the legal system of Israel.The external influences and the internal factors in the life of Israel were one of the pivotal factors in the growth and development of the Israelite Law system. Though the Biblical law is perceived to be of divine origin and the neighboring nation's laws had their source in the king, and they have differences, but a closer reading reveals of a strong influence of neighboring nations in the life and legal practice of Israel.

The Book of Exodus is generally understood as a book advocating liberation. But a closer reading of the book reveals that it carries an androcentric view. So, understanding the book as

777 Ronald J. Ricci Robert D. Taylor, "Three Biblical Models of Liberty and Some Representative Laws," *Ex auditu* 11 (1995): 120.

a book of liberation appears to be highly problematic, as the law codes support the establishment and the stabilization of a male dominated hierarchical society. The subordination of women is not merely a religio-cultural and patriarchal subordination but rather a subordination of politics. The role of colonialism is heavily present.

Women are not given the rights of freedom. They are only portrayed in gender specific roles. The law though understood as divine, advocates and supports for the marginalization of female. Though God frees the Israelites from Egyptian slavery, the freedom in reality is for male and not for female. This aspect is however to some extent opposed in Deuteronomic code where freedom is entitled both for male and female.

Israel being a nomad grew and developed as a nation seeing and observing the surrounding nations, whose aim was to accumulate land and subjugate other nation/s. Israel too mimicked the surrounding nations by adopting their strategies. Israel adopted the laws of AWA, which was secular in color. They adopted the agricultural practice of Mesopotamia to boom their economic position. By doing so, they not only assimilated the culture and practice of her neighboring nations, but also brought ambivalence within her system. An imbalance approach can be seen between the free woman and the slave.

Ancient West Asian powers such as Assyria, Babylon and Persia were dominant nations with 'power over others'. The law codes in Pentateuch were a product from a context of interaction between imperial cultures and local Jewish culture. Other than power from outside there was also strong relations between the centre/elite and the periphery/others in terms of social class (rich/poor), sex (male/female) and ethical/racial boundaries. The domination by the core group and the subordination of the periphery/marginalia can be clearly seen in the law codes especially in the book of the Covenant Code. Hence, it is highly possible that the legal codes emerged from the interaction of imperial cultures and local culture, and also from the elite/dominant group. The traditional understandings of Mosaic authorship must be seriously relooked. The Israelite law went through major changes in her history. The Book of the Covenant Code had a strong influence of 8th century BCE, which made a gap between the rich/elite (centre) and the weaker sections specially the women (periphery). The Deuteronomic Code of 7th century BCE is a progressive law addressing the needs of all community. The Holiness Code of 6th century BCE falls closer to the book of the Covenant Code. In short, all the three codes though had laws of earlier times but had a strong influence of the respective centuries.

God is the one who subverts all that marginalizes the people irrespective of their class, color or gender and subverts imperialistic power. God who curtailed the power of Pharaoh over Israel expects the people of Israel to serve each other but unfortunately the laws in Exodus support the vested interest of those who subvert the marginalized. When we compare the Deuteronomic Code with the Book of the Covenant Code, we learnt that the Deuteronomic code favors the whole strata of society irrespective of who they are.The most remarkable and unique feature of the Deuteronomic Code is its deep concern for the welfare of all individuals irrespective of class and gender. For Deuteronomy justice is not to be administered solely in accordance with his/her position or voice in the community/society, rather it is concerned with every individual according to his/her need. The laws in Deuteronomy safeguard the poor, weak, marginalized and the defenseless. There is no separation of freedom and welfare based on class and gender. The revolution of freedom, equality and justice for all is one of the prominent threads in Deuteronomic legislation.

Human Dignity and Human Right

The struggle for the recognition of the rights of the weaker sections of the society, especially the women must be taken due consideration. The restoration of full dignity of women in front of others must be affirmed and acknowledged. The law must address the religio-socio-economic- political reality of each individual irrespective of his or her social standings. Law must address to the issues of both human dignity and human rights. Law must give room to each and every individual to protest against the dehumanization in the context of oppression and dehumanization.

Womanism and Postcolonial Womanism: A fight against patriarchal and colonial ideologies

Womanism questions the discrimination of gender and race in the area of politics, economic, social and religion. A postcolonial womanist reading not only tackles the issue of gender discrimination, but also goes beyond and investigates the reason behind the gender discrimination. The reason behind gender discrimination is not merely patriarchal, rather the issue of power. The powerful nations in order to maintain their domination over the weaker nations inculcated the strategy of gender discrimination. The laws of rape, seduction, adultery and slavery were to delimit the power of the weaker nations. This form of strategy can be seen in the context of war. For example, when America and the allies were in war against Iraq, they not only destroyed the Iraqi regime but also committed crime against the Iraqi women. The same strategy was used by Muammar Gadaffi[778] in Libya, where he gave freedom to rape wife and daughters of those men who is opposing his rule.

The nation of Israel was new in comparison to her neighboring nations. Hence, it was necessary and mandatory to have a law of her own to govern her people. It was not possible to function with a law meant only for nomadic herders. It was necessary for the law to have been modified as the social situation of the people changed. It appears that when Israel became villagers and moreover urban dwellers, they got influenced by her neighboring nations and perhaps mimiticized the strategy, culture and policy patterns of powerful

778 The times of India reported about slain Libyan dictator entitled 'Gadaffi kept schoolgirls as sex slaves'. Gadaffi beat and raped a 15 year old kidnapped school girl named Soraya, who was chosen to give him a bouquet when he visited her school. She was driven by the kidnappers for hours through the desert, her breasts measured before being stripped and shaved. She was escorted to Gadaffi's bedroom and was shocked to find him naked. Gadaffi said, 'Don't be afraid. I 'm your papa…but I'm also your brother and your lover.' He repeatedly raped, beat and urinated on this teenager during her five years in captivity. He had many other slave girls who were forced to perform oral sex, wear lacy underwear and watch porn films. The paper reports that Gadaffi had 'needed' several girls every day. According to the paper, Gadaffi's sex slave victims are still suffering after being rejected by their families for having sex when they were not married [The Times of India (Delhi), 25 September, 2012]

nations to project herself as a equally competent nation, which resulted into an imbalance in the status between the powerful and powerless and discrimination against sexes. On the other hand, the powerful nations in order to dominate and to have control over other nations, exploited women of all classes both within and outside their nation. Hence, the laws which were both patriarchal and colonial and transmitted from one nation to another must be relooked to address the needs and welfare of all. The powerful representing the powerless and male representing female should be challenged. Respecting and considering the identity and dignity of each individual irrespective of class and gender must be given prime importance. By reading the whole of the laws (pro-colonial covenant code, anti-colonial deuteronomic code and ambivalent holiness code) one could create public opinion against the power of the colonial empire/s through a postcolonial womanist approach.

Summing up, the Covenant Code probably came to its final shape in 8th century BCE, a time when Assyrian empire was weak (783-745 BCE)[779] and Israel as a nation was emerging equally competent with the other neighboring nations. The nation Israel in order to compete with other nations probably modified the legislation which created an immense gulf between the powerful and powerless, which in turn affected the weaker sections especially women. The Deuteronomic Code reached its present form in the seventh century BCE, when Assyrian Empire was declining. The kings of Judah particularly Manasseh and Josiah took this opportunity to reform the entire system including the legislation. It narrowed down the gap between the rich and the poor. The weaker section particularly the women was benefited as they too received their rights. The Holiness Code came to its present form during Persian Imperialism. The Persian Empire unlike Assyria and Babylon granted the captive people the right to worship and the people of Judah regained their former strength. The Persian strategy was to extend their boundaries and to have leaders of the captive group, which would further strengthen their empire. The governor and high priest of Judah were given power over the Judean community. This privilege created a

779 C.f. Page 19, section on the 'Probable date of the codes (The Covenant Code)' in the "introductory" chapter.

gulf between the religious leaders and the common people. Holiness and strict regulations were imposed on the people. It affected the common people, specially the women. Hence, the Holiness Code is ambivalent in nature.

Like AWA and Israel, Hinduism too is affected by gender, class and caste system. In several hymns of Rig Veda[780], the theme is the struggle between the Aryans and the *Dasas*. The manner in which Aryans came in India, and attacked the aboriginal groups or Dravidians is quite familiar to us. Manusmriti marks Dalits as untouchables and unseeable, whose touch, shadow and even sight pollute the people of other castes. The most affected group is the Dalit women. They are the victims of unjust system of patriarchy, capitalism and casteism. As a result, their lives are subjected to subordination, violence and sexual exploitation.

On the one hand, women are given due respect in India, but on the other hand, they are subjugated and deprived of social justice. The increasing incidences of violence against women can be seen in 'shinning India.'

According to Rameshwari Pandya,

> Women have been idiolised in India yet they have also been exploited and denied social justice. Police officials, lawyers, social workers, policy makers and educationalists are of the opinion that only a small numbers of incidents, especially those of involving severe injury or death, get newspapers and media coverage.[781]

The Indian law though guarantees equality to all citizens of India irrespective of gender, but in reality they are way behind to men and they are pushed into a low and inferior place. The laws are

---

780 The Rig Veda praises the gods 'who made the Manus superior to the *Dasas*' and extols Indra for having in hundred ways 'preserved the Aryan worshipper… and subjected the dusty skinned to the Manus' (Rig Veda I, 130, 8). The Rig Veda indicates the superiority of the white Aryans over the dark skinned *Dasas* (Rig Veda I, 179, 6; II, 12, 4, III 34, 9; IV 16, 13; IX 71, 2). The encounter between the Aryans and *Dasas* brought face to face the two cultural approaches and religious attitudes. The most disadvantage group are the women.

781 Rameshwari Pandya, *Women and Law* (Haryana: Madhav Books, 2009), 1.

not implemented properly. There is a big gap between the passing of the law and the benefits reaching to the women. It is not merely due to the lack of awareness or knowledge among women, but due to social, cultural and economic factors. The women need to come out of these ideological differences and its framework and develop a self-identity leading to a life of dignity.

Bibliography

Primary Sources

Alt, A, *et.al. Biblia Hebraica Stuttgartensia*. Stuttgart: Deutsche Bibelgesellschaft, 1977.

Brown, Francis, *et.al. The Brown-Driver-Briggs Hebrew and English Lexicon*. Massachusetts: Hendrickson Publishers, 2000.

Kramer, S. N. "Lipit-Ishtar Lawcode." In *Ancient Near Eastern Texts Relating to the Old Testament*, ed. James B. Pritchard, 159-161. Princeton: Princeton University Press, 1950.

Meek, Theophile J. "The Middle Assyrian Laws." In *Ancient Near Eastern Texts: Relating to the Old Testament*, ed. James B. Pritchard, 180-188. Princeton: Princeton University Press, 1969.

Meek, Theophile J. "The Code of Hammurabi." In *Ancient Near Eastern Texts*, ed. James B. Pritchard, 167-170. New Jersey: Princeton University Press, 1955.

William F. Arndy, F. Wilbur Gingrich. *A Greek-English Lexicon of the New Testament and Other Early Christian Literature*. Chicago: The University of Chicago Press, 1957.

Secondary Sources

A. T. Chapman, A. W. Streane. *The Book of Leviticus*. Cambridge: University Press, 1914.

Abrams, M. H. *The Mirror and the Lamp: Romantic Theory and the Critical Tradition*. New York: OUP, 1953.

Alt, A. "The Origins of Israelite Law." In *Essays on Old Testament History and Religion*. Oxford: Oxford University Press, 1966.

Andermahr, Sonya. *A Glossary of Feminist Theory*. New York: Oxford University Press, 2000.

Anderson, Cheryl B. *Ancient Laws and Contemporary Issues*. Oxford: Oxford University Press, 2009.

Balentine, Samuel E. "Leviticus." In *Interpretation*, ed. Patrick D. Miller. Louisville: John Knox Press, 2002.

Bartholomew, Craig G. "Deconstruction." In *Dictionary for Theological Interpretations of the Bible*, ed. Kevin J. Vanhoozer, 163-165. Grand Rapids, Michigan: Baker Academic, 2005.

________. "Postmodernity and Biblical Interpretation." In *Dictionary for Theological Interpretation of the Bible*, ed. Kevin J. Vanhoozer, 600-607. Grand Rapids, Michigan: Baker Academic, 2005.

Barton, George A. *Archaeology and the Bible*. Philadelphia: American Sunday School Union, 1916. Reprint, 1941.

Berquist, Jon L. *Judaism in Persian's Shadow: A Social and Historical Approach*. Eugene, Origen: Wipf and Stock Publishers, 1995.

Beyer, Bill T. Arnold and Byran E., ed. *Readings from the Ancient near East*. Grand Rapids, Michigan: Baker Academic, 2002.

Bhabha, Homi K. *The Location of Culture*. New York: Routledge, 1994.

________. "Of Mimicry and Men: The Ambivalence of Colonial Discourse." In *The Location of Culture*, 85-92. London, 1994.

________. "Of Mimicry and Man: The Ambivalence of Colonial Discourse." In *Postcolonialisms: An Anthology of Cultural Theory and Criticism*, ed. Gaurav Desai and Supriya Nair, 125-133. New Jersey, 2005.

Bird, Phyllis A. *Missing Persons and Mistaken Identities: Women and Gender in Ancient Israel*. Minneapolis: Fortress Press, 1997.

Blunt, Alison. *Travel Gender and Imperialism: Mary Kingsley and West Africa*. New York: Guildford, 1994.

Bottero, Jean. "The First Semitic Empire." In *Delacorte World History-the near East: The Early Civilizations*, ed. and Elena Cassin Jean Bottero, and Jean Vercoutter, 2, 91-132. New York: Delacorte Press, 1967.

Bright, John. "Modern Study of the Old Testament Literature." In *The Bible and the Ancient near East*, ed. G. E. Wright. Indiana: Winona Lake, 1961.

________. *A History of Israel.* London: SCM Press, 1980.

Cairns, Ian. "Word and Presence: A Commentary on the Book of Deuteronomy." In *International Theological Commentary*, ed. Fredrick Carlson Holmgren and George A. F. Knight. Edinburgh: The Handsel Press Ltd, 1992.

Carmody, Denise Lardner. *Biblical Woman: Contemporary Reflection on Scriptural Texts*. New York: Crossroad, 1992.

Cassuto, U. *A Commentary on the Book of Exodus*. Jerusalem: The Magness Press, 1967.

Chambliss, Rollin. *Social Thought: From Hammurabi to Comte*. New York: The Dryden Press, 1954.

Chanda, Ramaprasad. *The Indo-Aryan Races: A Study of the Origin of Indo-Aryan People and Institutions*. Calcutta, 1969.

Chatterji, Suniti Kumar. *Indo-Aryan and Hindi*. Calcutta, 1969.

Chettimatam, John B. *Dialogue in Indian Tradition*. Bangalore: Dharmaram College, 1969.

Childs, Brevard S. *The Book of Exodus*. London: SCM Press Ltd, 1974.

Chopp, Rebecca. "Eve's Knowing: Feminist's Theology's Resistance to Malestream Epistemological Frameworks." In *Concilium 1996/1: Feminist Theologies in Different Contexts*, ed. Elisabeth Schussler Fiorenza and Mary Shawn Copeland. New York: Orbis Books, 1996.

Chrisman, Laura. "Postcolonial Studies." In *New Dictionary of the History of Ideas*, ed. Maryanne Cline Horowitz, 5, 1857-1859. London: Gale Cengage Learning, 2005.

Christensen, Duane L. "Deuteronomy 1:1-21:9." In *Word Biblical Commentary*, ed. John D. W. Watts, 6A. Nashville: Thomas Nelson Publishers, 2001.

________. "Deuteronomy 21:10-34:12." In *Word Biblical Commentary*, ed. John D. W. Watts, 6B. Nashville: Thomas Nelson Publishers, 2002.

Clements, R. E. "Deuteronomy." In *Old Testament Guides*, ed. R. N. Whybray. Sheffield: JSOT Press, 1989.

Clements, Ronald E. *Exodus*. Cambridge: Cambridge University Press, 1972.

________. "The Book of Deuteronomy." In *The New Interpreter's Bible*, ed. Leander E. Keck, II. Nashville: Abingdon Press, 1998.

Clifford, Anne M. *Introducing Feminist Theology*. New York: Orbis Books, 2001.

Clines, D. J. A. *What Does Eve Do to Help? And Other Readerly Questions to the Old Testament*. Sheffield: JSOT Press,1990.

Cole, Alan. *Exodus: An Introduction and Commentary*. England: Inter-Varsity Press, 1973.

Contenau, Georges. *Everyday Life in Babylon and Assyria*. London: Edward Arnold Publishers Ltd, 1955.

Coogan, Michael D. *The Old Testament: A Historical and Literary Introduction to the Hebrew Scriptures*. New York/Oxford: Oxford University Press, 2006.

Craige, Peter C. *The Book of Deuteronomy*. Grand Rapids, Michigan: William B. Eerdmans Publishing Company, 1976.

Crusemann, Frank. *The Torah: Theology and Social History of Old Testament Law*. Translated by Allan W. Mahnke. Edinburgh: T&T Clark, 1996.

Cunliffe-Jones, H. "Deuteronomy." In *Torch Bible Commentaries*, ed. Alan Richardson John Marsh, R. Gregor Smith. London: SCM Press Ltd, 1951.

Dandamayev, Muhammad A. "Slavery (Ancient near East)." In *Anchor Bible Dictionary*, ed. David Noel Freedman, 6, 58-62. New York: Double day, 1992.

________. "Slavery (Old Testament)." In *Anchor Bible Dictionary*, ed. David Noel Freedman, 6, 62-65. New York: Double day, 1992.

Daube, D. *Studies in Biblical Law*. Cambridge: Cambridge University Press, 1947.

Davies, G. Henton. *Exodus*. London: SCM Press Ltd, 1967.

Devasahayam, V. "Pollution, Poverty and Powerlessness." In *A Reader in Dalit Theology*, ed. Arvind P. Nirmal, 1-22. Madras: Gurukul Lutheran Theological College and Research Institute, n.d.

Dirks, Nicholas. "Colonialism." In *New Keywords: A Revised Vocabulary of Culture and Society*, ed. Lawrence Grossberg Tony Bennett, and Meaghan Morris. UK/ USA/ Australia: Blackwell Publishing, 2005.

Dobson, John H. *A Guide to the Book of Exodus*. London: SPCK, 1977.

Donaldson, Laura. *Decolonizing Feminisms: Race, Gender and Empire Building*. Chapel Hill: University of the North Carolina Press, 1992.

Donna Landry, Gerald Maclean, ed. *Selected Works of Gayatri Chakravorty Spivak*, The Spivak Reader. New York and London: Routledge, 1996.

Douglas, Mary. *Purity and Danger*. London: Routledge, 1966.

Dozeman, Thomas B. *Commentary on Exodus* The Eerdmans Critical Commentary, ed. David Noel Freedman. Cambridge: William B. Eerdmans Publishing Company, 2009.

Driver, S. R. *A Critical and Exegetical Commentary on Deuteronomy*. Edinburgh: T&T Clark, 1902.

________. "Deuteronomy: A Critical and Exegetical Commentary." In *The International Critical Commentary*, ed. A. Plummer, C. A. Briggs and S. R. Driver. Edinburgh: T&T Clark, 1996.

Driver, S. R. *The Book of Exodus*. Cambridge: Cambridge University Press, 1929.

Dube, Musa W. *Other Ways of Reading: African Women and the Bible*. Atlanta: Society of Biblical Literature, 2001.

________. "Reading for Decolonization (John 4.1-42)." In *John and Postcolonialism: Travel, Space and Power*, ed. Musa W. Dube and Jeffrey L. Staley. Sheffield: Sheffield Academic Press, 2002.

Durham, John I. "Exodus." In *Word Biblical Commentary*, ed. John D. W. Watts and James W. Watts, 3. USA: Nelson Reference & Electronic, 1987.

Edzard, Dietz Otto. "The Early Dynastic Period." In *Delacorte World History-the near East: The Early Civilizations*, ed. Elena Cassin Jean Bottero, and Jean Vercoutter, 2, 52-90. New York: Delacorte Press, 1967.

________. "The Third Dynasty of Ur- Its Empire and Its Successor States." In *Delacorte World History-the near East: The Early Civilizations*, ed. Elena Cassin Jean Bottero, and Jean Vercoutter, II, 133-176. New York: Delacorte Press, 1967.

Epsztein, Leon. *Social Justice in the Ancient near East and the People of the Bible*. London: SCM Press Ltd, 1986.

Fiorenza, Elisabeth Schussler. "Feminist Hermeneutics." In *Anchor Bible Dictionary*, ed. David Noel Freedman, 2, 783-795. New York: Doubleday, 1992.

Floss, Johannes P. "Form, Source and Redaction Criticism." In *The Oxford Handbook of Biblical Studies*, ed. J. W. Rogerson and Judith M. Lieu, 591-614. Oxford: Oxford University Press, 2006.

Frymer-Kensky, Tikva. "Deuteronomy." In *Women's Bible Commentary*, eds. Carol A. Newsom and Sharon H. Ringe, 57-68. Kentucky: John Knox Press, 1998.

G. R. Driver, John C. Miles. *The Babylonian Laws*. Vol. I. Oxford: Clarendon Press, 1960.

Gadamer, Hans-Georg. *Truth and Method*. London: Sheed and Ward, 1981.

Gandhi, Leela. *Postcolonial Theory: A Critical Introduction*. Delhi: Oxford University Press, 1999.

Gaster, T. H. *Myth, Legend and Custom in the Old Testament*. New York: Harper, 1969.

Gerstenberger, Erhard S. "Leviticus." In *The Old Testament Library*, ed. Carol A. Newsom, David L. Petersen and James L. Mays. Kentucky: Westminster John Knox Press, 1996.

Gnuse, Robert. *You Shall Not Steal: Community and Property in the Biblical Tradition* New York: Orbis Books, 1985.

Goldingay, J. "Hermeneutics." In *Dictionary of the Old Testament Pentateuch*, ed. T. Desmond Alexander and David W. Baker, 387-401. Secunderabad: OM Authentic Books, 2003.

Gorman, Frank H. "Divine Presence and Community: A Commentary on the Book of Leviticus." In *International Theological Commentary*, ed. Fredrick Carlson Holmgren and George A. F. Knight. Edinburgh: The Handsel Press Ltd, 1997.

Gottwald, Norman. *The Tribes of Yahweh: A Sociology of the Religion of Liberated Israel 1250-1050 B.C.E.* London: SCM Press 1980.

Gramsci, Antonio. *Selection from Prison Notebooks.* Translated by Quintin Hoare and Geoffrey Nowell Smith. London: Lawrence and Wishart, 1978.

Grayson, A Kirk. "Assyrian Rule of Conquered Territory in Ancient Western Asia." In *Civilizations of the Ancient near East*, ed. Jack M Sasson, I & II, 959-968. Massachusetts: Hendrickson Publishers, 1995.

Greengus, Samuel. "Law." In *Anchor Bible Dictionary*, ed. David Noel Freedman, 4, 242-252. New York: Double day, 1992.

________. "Legal and Social Institutions of Ancient Mesopotamia." In *Civilizations of the Ancient near East*, ed. Jack M Sasson, I& II, 469-484. Massachusetts: Hendrickson Publishers, 1995.

Gupta, Sobhanlal Datta. "Imperialism and Colonialism: Towards a Postcolonial Understanding "In *History of Science, Philosophy and Culture in Indian Civilization: Science, Technology, Imperialism and War*, ed. D. P. Chattopadhyaya, 15, 423-466. Delhi: Centre For Studies In Civlizations, 2007.

Hammack, Jacqueline K. "Women in Ancient Mesopotamia: The Mothers of Female Subordination." 1-8. USA: Jackson State University, 2007.

Handcock, Percy. *The Code of Hammurabi*. London: Society for Promoting Christian Knowledge, 1932.

Hartley, John E. "Leviticus." In *Word Biblical Commentary*, ed. John D. W. Watts, 4. Texas: Word Books, 1992.

Hoffman, D. *Das Buch: Leviticus*. Berlin: Poppelaver, 1906.

Hoffner, Harry A. "Legal and Social Institutions of Hittite Anatolia." In *Civilizations of the Ancient near East*, ed. Jack M. Sasson, I & II, 555-569. Massachusetts: Hendrickson Publishers, 1995.

Hooke, S. H. *Babylonian and Assyrian Religion*. London: Hutchinson's University Library, 1953.

Hooks, Bell. *Ain't I a Woman: Black Woman and Feminism*. Boston: South End Press, 1981.

________. *Feminist Theology from Margin to Center*. Boston: South End Press, 1984.

Houtman, Cornelis. "Exodus." In *Historical Commentary on the Old Testament*, ed. Gert T. M. Prinsloo Cornelis Houtman, Wilfred G. E. Watson and Al Wolters, 3. Leuven: Peeters, 2000.

Huddart, David. *Homi K. Bhabha*. London and New York: Routledge, 2006.

Hyatt, J. P. *Exodus*. London: Oliphants, 1971.

Imparati, Fiorella. "Private Life among the Hittites." In *Civilizations of the Ancient near East*, ed. Jack M. Sasson, I & II, 571-586. Massachusetts: Hendrickson Publishers, 1995.

Jeremias, Alfred. *The Old Testament in the Light of the Ancient East: Manual of Biblical Archaeology*. Vol. II Theological Translation Library, ed. Canon C. H. W. Johns. New York: William & Norgate, 1911.

Kaiser, Walter C. *Towards Old Testament Ethics*. Grand Rapids, Michigan: Zondervan Publishing House, 1983.

________. "The Book of Leviticus." In *The New Interpreter's Bible*, ed. Leander E. Keck, I. Nashville: Abingdon Press, 1994.

Keil, C. F. "The Pentateuch." In *Commentary on the Old Testament*, ed. C. F. Keil and F. Delitzsch, I. Massachusetts: Hendrickson Publishers, 2001.

Khare, R. S. "Elusive Social Justice, Distant Human Rights: Untouchable Women's Struggles and Dilemmas in Changing India." In *Changing Concepts of Rights and Justice in South Asia*, ed. Michael R. Anderson and Sumit Guha, 188-204. Delhi: Oxford University Press, 1998.

Kilian, R. *Literarkritische Und Formgeschichtiche Untersuchung Des Heiligkeitsgesetzes*. Bonn: Hanstein, 1963.

Kim, Hyun Sook. "The Politics of Border Crossings: Black, Postcolonial, and Transnational Feminist Perspectives." In *Handbook of Feminist Research: Theory and Praxis*, ed. Sharlene Nagy Hesse-Biber, 107-122. New Delhi/London: SAGE Publications/Thousand Oaks, 2007.

King, Richard. *Orientalism & the Myth of Modern Hinduism*. New Delhi: Critical Quest, 2008.

Kline, Meredith G. *Treaty of the Great King*. Grand Rapids, Michigan: William B. Eerdmans Publishing Company, 1963.

Klingbeil, G. A. "Historical Criticism." In *Dictionary of the Old Testament Pentateuch*, ed. T. Desmond Alexander and David W. Baker, 401-420. Secunderabad: OM Authentic Books, 2003.

Knight, Douglas A. "Village Law and the Book of the Covenant." In *A Wise and Discerning Mind: Essays in Honor of Burke O. Long, ed. Saul M. Olyan and Robert C. Culley*, 103-119. RI: Brown Judaic Studies, 2000.

Knight, George A. F. *Leviticus*. Philadelphia: The Westminster Press, 1981.

L. Finkelstein. "An Eye for an Eye." *The Menorah Journal* 24 (1936): 207-218.

Lalfakzuala. *Human Rights in Deuteronomy: A Sociological Approach*. Delhi: ISPCK, 2004.

Lambert, W. G. "Ancient near Eastern Studies: Mesopotamia." In *The Oxford Handbook of Biblical Studies*, ed. J. W. Rogerson and Judith M. Lieu, 74-88. Oxford: Oxford University Press, 2006.

Lategan, Bernard C. "Hermeneutics." In *The Anchor Bible Dictionary*, ed. David Noel Freedman, 3, 149-154. New York: Doubleday, 1997.

Lerner, Gerda. *The Creation of Patriarchy*. New York: Oxford University Press, 1986.

Levine, Baruch A. "Leviticus." In *The Jewish Publication Society Torah Commentary*, ed. Nahum M. Sarna. Jerusalem: The Jewish Publication Society, 1989.

Loomba, Ania. *Colonialism/Postcolonialism*. New York: Routledge, 2007.

Manley, G. T. *The Book of the Law*. London: The Tyndale Press, 1957.

________. *The Book of the Law: Studies in the Date of Deuteronomy*. London: The Tyndale Press, 1957.

Marsman, Hennie J. *Women in Ugarit and Israel: Their Social and Religious Position in the Context of the Ancient near East*. Leiden: Brill, 2003.

Matthews, Victor H. *Manners and Customs in the Bible*. Massachusetts: Hendrickson Publishers, 1991.

Mayes, A. D. H. "Deuteronomy." In *New Century Bible Commentary*, ed. Ronald E. Clements. Grand Rapids, Michigan: Wm. B. Eerdmans Publishing Company, 1979.

Mendelsohn, I. "The Family in the Ancient near East." *The Biblical Archaeologist* 11, no. 2 (1948): 24-40.

________. "Slavery in the Old Testament." In *Interpreter's Dictionary of the Bible*, ed. George Arthur Buttrick, 4, 383-391. New York: Abingdon Press, 1962.

Mendelsohn, Isaac. *Slavery in the Ancient near East*. New York: Oxford University Press, 1949.

Merrill, Eugene H. "Deuteronomy." In *The New American Commentary*, ed. E. Ray Clendenen, 4. USA: Broadman & Holman Publishers, 1994.

Milgrom, Jacob. "Leviticus 1-16." In *The Anchor Bible*, ed. William Foxwell Albright and David Noel Freedman, 3. New York: Doubleday, 1991.

________. "Leviticus 17-22." In *The Anchor Bible*, ed. David Noel Freedman William Foxwell Albright, 3A. New York: Doubleday, 2000.

________. "Leviticus 23-27." In *The Anchor Bible*, ed. William Foxwell Albright and David Noel Freedman, 3B. London: Yale University Press, 2001.

________. *Leviticus: A Book of Ritual and Ethics*. Minneapolis: Fortress Press, 2004.

Moore-Gilbert, Bart. *Post-Colonial Theory: Contexts, Practices, Politics*. London: Verso, 1997.

Morenz, Siegfried. *Egyptian Religion*. Translated by Ann E Keep. London: Methuen & Company Ltd, 1973.

Morton, Stephen. *Gayatri Chakravorty Spivak*. London and New York: Routledge, 2003.

Muthunayagom, Daniel Jones. "Globalization, Debt Burden and Debt Slavery: Response from a Biblical Perspective." In *Bible Speaks Today: Essays in Honour of Gnana Robinson*, ed. Daniel Jones Muthunayagom, 114-133. Delhi: ISPCK, 2000.

________. "Contemporary Approaches to Old Testament Interpretation." In *Interweaving Methodology and Praxis- Exploring Disciplinary Options in Today's World*, ed. Indukuri John Mohan Razu, 169-204. Bangalore: BTESSC/SATHRI, 2007.

Nelson, Richard D. "Deuteronomy: A Commentary." In *The Old Testament Library* ed. Carol A. Newsom, David L. Petersen and James L Mays. London: Westminster John Knox Press, 2004.

North, R. *Sociology of the Biblical Jubilee*. Rome: Pontifical Biblical Institute, 1954.

Noth, Martin. *The History of Israel*. London: Adam and Charles Black, 1960.

________. *Exodus*. London: SCM Press Ltd, 1962.

________. *Leviticus*. Philadelphia: Westminster Press, 1965.

________. *The Laws in the Pentateuch and Other Studies*. Edinburgh: Oliver & Boyd, 1966.

Otto, Eckart. "False Weights in the Scales of Biblical Justice? Different Views of Women from Patriarchal Hierarchy to Religious Equality in the Book of Deuteronomy." In *Gender and Law in the Hebrew Bible and the Ancient near East*, ed. Bernard M. Levinson Victor

H. Matthews, and Tikva Frymer-Kensky, 128-146. Sheffield: Sheffield Academic Press, 1998.

Pandya, Rameshwari. *Women and Law*. Haryana: Madhav Books, 2009.

Parry, Robin. "Reader-Response Criticism." In *Dictionary for Theological Interpretation of the Bible*, ed. Kevin J. Vanhoozer, 658-661. Grand Rapids, Michigan: Baker Academic, 2005.

Patrick, Dale. *Old Testament Law*. Atlanta: John Knox Press, 1985.

Paul, S. M. *The Book of the Covenant: Its Literary Setting and Extra-Biblical Background*. Michigan: Ann Arbor, 1966.

Perdue, Leo C. *Reconstructing Old Testament Theology: After the Collapse of History*. Minneapolis: Fortress Press, 2005.

Philips, Anthony. *Deuteronomy* The Cambridge Bible Commentary, ed. A. R. C. Leaney P. R. Ackroyd, J. W. Packer. Cambridge: University Press, 1973.

Porter, J. R. "Leviticus." In *The Cambridge Bible Commentary*, ed. A. R. C. Leaney, P. R. Ackroyd and J. W. Packer. London: Cambridge University Press, 1976.

Preiser, W. "Vergeltung Und Sühne Im Altisraelitischen Strafrecht." *Festschrift für Eberhard Schmidt* (1961).

Premnath, D. N. *Eighth Century Prophets: A Social Analysis*. St. Louis: Chalice Press, 2003.

Propp, William H. C. *Exodus 19-40* The Anchor Bible, ed. William Foxwell Albright and David Noel Freedman. New York: Doubleday, 2006.

Pui-lan, Kwok. *Introducing Asian Feminist Theology*. Sheffield: Sheffield Academic Press, 2000.

R. Osborne, Grant. "Redaction Criticism." In *Dictionary for Theological Interpretation of the Bible*, ed. Kevin J. Vanhoozer, 663-666. Grand Rapids, Michigan: Baker Academic, 2005.

Rad, Gerhard von. *Studies in Deuteronomy*. London: SCM Press, 1948. Reprint, 1961.

________. *Studies in Deuteronomy*. London: SCM Press Ltd, 1953.

________. *Deuteronomy*. London: SCM Press Ltd, 1966.

Raja, A. Maria Arul. "Dalit Layers of Consciousness in Dialogue with Biblical World." In *Dalit-Tribal Theological Interface: Current Trends in Subaltern Theologies*, ed. James Massey and Shimreingam Shimray, 195-217. Jorhat, New Delhi: TSC and CDS, 2007.

Rao, Chilkuri Vasantha. *Ecological and Theological Aspects of Some Animal Laws in the Pentateuch*. Delhi: ISPCK, 2005.

Ravindran, T. K. Sundari. *Subverting Patriarchy: Workshops for Rural Women*. Chennai: Rural Women's Social Education Centre, 1999.

Ricoeur, Paul. *Hermenuetics and the Human Sciences*. Cambridge: Cambridge University Press, 1981.

Ringgren, Helmer. "The Impact of the Ancient near East on Israelite Tradition." In *Tradition and Theology in the Old Testament*, ed. Douglas A. Knight, 31. Philadelphia: Fortress Press, 1977.

Rofe, Alexander. *Deuteronomy: Issues and Interpretation,* Old Testament Studies, ed. David J. Reimer. London: T&T Clark, 2002.

Rooker, Mark F. "Leviticus." In *The New American Commentary*, ed. E. Ray Clendenen, 3A. Nashville: Broadman & Holman Publishers, 2000.

Ross, Allen P. *Holiness to the Lord*. Grand Rapids, Michigan: Baker Academic, 2002.

Saggs, H. W. F. *The Greatness That Was Babylon*. New York and Toronto: The New American Library, 1962.

Said, Edward W. *Orientalism*. New York: Vintage Books, 1978.

________. *Orientalism*. Penguin: Harmondsworth, 1985.

________. *Culture and Imperialism*. New York: Alfred A. Knopf, 1993.

Sarna, Nahum M. "Exodus." In *The Jerusalem Publication Society Torah Commentary*, ed. Nahum M. Sarna. Jerusalem: The Jewish Publication Society, 1991.

Schmidt, Werner H. *Old Testament Introduction*. Mumbai: St. Pauls Publication, 1997.

Scholz, Susanne. "The Complexities of 'His' Liberation Talk: A Literary Feminist Reading of the Book of Exodus." In *Exodus to*

Deuteronomy, ed. Athalya Brenner, 5, 20-40. Sheffield: Sheffield Academic Press, 2000.

Schultz, Richard L. "Form Criticism and the Old Testament." In *Dictionary for Theological Interpretation of the Bible*, ed. Kevin J. Vanhoozer., 233-237. Grand Rapids, Michigan: Baker Academic, 2005.

Segal, M. H. *The Pentateuch and Other Biblical Studies*. Jerusalem: The Magnes Press, 1967.

Setel, Drorah O' Donnel. "Exodus." In *Women's Bible Commentary*, eds. Carol A. Newsom and Sharon H. Ringe, 30-39. Kentucky: John Knox Press, 1998.

Seters, John van. *A Law Book for the Diaspora: Revision in the Study of the Covenant Code*. New York: Oxford University Press, 2003.

Sim, Stuart. "Homi K. Bhabha." In *The Routledge Critical Dictionary of Postmodern Thought*, ed. Stuart Sim, 200-201. New York Routledge, 1999.

________. *The Routledge Critical Dictionary of Post Modern Thought*. New York: Routledge, 1999.

Snaith, N. H. "Leviticus and Numbers." In *The Century Bible*, ed. H. H. Rowley. London: Thomas Nelson and Sons Ltd, 1967.

Soggin, J. Alberto. *Introduction to the Old Testament*. London: SCM Press, 1976.

Spivak, Gayatri Chakravorty. "Can the Subaltern Speak?" In *Marxism and the Interpretation of Culture*, ed. Cary Nelson and Larry Grossberg, 271-313. Urbana: University of Illinois Press, 1988.

________. *In Other Worlds: Essays in Cultural Politics*. New York: Routledge, 1988.

________. *The Postcolonial Critic: Interviews, Strategies, Dialogues*, ed. Sarah Harasym. New York: Routledge, 1990.

________. *Outside in the Teaching Machine*. New York: Routledge, 1993.

________. *A Critique of Postcolonial Reason: Toward a History of the Vanishing Present*. Cambridge: Harvard University Press, 1999.

________. "Postcolonial Theory and Literature." In *New Dictionary of the History of Ideas*, ed. Maryanne Cline Horowitz, 5, 1859-1897. London: Gale Cengage Learning, 2005.

Staley, Musa W. Dube and Jeffrey L. "Descending from and Ascending into Heaven: A Postcolonial Analysis of Travel. Space, and Power in John." In *John and Postcolonialism: Travel, Space and Power* ed. Musa W. Dube and Jeffrey L. Staley. Sheffield: Sheffield Academic Press, 2002.

Stol, Marten. "Private Life in Ancient Mesopotamia." In *Civilizations of the Ancient near East*, ed. Jack M. Sasson, I&II, 485-501. Massachusetts: Hendrickson Publishers, 1995.

Sugirtharajah, R. S. *The Bible and Empire: Postcolonial Explorations*. Cambridge: Cambridge University Press, 2005.

Taylor, R. A. "Form Criticism." In *Dictionary of the Old Testament Pentateuch*, ed. T. Desmond Alexander and David W. Baker, 336-343. Secunderbad: OM Authentic Books, 2003.

Teddy Kollek, Moshe Pearlman. *Jerusalem, Sacred City of Mankind: A History of Forty Centuries*. London: Weidenfeld and Nicolson, 1968.

Tetlow, Elisabeth Meier. *Women, Crime and Punishment in Ancient Law and Society*. Vol. 1 The Ancient near East. New York: Continuum, 2004.

Thiselton, Anthony C. *New Horizons in Hermeneutics*. Grand Rapids, Michigan: Zondervan Publishing House, 1992.

Thompson, J. A. *Deuteronomy: An Introduction and Commentary* The Tyndale Old Testament Commentaries, ed. D. J. Wiseman. England: Inter-Varsity Press, 1974.

________. "Deuteronomy." In *The Tyndale Old Testament Commentaries*, ed. D. J. Wiseman. England: Inter-Varsity Press, 1976.

Thorat, Sukhaedeo. "Dalit Reality: From an Economic Perspective." In *Dalits and Women*, ed. V. Devasahayam, 23-49. Chennai: Gurukul - Department of Research and Publications, 1992.

Tigay, Jeffrey H. "Deuteronomy." In *The Jewish Publication Society Torah Commentary*, ed. Nahum M. Sarna. Jerusalem: The Jewish Publication Society, 1996.

Vattaparackel, Joy Joseph. ""Re-Lecturing" Of Deuteronomy (Chapter 12-26) in the Post-Exilic Period." München, 1997.

Vaux, Roland De. *The Bible and the Ancient near East*. Translated by Damian Mchugh. New York: Doubleday & Company, 1971.

Walker, Alice. "To the Editors of Ms Magazine." In *Search of Our Mothers' Gardens*. New York: Harcourt Brace Jovanovick, 1983.

Wallis, Hale G. "Chāmadh." In *Theological Dictionary of the Old Testament*, ed. G. Johannes Botterweck and Helmer Ringgren, 452-461. Grand Rapids, Michigan: William B. Eerdmans Publishing Company, 1980.

Weinfeld, Moshe. *Deuteronomy and the Deuteronomic School*. Oxford: Clarendon Press, 1972.

Weinsheimer, Joel C. *Gadamer's Hermeneutics: A Reading of 'Truth and Method'*. New Haven: Yale University Press, 1985.

Welch, A. C. *The Code of Deuteronomy: A New Theory of Its Origin*. London, 1924.

Wenham, Gordon J. "The Book of Leviticus." In *The New International Commentary on the Old Testament*, ed. R. K. Harrison. Grand Rapids, Michigan: William B. Eerdmans Publishing Company, 1979.

Williams, P. J. "Textual Criticism." In *Dictionary of the Old Testament Pentateuch*, ed. T. Desmond Alexander and David W. Baker, 834-841. Secunderabad: OM Authentic Books, 2003.

Wolff, H. W. *Anthropology of the Old Testament*. London: SCM Press, 1974.

Wright, Christopher J. H. "Deuteronomy." In *New International Biblical Commentary*, ed. Robert K. Johnston Robert L. Hubbard Jr. . USA: Paternoster Press, 1996.

Articles

Alt, A. "Die Ursprunge Des Israelitischen Rechts." *BSAW* 86, no. 1 (1934): 101-171.

Balasundaram, Franklyn J. "Dalit Struggle and Its Implications for Theological Education." *Bangalore Theological Forum* 29, no. 3 & 4 (1997): 69-91.

Barton, John. "Classifying Biblical Criticism." *JSOT* 29 (1984): 19-35.

Bartor, Assnat. "The Representation of Speech in the Casuistic Laws of the Pentateuch: The Phenomenon of Combined Discourse." *JBL* 126, no. 2 (2007): 231-249.

Carmichael, Calum M. "A Ceremonial Crux: Removing a Man's Sandal as a Female Gesture of Contempt." *JBL* 96, no. 3 (1977): 321-336.

Chackalackal, Saju. "Religion and Law - Forces of Liberation?" *Journal of Dharma* 32 (2007): 221-240.

Chakkalackal, Pauline. "Law and Religion: A Feminist Biblical-Theological Critique." *Journal of Dharma* 32, no. 3 (2007): 241-255.

Finkelstein, J. J. "Ammisaduqa's Edict and the Babylonian 'Law Codes'." *JCS* 15 (1961): 91-104.

Fiorenza, Elisabeth Schussler. "The Ethics of Biblical Interpretation: De-Centering Biblical Scholarship." *JBL* 107 (1988): 3-17.

Heger, Paul. "Source of Law in the Biblical and Mesopotamian Law Collections." *Biblica* 86, no. 3 (2005): 324-342.

Herron, Roy Brasfield. "The Land, the Law, and the Poor." *Word and World* 6, no. 1 (1986): 76-84.

Isser, Stanley. "Two Traditions: The Law of Exodus 21:22-23 Revisited." *The Catholic Biblical Quarterly* 52 (1990): 30-45.

Jackson, Bernard S. "Problem of Exodus 21:22-5, Ius Talionis." *Vetus Testamentum* 23, no. 4 (1973): 273-304.

Joy, C. I. David. "The Social and Religious Origins of the Gospel of Mark and Its Hermeneutical Implications: A Post-Colonial Critique." *Bangalore Theological Forum* 33, no. 1 (2001): 1-24.

Kim, Jean K. "Uncovering Her Wickedness: An Inter(Con) Textual Reading of Revelation 17 from a Postcolonial Feminist Perspective." *JSNT* 73 (1999): 61-81.

Kopf, David. "Hermeneutics Versus History." *Journal of Asian Studies* 39, no. 3 (1980): 498-505.

L. Finkelstein. "An Eye for an Eye." *The Menorah Journal* 24 (1936): 207-218.

Laney, J. Carl. "Deuteronomy 24:1-4 and the Issue of Divorce." *Bibliotheca Sacra* 149, no. 593 (1992): 3-15.

Lemche, N. P. "Manumission of Slaves-the Fallow Year-the Sabbatical Year-the Jubilee Year." *Vetus Testamentum* 26, no. 1 (1976): 38-59.

Lemche, N. P. "The Hebrew Slave: Comments on the Slave Law Exodus 21:2-11." *Vetus Testamentum* 25 (1975): 124-144.

Limburg, James. "Human Rights in the Old Testament." *Concillium* (1979).

Lindenberger, James M. "How Much for a Hebrew Slave? The Meaning of Misneh in Deut 15:18- Critical Notes." *JBL* 110, no. 3 (1991): 479-498.

McCarthy, D. J. "Treaty and Covenant." *AnBib* 21 (1963).

Mendelsohn, I. "The Conditional Sale into Slavery of Free-Born Daughters in Nuzi and the Law of Exodus 21:7-11." *JAOS* 55 (1935): 190-195.

________. "The Family in the Ancient Near East." *The Biblical Archaeologist* 11, no. 2 (1948): 24-40.

Mendenhall, G. E. "Law and Covenant in Israel and the Ancient Near East." *BA* 17 (1954): 26-46.

Menezes, Rui de. "Was There Slavery in Ancient Israel?" *Vidya Jyothi Journal of Theological Reflection* 63 (1999): 799-811.

Mulloor, Augustine. "Development of Biblical Studies in the Second Millennium: Historical Moments and Trend-Setting Shifts." *Jeeva Dhara* 29, no. 173 (1999): 341-354.

Muthunayagom, Daniel Jones. "Theologizing in India Today: Challenges and Perspectives from Biblical Interpretative Process." *Bangalore Theological Forum* 39, no. 2 (2007): 137-150.

Parry, Benita. "Problems in Current Theories of Colonial Discourse." *Oxford Literary Review* 9, no. 1-2 (1987): 27-58.

Paul, Shalom. "Studies in the Book of the Covenant in the Light of Cuneiform and Biblical Law." *VTS* 18 (1970): 78-83.

Philips, Anthony. "Another Look at Adultery." *JSOT* 20 (1981): 10.

________. "The Laws of Slavery: Exodus 21:2-11." *JSOT* 30 (1984): 51-66.

R. Yaron. "The Middle Assyrian Laws and the Bible." *Biblica* 51 (1970): 549-557.

Robert D. Taylor, Ronald J. Ricci. "Three Biblical Models of Liberty and Some Representative Laws." *Ex auditu* 11 (1995): 111-127.

Rohrlick, Ruby. "State Formation in Sumer and the Subjugation of Women." *Journal of Feminist Studies* 6 (1980): 83-102.

Rost, L. "Das Bundesbuch." *ZAW* 77 (1965): 225-259.

Singh, Ivy. "Feminism: Various Approaches and Its Values." *Indian Journal of Theology* 37, no. 1 (1995): 58-67.

Vasholz, Robert I. "A Legal 'Brief' on Deuteronomy 22: 13-21." *Presbyterion* 17, no. 1 (1991): 62.

Wells, Bruce. "Sex, Lies, and Virginal Rape: The Slandered Bride and False Accusation in Deuteronomy." *JBL* 124, no. 1 (2005): 41-72.

________. "What Is Biblical Law? A Look at Pentateuchal Rules and near Eastern Practice." *The Catholic Biblical Quarterly* 70 (2008): 223-243.

Westbrook, R. "Jubilee Laws." *Israel Law Review* 6 (1971): 209-226.

Wilfred, Felix. "Towards a Subaltern Hermeneutics: Beyond the Contemporary Polarities in the Interpretation of Religious Tradition." *Jeeva Dhara* 26, no. 151 (1996): 45-62.

Williams, Delores S. "Womanist-Feminist Dialogue: Problems and Possibilities." *Journal of Feminist Studies in Religion* 9, no. 2 (1993): 67-73.

Wiseman, D. J. "The Laws of Hammurabi Again." *JSS* 7 (1962): 161-172.

News Papers and Unpublished works

The Hindu (Bangalore), 7 March 2009.

Deccan Herald (Bangalore), 9 March 2009.

The Hindu (Bangalore), 28 July 2009.

The Hindu (Bangalore), 29 July 2009.

The Hindu (Bangalore), 28-29 July 2009

The Hindu (Bangalore), 30 July 2009.

The Hindu (Bangalore), 11 April 2010.

The Hindu (Bangalore), 24 August 2010.

The Times of India (Chennai), 27 August 2010.

The Hindu (Bangalore), 10 September 2010.

The Times of India (Bangalore), 21 October 2010.

The Hindu (Bangalore), 7 February 2011.

The Hindu (Bangalore), 11 February 2011.

Abraham, Joseph. "Re-Reading the Old Testament: A Study of Feminist Readings of Genesis 1-3." UK: Coventry University through Wycliffe Hall Oxford, 1996.

George Oommen, *A Historian's Interaction with Postcolonialism and Subaltern Theories, UTC, Bangalore, 2004.*

Thomas, V. V. "Research Methodology: History of Christianity." In *DTh Methodology Seminar*. Bangalore: SATHRI, 2008.

Webliography

Jessica Bieda, "Women in Ancient Mesopotamia", *http://www. assyrian voice.net/forum/index.php? topic=16767.5.*

Index of Subjects

D

E

F

G

H

I

R

S

T

Index of Authors